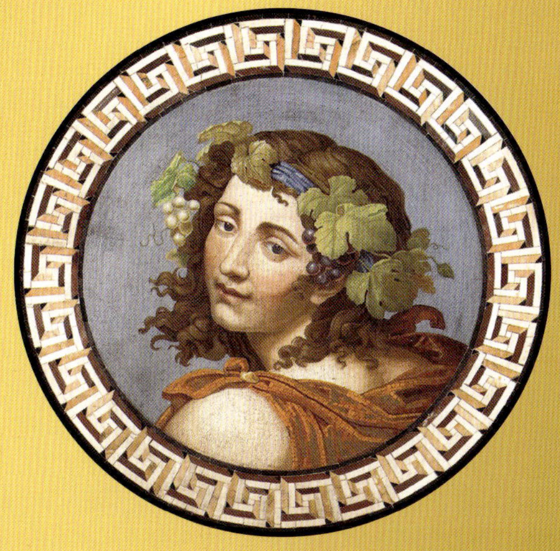

THE *David Roche* FOUNDATION

ROBERT REASON

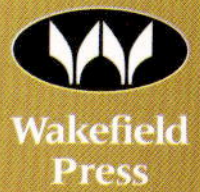

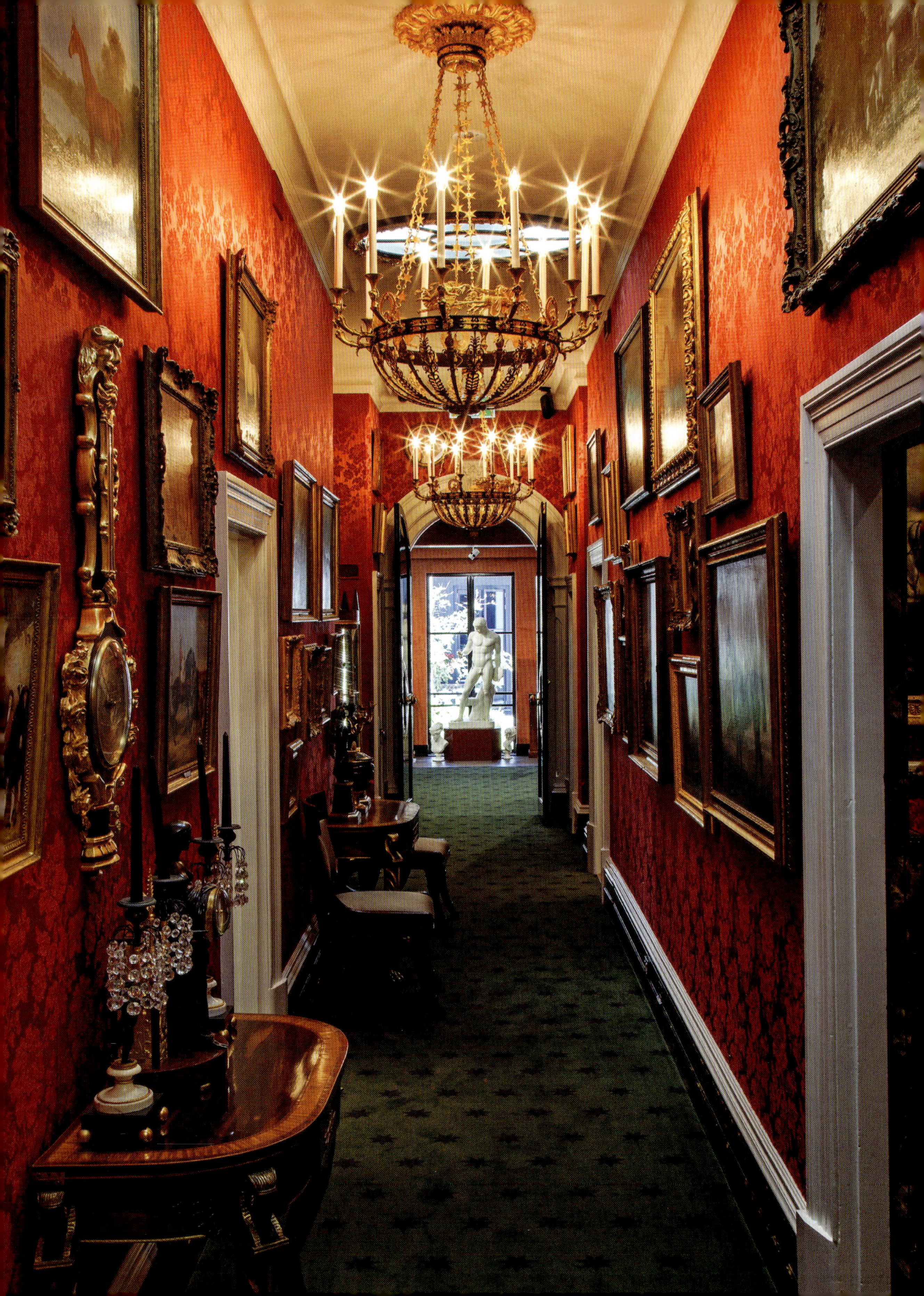

CONTENTS

FOREWORD

David Roche's home, Fermoy House, was set amidst a series of nine house blocks, all of which were once owned by David, and which altogether equalled the size of the Adelaide Town Hall and Parliament House combined. At its height, the grounds of Fermoy House were home to not only his house and collection, but also to his kennels, which housed up to 40 dogs at any one time. Although the kennels are now gone and the landholding reduced, the house and collection still remain as a testament to David Roche.

This guidebook, prepared by our Senior Curator, Robert Reason, allows visitors to visualise, in vivid detail, this incredible gift to South Australia by this most shy, yet generous man. As Robert describes each room, it is as if you are being taken on a tour through Fermoy and the wonderful collection housed therein. Having had the benefit of having Robert's book read to me, I was able to close my eyes and picture every piece and its merits.

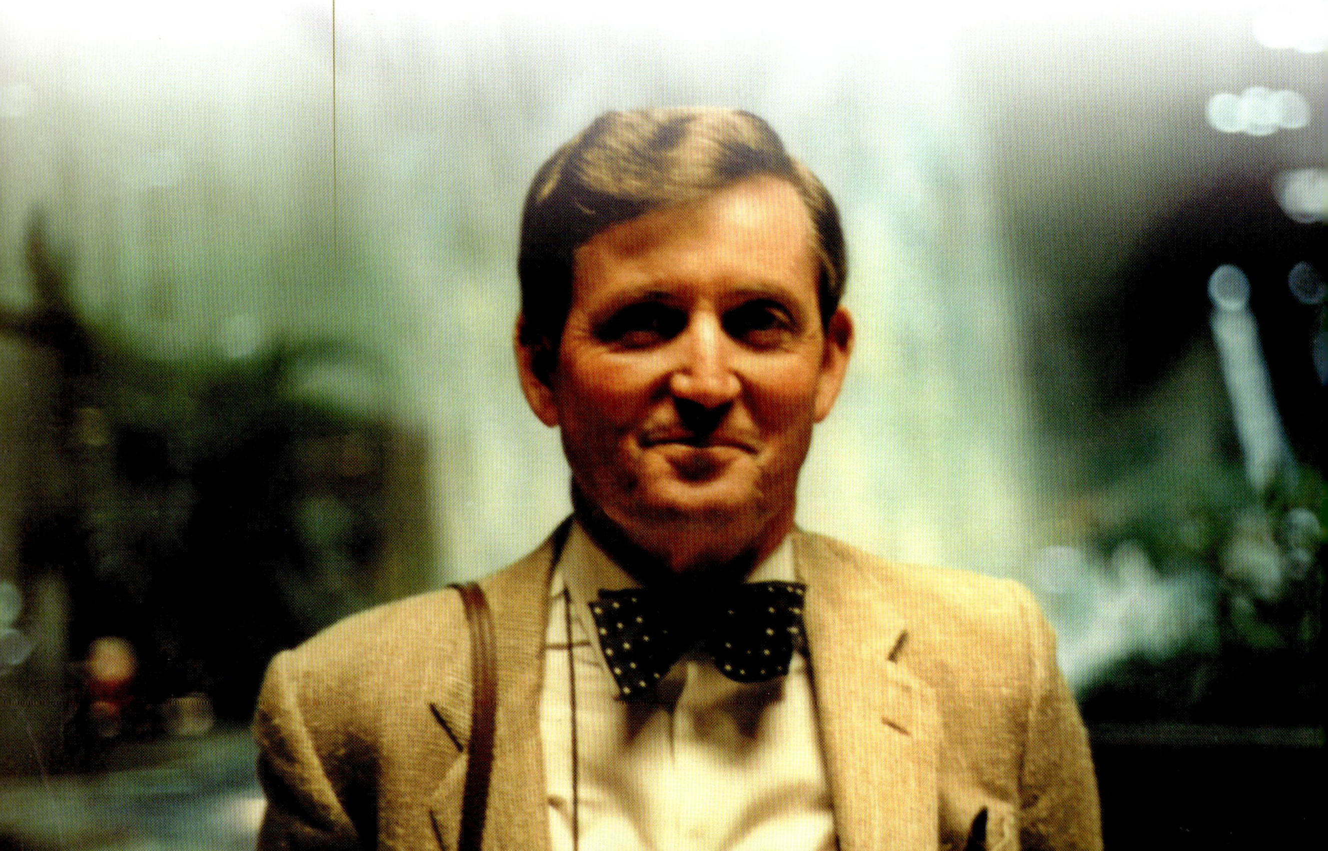

The book also provides a brief biography of his life (as David would have wanted), as well as a wonderful essay by Judy Chapman recounting David's lifelong passion for dogs, his Fermoy Kennels and his successes in the dog world over the years.

David was a fastidious and considered collector of art with a particular love of English Regency and French and Russian Empire works, and the main aim of his life was to leave something to benefit Adelaide and his beloved state of South Australia.

From a very early age David was a collector and that continued right up until his death. The collection was solely funded by David from David's own resources, and as a result of his fastidiousness, the many purchases that he made have increased the collection's value.

I had the great pleasure and honour to be David's friend for over 30 years, and we travelled together regularly. I believe that as a friend and as a travelling companion, you could not want one better or more generous.

The collection is now in the care of his foundation, and I am very proud – as are all the people who work here – of its direction going into the future and, in particular, of how it continues to be a monument to the life, love and generosity of David Roche. No matter what the future holds, it will always be The David Roche Collection.

Robert's catalogue has been thoroughly and meticulously researched and he has turned up some fascinating details that provide all who read the book with an insight into the character and vision of David Roche (though if you think something is missing, it may well be the 10 panelled doors that have been removed to allow for easy access). I am certain that all who acquire a copy of this book will be both greatly fascinated and entertained by it for many years.

His life was a joyous one and we are all fortunate to benefit from The David Roche Foundation, his singular and ongoing gift to the people of Adelaide and South Australia.

Martyn Cook
Museum Director

Previous page:
The Red Hallway, 2018.

Opposite page:
David Roche c. 1980.

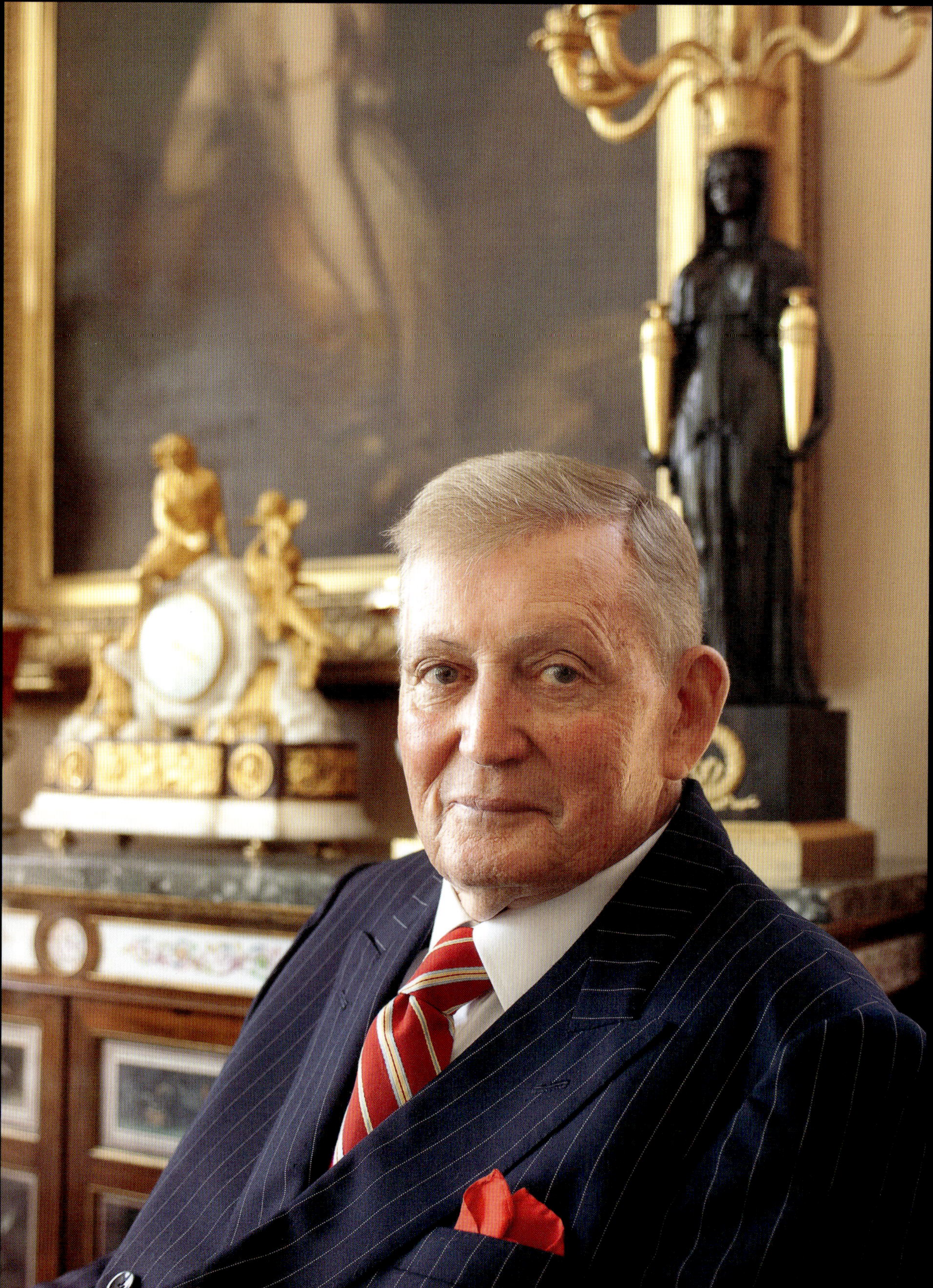

INTRODUCTION

The Man

DAVID JEROME ROCHE, AM (1930–2013)

Opposite page:
David Roche seated in the Roman room, 2008.

David Roche, an intensely private man in many ways, did not boast about his wealth, art collection or pedigree dogs. He would be the first to admit to close friends that antique collecting was both a joy and a worry, whereas his dogs were his primary love. This dual aspect to David's life makes for a fascinating man who was at once confident in the judging ring anywhere in the world, yet shy about inviting people into his home where his collection surrounded him. In David's 83 years he lived a full life that saw him travel widely and in style, meeting remarkable people, judging and exhibiting in the best dog shows and making great friendships. Most importantly, he created Fermoy House in North Adelaide as his legacy to Australia.

David did not keep journals documenting his life or diaries of his travels, letters he received were discarded over time and he was not terribly fond of being photographed. Friends in the dog world tried to capture this part of his life, but a planned publication sadly did not eventuate. The closest that David came to creating a short biography was with Christopher Menz, Director of the Art Gallery of South Australia in 2008, in preparation for the publication and exhibition *Empires & Splendour: The David Roche Collection*. It remains an important source of information, including a foreword written by David. In his own words, he writes: 'I attended my first dog show at the age of nine, and owned my first antique at seventeen . . . I have come to realise that my two great passions [dogs and antiques] have much in common. The "eye" that is required to be a top dog judge can be equally applied to antiques. With the eye comes the ability to assess things quickly and easily.' It was a skill that stood David in good stead, selecting the best antiques, followed by the consequence of worrying about finding the money!

David made close friends through the antique trade – Carlton Hobbs of London and New York, and Martyn Cook of Sydney. They shared his passion and enthusiasm, found the most wonderful things, and more importantly encouraged him to 'think big'. David wrote: 'At the beginning [1999], I was very hesitant about setting up a foundation. It took much persuasion for me to believe that my little collection was good enough to do more than give me pleasure. It was visits to small, now famous, collections such as the Mario Praz Collection in Rome that made me think it might be possible. Eventually convinced, I set out as never before to upgrade the collection to the point where I was happy and not reticent about sharing what I had assembled. The joy I have experienced could now be shared with many people.' The quote reveals the commitment David had toward his collection, but also his modesty, as he owned around 3,500 items by some of the finest European makers and designers of the 18th and 19th centuries.

An unintended consequence from David's perspective would be the visitor's interest in him. Viewing Fermoy House Museum is an intense visual and physical experience. Never afraid of pattern or colour (as Martyn Cook would say), for David there was 'simply no room in my house for minimalism', and as a result, you cannot help but feel slightly overwhelmed. Each room is densely hung with paintings, vitrines are full, furniture abounds, and wallpapers, curtains and soft furnishings all cry out for your attention. Not surprisingly, the stories about David living in the home, of how and where things were bought and why for that room, are as important as the works of art. It is as much about David as the object. As a private collector for over 60 years he looms large, but this history is fragile, as David did not document it, think it important, or necessary to the museum experience. His private life was exactly that, and in many ways he has entrusted his memory to those who knew him, especially Martyn Cook, who joined the Foundation Board in 1999 and has been both the inaugural curator and director of the museum.

This house book takes you on a tour of David's home, pointing out the many fine things you will see as well as how David created and used the rooms, plus a few interesting anecdotes on individual pieces. But before this, we need to know a little more about David.

David was born in 1930, the fourth of six children, two boys and four girls, to John D.K. (Jack) Roche (1901–1958) and Dorinda Elfreda Thomas (1904–1986). Financed by his father, John Joseph (d. 1933), Jack moved from Melbourne to Adelaide in the early 1920s buying land and establishing the Adelaide Development Company (ADC). Many years later, and with a portfolio of land and housing subdivisions in Adelaide and Perth, David would inherit a 25% share of the family firm. We learn from a 30 January interview with David in 1981 for the *Indian Express* newspaper that at age six, his father bought him a cocker spaniel, and 'later he saved his pocket money and bought a Kerry blue for three guineas. Even when he was away from home in Geelong Grammar School in Victoria his heart was in Adelaide where his dogs were'. At age nine, David remembers touring Europe with the whole family and rather frighteningly, leaving Austria as the Germans advanced. More travel would follow after the war and introductions to masterpieces by museum directors at the behest of his father.

Geelong Grammar School was an unusual choice for David's schooling since the Roches were Catholic. David was in Cuthbertson House (1944–1948) during the period James Darling was principal and Ludwig Hirschfeld-Mack

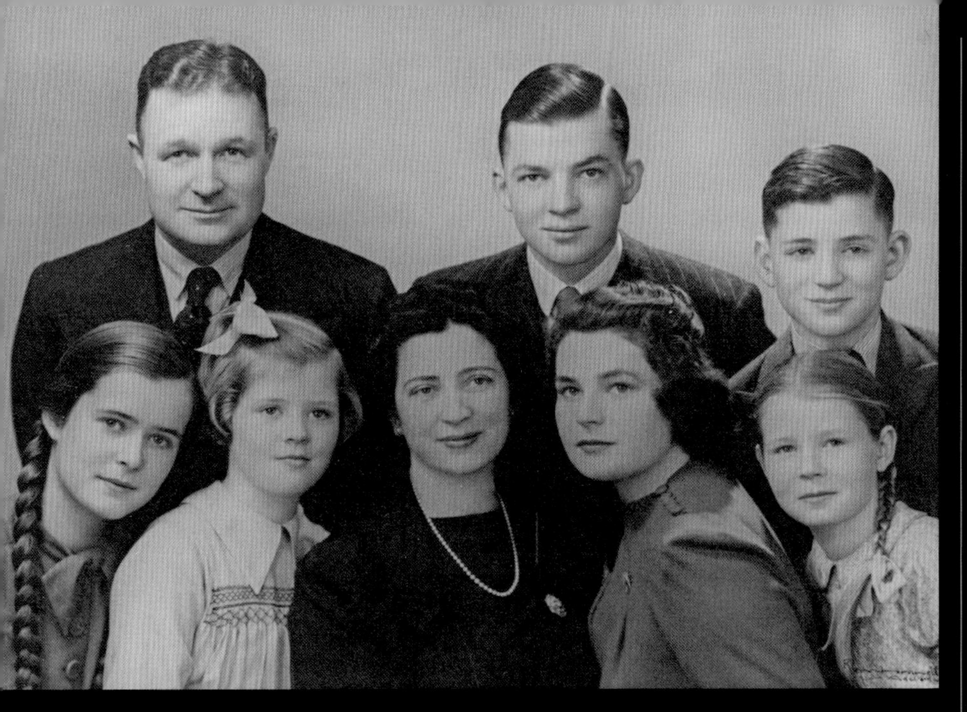

Clockwise from top:
The Roche family, left to right. Back: Jack (father), John, and David.
Front: Judith, Jennifer, Dorinda (mother), Diana, Josephine c. 1940.

David Roche with his poodles, c. 1955.

David Roche en route to Europe with his family, 1939.

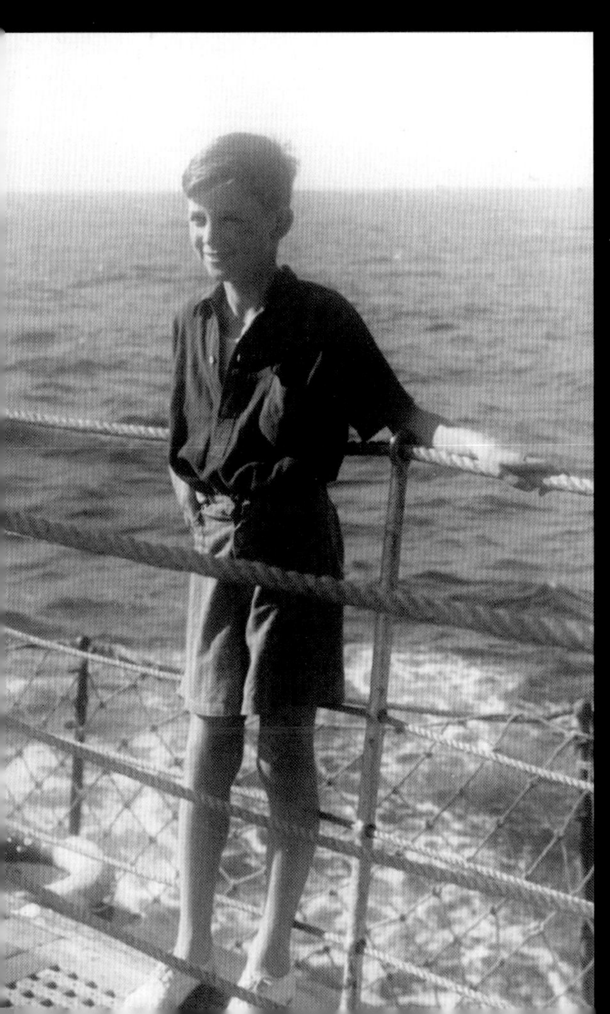

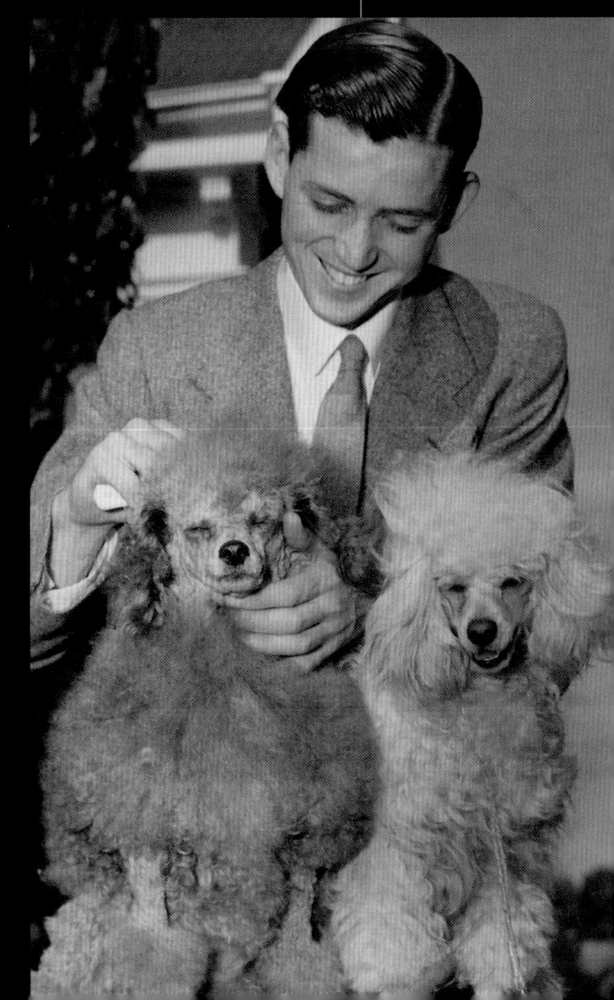

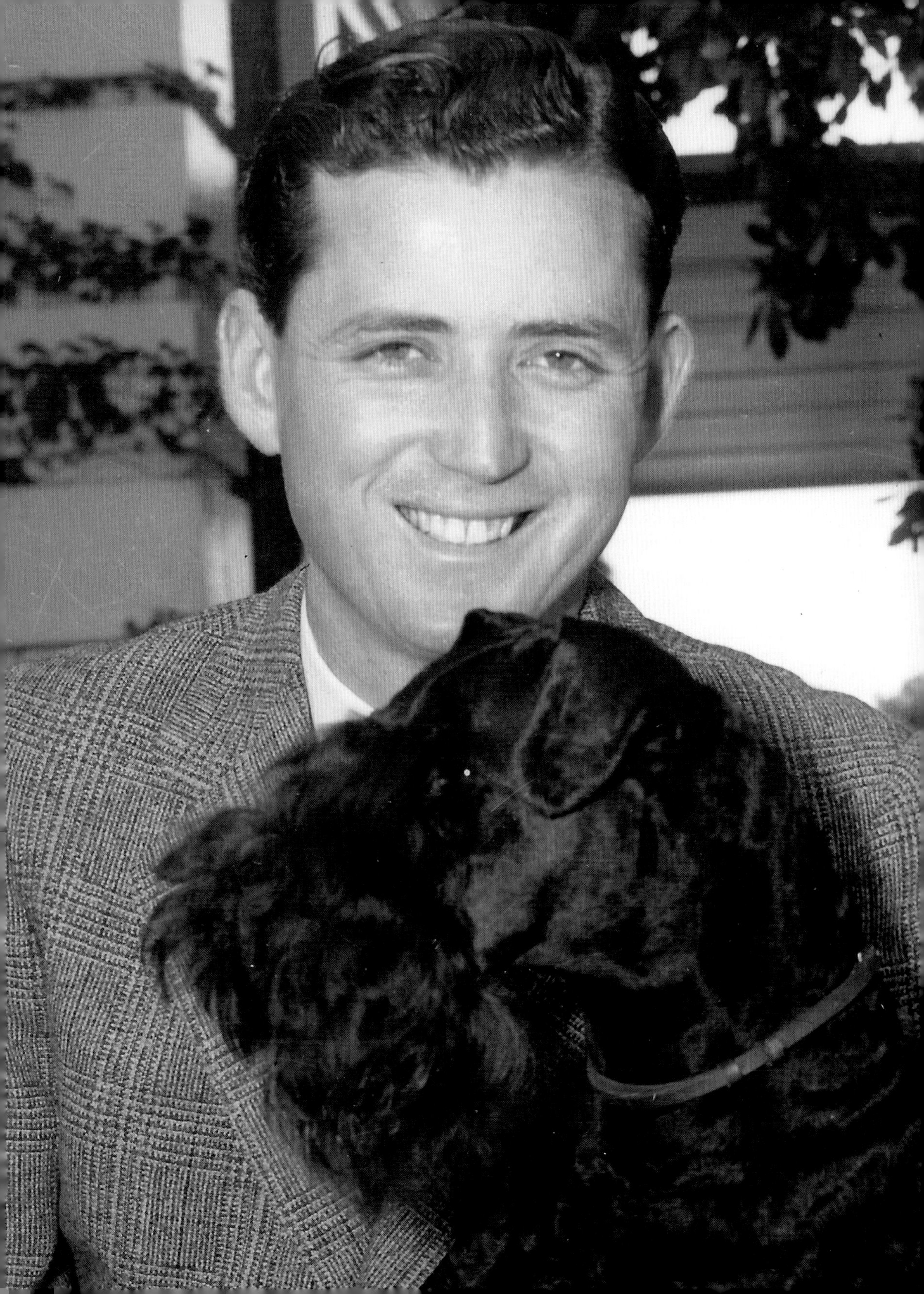

(Germany/Australia 1892–1965) was teaching the Bauhaus art method. An old schoolbook with addresses in the front show holidays spent either back at the family home in Brougham Place, North Adelaide, or their Sydney home Cranford in Edgecliff. At school, David took part in both sport and the arts. Athletics and boxing feature, and in the school production of Shakespeare's *Julius Caesar* he played Clitus, a soldier of Brutus and Cassius. The production, which toured rural Victoria in September 1945, also featured a young Rupert Murdoch (b. 1931) who played Lucius, servant boy of Brutus. David kept the handsome photographic book of the play, which had the students in classical garments inhabiting pared back Roman architectural props and furniture by Hirschfeld-Mack and T.H. Banfield. It is tempting to think it left a lasting impression on David's collecting taste for neoclassicism, which draws heavily from ancient Rome and Greece.

Following his schooling David went to work briefly outside Perth at a family property, but soon returned to Adelaide, joining the Adelaide Development Company in the late 1940s and working there into the early 1950s. With a job came the opportunity to start buying antiques, mainly English Regency and 19th century French furniture. At the same time, David began buying books on antiques and collecting auction catalogues, and he returned to exhibiting dogs. In 1952, David became Australia's youngest All Breeds qualified judge at the age of 22. He was a tall, good-looking young man who, along with his sisters, regularly made the social pages of newspapers and magazines in Adelaide and Sydney in the 1950s. He enjoyed dancing, particularly the Scottish reel, and attended society events, including Sir Lavington Bonython and Lady Bonython's party at their home, St Corantyn. Years later, he would always speak fondly of meeting Bill and Ursula Hayward at one of their legendary parties at Carrick Hill. David was so excited to attend that he unconsciously over-dressed but was put at ease immediately by Bill. David also met 'Johnnie' (John) Spencer (later 8th Earl Spencer 1924–1992) when he served as Aide-de-Camp (1947–1950) to His Excellency Lieutenant-General Sir Willoughby Norrie (1893–1977), Governor of South Australia. David also played ten-pin bowling, joining the Goodwood club c. 1960 and a team called the 'Goodie boys'.

In December 1951 David joined his parents and two of his sisters on a world tour for 11 months. They stayed at the Ritz London and toured England and Scotland, spending time at the Duke of Sutherland's Highlands estate. David travelled to the United States separately, while the rest of the family toured South America. Back in Adelaide, he started a lifelong commitment to canine judging nationally and internationally, and for the next six decades would travel regularly to Britain and the United States as well as over 20 other countries. Buying his home at 241 Melbourne Street, North Adelaide, in 1954 was a significant moment in his life. It gave him a blank canvas to

Opposite page:
David Roche with Wulfreda Rhapsody (Kerry blue terrier), late 1950s.

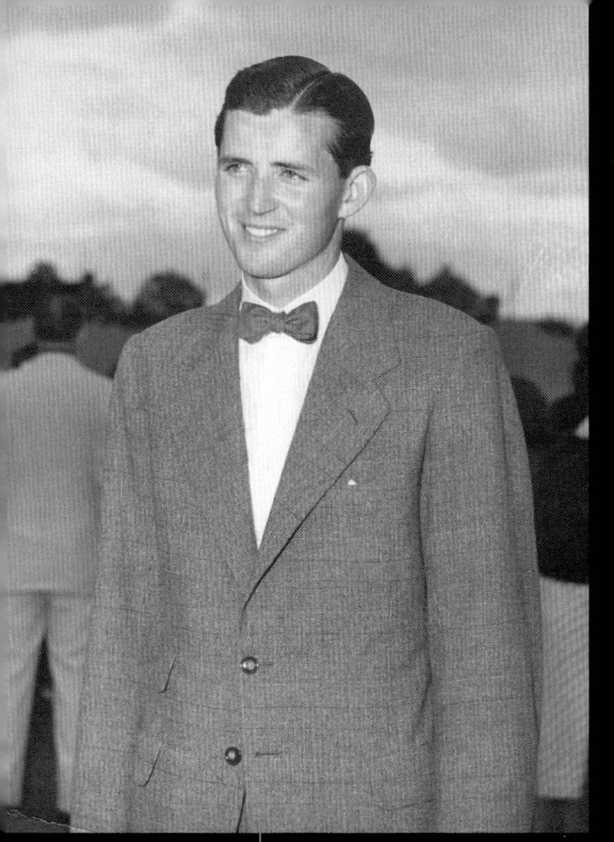

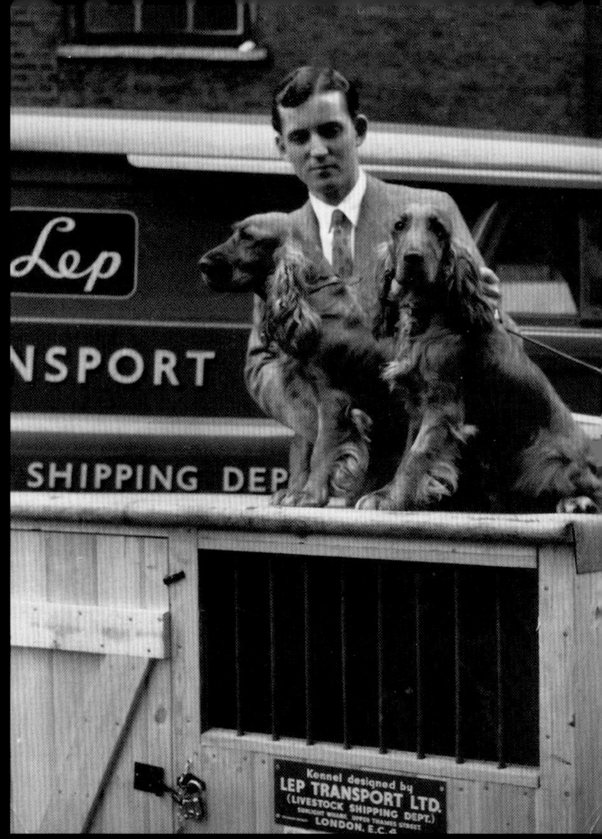

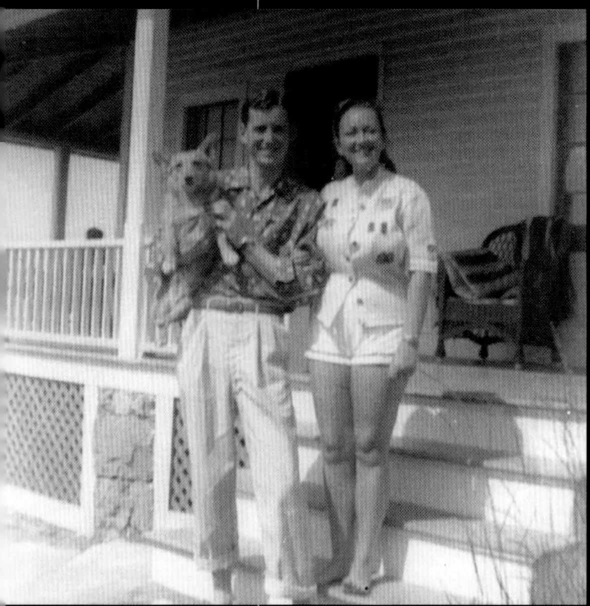

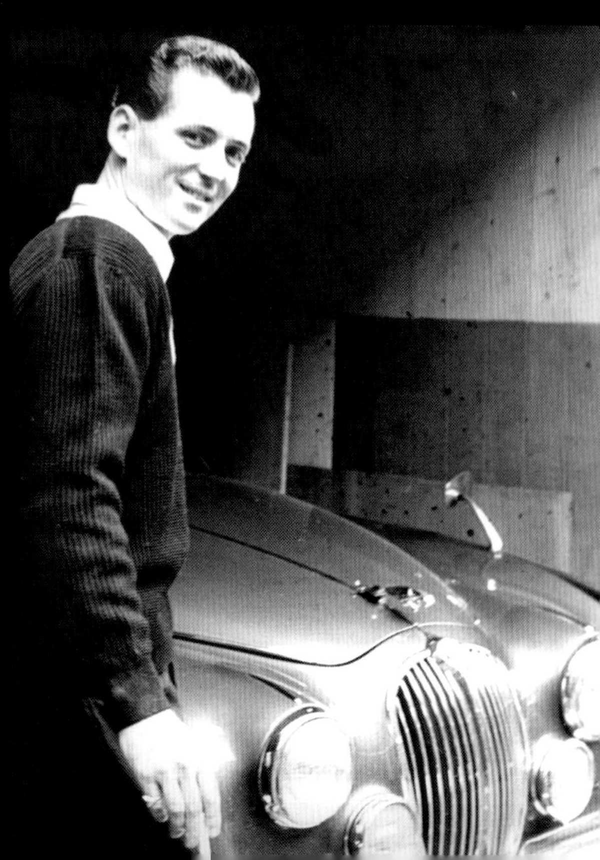

Clockwise from top left: David Roche at his first judging appointment, Goshen, New York, 1952.

David Roche with his English cocker spaniels, London, early 1950s.

David Roche standing next to his new Jaguar MK II, c. 1963.

David Roche with an unidentified friend, probably in the United States, c. 1960.

redesign and slowly fill with antique furniture, porcelain, pottery, sculpture, fine metalware, lighting and paintings; an effort which continued until 2013 when David passed away. His parents' home in Tranmere had been named Fermoy Court and David chose Fermoy House. The name 'Fermoy' refers to their Irish antecedents at Fermoy of County Cork, Ireland. David then built substantial kennels next door and over the decades the name Fermoy Kennels would become internationally acclaimed.

While finding his way as a young man in the world, David came to the difficult realisation that he was homosexual at a time of intolerance and hate. It was not something David spoke about for many years, as homosexuality was not decriminalised in South Australia until 1975, when David was 45. He would be the first to admit that he was not a gay activist, however, he did not marry for convenience; he got on with his life and being gay did not define David. It was his private life, which later included partners and the very occasional Sydney Mardi Gras. In respecting David's wishes, his personal life remains just that, whereas his home and collection are a wonderful, rich expression of his aesthetic and taste. They speak volumes and are what David wished people to remember.

Although David's passports do not exist before 1973 (and 1983–1989 is missing), he clearly enjoyed travelling regularly and for several months at a time. From 1973 onward, he was in England every other year, and every year between 1990 and 1998. He frequently travelled to the United States before and after 1973 and at least four times to Canada after 1978. France was a popular destination after 1990 and of course many countries throughout Europe. He went to South Africa and Spain in 1980; India in 1981 and 1993; Russia in 1994, 1997 and 1999; Japan in 1996 and 1999; Turkey in 2002, and had many stopovers in Singapore, Hong Kong, Malaysia and Hawaii. He also had the opportunity to fly Concorde between London and New York, meeting the odd celebrity such as Sophia Loren.

Travel was for pleasure, to meet friends, attend important canine shows and visit museums. We do know something of one of his earlier overseas trips in 1963, when he travelled with three friends to England and Europe for an extended period of 18 months. David bought a blue Jaguar MK II in which they toured England, France, Italy and Greece, sometimes retracing an earlier Roche family trip and visiting places like the Palace of Versailles. He even brought the car back to Adelaide. Considerable time was spent looking at menswear and shoes and David did some modelling of mainly handsome coats from Savile Row tailors of London. The large format photographs remain.

On returning to Adelaide, David remodelled a back area in Gawler Chambers, a building owned by the ADC, and in 1965 opened The Cock's Feathers menswear shop. Accessed from a laneway off Gawler Place, David sold luxury English clothes from DAKS and Aquascutum of London, Burberrys Irish Tweed overcoats, as well as Italian and Bally shoes. Shirts, shorts and ties were manufactured in Adelaide, the shirts featuring the Cock's Feathers logo of a pheasant and most stock carried his label 'The Cock's Feathers Adelaide'. The quick trip from North Adelaide to the shop was often made on the back of a friend's Italian Lambretta scooter. David's most well known client was the Premier of South Australia, Don Dunstan (1926–1999), who was a regular customer until the shop closed in about 1970.

From the 1980s onward, the role of seeking antiques for his collection grew significantly in his primary collecting areas of English Regency, French and Russian Empire. Frequently accompanying David on these buying trips was Martyn Cook, who recalls – 'A London hotel room would be booked as a base during May and June to attend the Chelsea Flower Show, Ascot races, the antiques fairs at Grosvenor House, Olympia, Chelsea; and the auction houses Christie's, Sotheby's and Bonham's, to name a few. All were paid a visit, as were the antique dealers from Portobello Road to Bond Street.' David toured England, Scotland and Ireland, enjoying visiting country houses, local antique shops and even car-boot sales. Prior to departing, 'Big Dave's shopping list', as he fondly called it, would be handwritten and faxed to Martyn. Auction catalogues accompanied David on the plane and his infamous red marker pen would circle items of interest, accompanied by notes. Many catalogues remain, peppered with dog-eared corners and his marker pen. David also had a penchant for saying 'hello handsome' to his reflection in the morning. Martyn, catching David out during these trips, would always get the same response, 'Well he's never told me otherwise!'

In France, David would visit every venue from the flea markets to the upmarket Rue du Faubourg, Saint Honoré. Bois de Boulogne exhibitions and the Biennale des Antiquaires at the Grande Palais were a regular fixture. Versailles, Malmaison, Fontainebleau and Vaux-le-Vicomte were greatly admired. A visit to Napoléon's death mask at Les Invalides became something of a ritual for David, who was fascinated by the true impression of the great man. A collector of the Napoléonic period, David asked that an impression of his face be taken upon his own death. Duly done by his executors, this mask now rests with his ashes inside a large Russian malachite-lidded urn. That aside, travels in Germany took in the architecture of Karl Schinkel and the Charlottenhof Palace complex. Russia was equally rewarding for David. St Petersburg and its surrounds were a treasure trove of palaces – Oranienbaum, Tsarskoye Selo, Peterhof and Pavlovsk, and of course the grand Hermitage which sent David into a temporary state of melancholia. How could anything compare?

Friends, acquaintances and staff in David's life were many and varied. Working at Fermoy House and kennels it was always 'Mr Roche', a formality

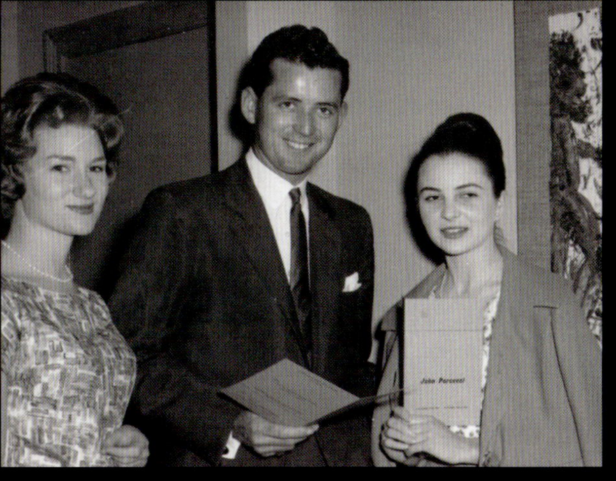

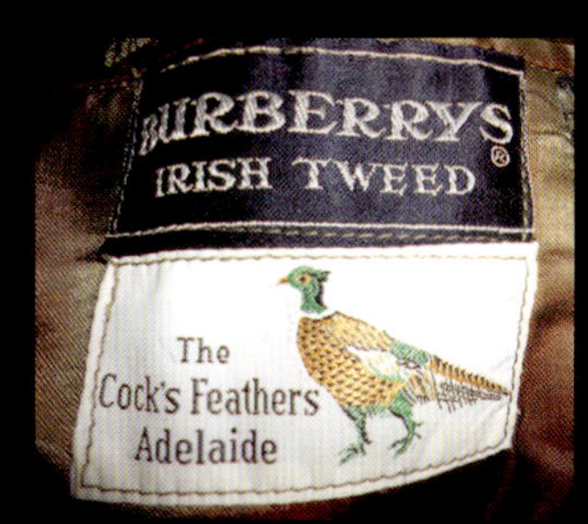

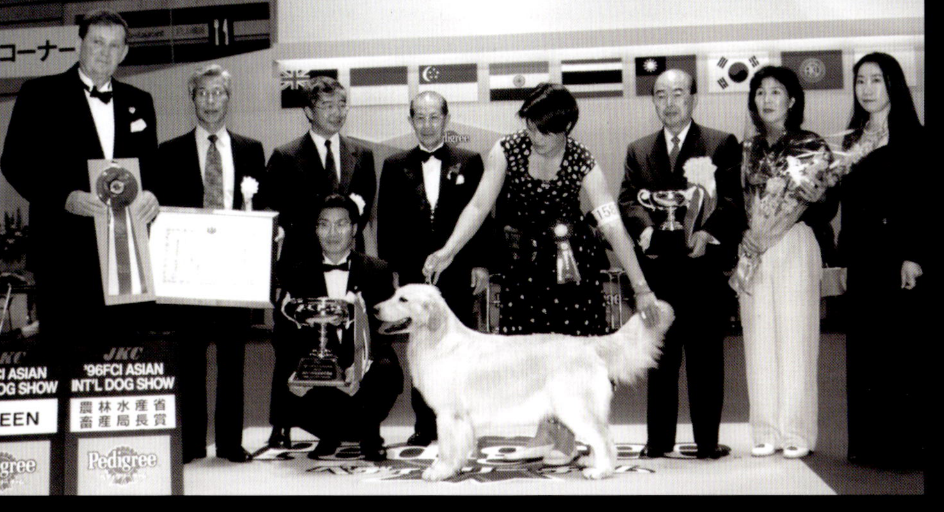

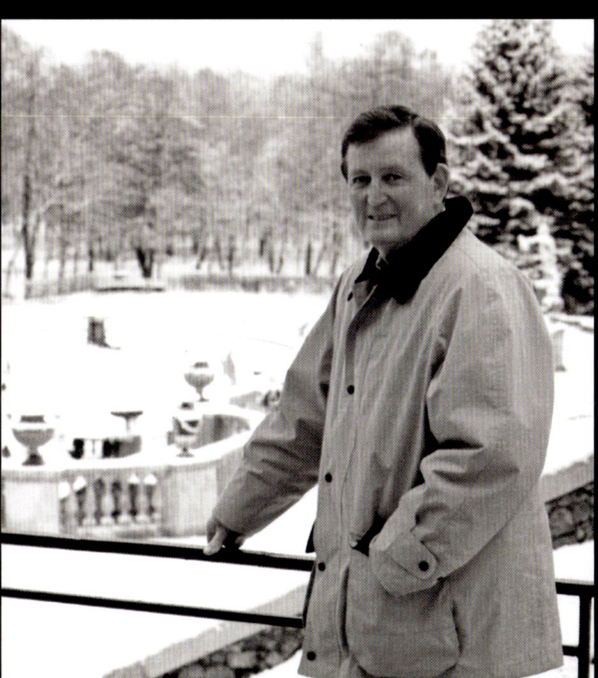

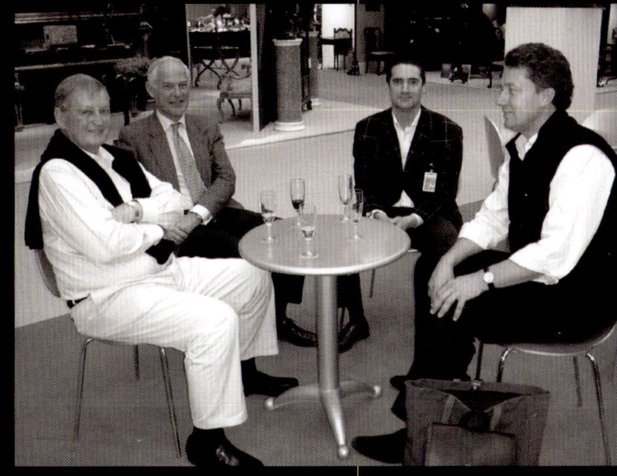

From top left:
(left to right) Sue Rymill, David Roche and Annabel Rymill attending a John Perceval exhibition, probably at Bonython Art Gallery, North Adelaide, 1967.

The Cock's Feathers label sewn into a garment purchased from David Roche's menswear shop.

David Roche awarding Best in Show at the Japanese Kennel Club, Asian International Dog Show, 1996.

David Roche outside Peterhof Palace, St Petersburg, Russia, 1994.

David Roche with Lanto Synge and Thomas Woodham Smith of Mallett Antiques, and Martyn Cook at the 'Olympia' Art and Antiques Fair, London, 2005.

that never ceased even though many of his staff worked there for a great many years. This led to the nickname 'Fermoy Island', as walking through the steel gate and behind the imposing brick walls onto Melbourne Street was like stepping into another domain. It was David's slice of Europe – art, sculpture and manicured gardens in North Adelaide, plus kennelling for 40 dogs. David's rule and routine never wavered and foremost were the three royal shows at Adelaide, Melbourne and Sydney to prepare for and attend every year. While working for David, the chances are you would have known his taste in music as it was piped through garden speakers. Although he culled his large vinyl collection, from those that remain he obviously loved movie soundtracks – *West Side Story*, *South Pacific*, *Hair*, *Oliver*, *The Sound of Music*, and *The King & I*, amongst others. Albums by individual singers included Mario Lanza, Pearl Williams, Al Martino, Ethel Merman, Sammy Davis Jnr, Neil Diamond, Maria Callas, and above all else the voice of American singer Johnny Mathis, with six albums.

Travel gave David freedom and canine judging opened doors. He met Thelma Gray (d. 1985) in the 1960s through the Crufts dog show and the pair became friends. Thelma bred corgis, beagles, chihuahuas (David's house dog) and assisted David many years later in finding 'BG' (Beau Geste), his trusted German shepherd. She was a consultant to HM Queen Elizabeth and the Windsor kennels, which David attended with her. David also counted Lavinia Fitzalan-Howard, Duchess of Norfolk (1916–1995) as a friend after meeting her regularly at dog shows. Also during the 1960s David met American Kay Finch (United States 1903–1994), who had the famous Crown Crest Afghan Kennels in California. They became good friends; David became equally famous for his Afghans and Kay gave him small ceramic and bronze Afghans for which she was well-known. David adored them and they still remain in the collection.

In the United States, David met Geraldine Rockefeller Dodge (1882–1973) through shows she judged and received a token of thanks – a metal 'D' key ring, probably after judging her prestigious Morris & Essex Show in 1955. In Italy, David knew Dr Giuseppe Benelli, Chairman of the Italian Kennel Club, whose kennels are at Il Monte, Galliano de Mugello. In India, David is still remembered for his canine services, meeting Nazeer Yar Jung, Nawab of Hyderabad, and his son, as well as Jaideep Singh, Maharaja of Baria (1929–c. 1987), Gudgerap State, and Chairman of the Kennel Club of India. He also knew Ayesha of Jaipur (born Princess Gayatri Devi 1919–2009). Outside canine circles, he enjoyed the company of David Easton (b. 1937), celebrated American interior designer and the Hon. David Nightingale Hicks (1929–1998), a celebrated English interior decorator and designer. They both visited David at Fermoy House but were not there to redesign his interiors.

After the establishment of his foundation in 1999, David occasionally invited experts to Adelaide to view his collection and give public seminars. This included Tatiana Fabergé (b. 1930), great-granddaughter of Carl Fabergé, with Russian art expert Alice Ilich in 2005, and then Henry (b. 1928) and John (b. 1959) Sandon, experts in English pottery and porcelain, in 2008. Martyn Cook presented regularly and by 2012 David had been encouraged to open a small viewing gallery of his collection next door to Fermoy House.

His philanthropic interests saw him donate funds in 2000 toward De Chazal De Chamerel's important *Portrait of Captain Matthew Flinders* 1806–1807, in memory of his father for the Art Gallery of South Australia. In 2004, he funded the purchase of a superb *Australian colonial sideboard* 1815–1820 in memory of his mother for the Powerhouse Museum in Sydney. He also lent many items to public collections, including the *HMS Resolution table*, c. 1810. Made to commemorate Captain James Cook (1728–1779), David acquired the table in 2003 and immediately arranged for its permanent display at the National Library of Australia in Canberra.

The majority of David's philanthropy in his lifetime was reserved, however, for animal welfare. He paid veterinary bills for people that otherwise would not have been able to save their pets. He gave funds to upgrade the dog park, known as the David Roche Park, in Kilburn, and at the Royal Adelaide Showgrounds, the dog pavilion has for many years been known as the David Roche Pavilion in gratitude for his support of the infrastructure for canine shows as well as trophies and prizes. David supplied many trophies over the years including The Sydney Cup for Breeder of Best in Show presented by the Sydney Kennel Club c. 2000; and Best in Show for the Santa Barbara Kennel Club, California, in 2005.

In recognition of David's service to the community as a benefactor to cultural institutions, a significant supporter and figure within the canine world, and for bequeathing his home and collection for the benefit of the state of South Australia, he was posthumously awarded an AM (Member in the General Division of the said Order of Australia) in June 2013, just months after he died on 27 March 2013, aged 83. David Roche leaves behind a remarkable legacy and a simple wish that each visitor would leave having found a favourite piece to remember.

Robert Reason
Senior Curator

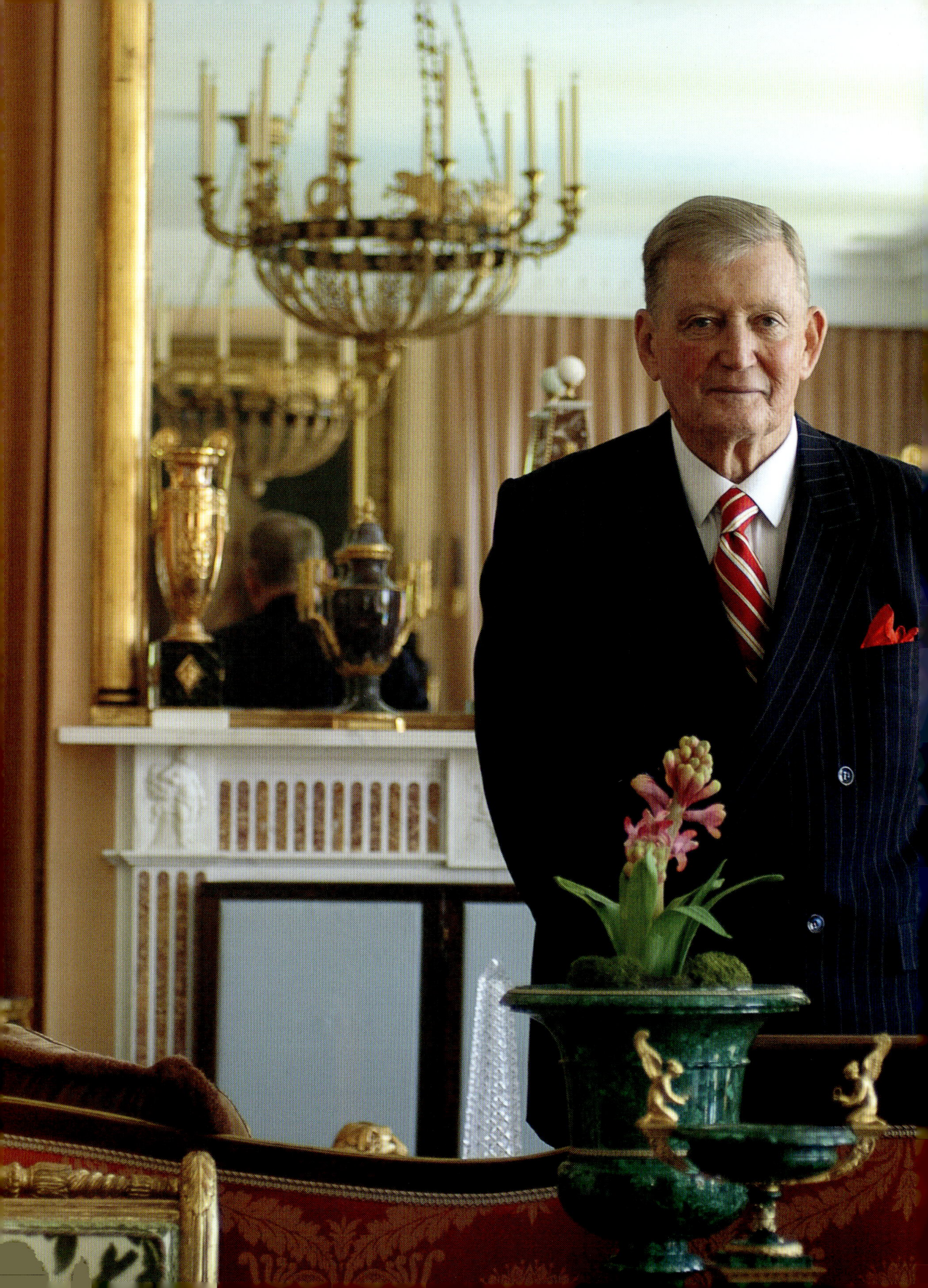

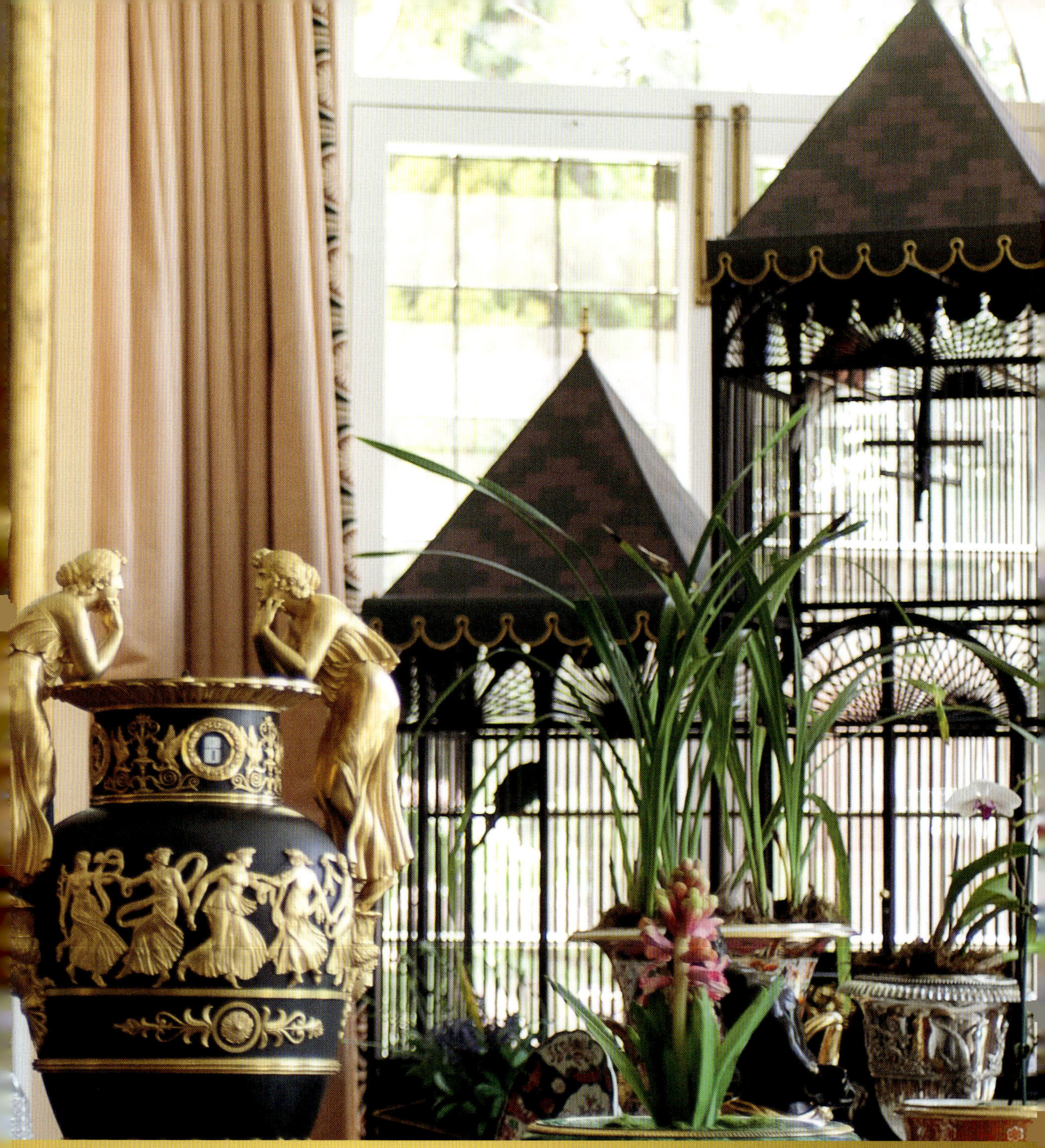

A TOUR OF *Fermoy House*

David Roche purchased his home at 241 Melbourne Street, North Adelaide, on 13 January 1954 from the Bevan sisters. He named it Fermoy House after his French-Irish grandparents. An early Australian Federation villa, David remodelled the front verandah to make it more Georgian in appearance and built the Roman room on the rear in the early 1970s.

THE INTERIOR

Previous spread: David Roche in the Roman room, 2008.

Opposite page: Top: the front garden at Fermoy House, 2013.

Bottom: David Roche in the Roman room, 2008.

Some 3,000 items are now on view throughout Fermoy House, which David Roche developed over a lifetime. The interiors and the collection have been transformed since the 1950s when the home had the character of most suburban residences. It was David's continuous cultivation of a deeper appreciation of art from the English Regency and French Empire periods that drove the change to more cohesive and impressive room settings beginning in the 1970s. Only 18th century porcelain and Staffordshire ware were a constant. His last great passion was for Russian art, which he began collecting in earnest after travelling to Russia in the 1990s. Frequent trips to Europe and England saw David visiting country houses, chateaus, palaces, museums and galleries from which he took elements for the interiors of his home. Aware of the difference in scale and volume, his suburban-sized Adelaide house slowly evolved into David's own compressed cabinet of curiosities of the finest sort.

A private and shy man around his collection with visiting dealers, experts or interested parties, he would never boast about his collection or what he had bought. Instead, he would weigh up people's answers and reactions and tailor the length of the stay to suit. Interior designers visited and offered opinions over the years. They were frequently met with a smile, but normally left empty-handed. David had his own vision and bought some marvellous papers and textiles on his international travels. An exception to the rule was Chrissie Jeffery of Stitches Soft Furnishings in Sydney, who worked with David to create some of his most dramatic window furnishings. In his lifetime there were a variety of long pile carpets covered with Persian rugs of differing styles, sizes and quality. Ever practical, he thought ahead to the future when it would be a museum and selected new carpets for the house. Today the interiors and the contents of each room continue to reflect how David used and lived in them.

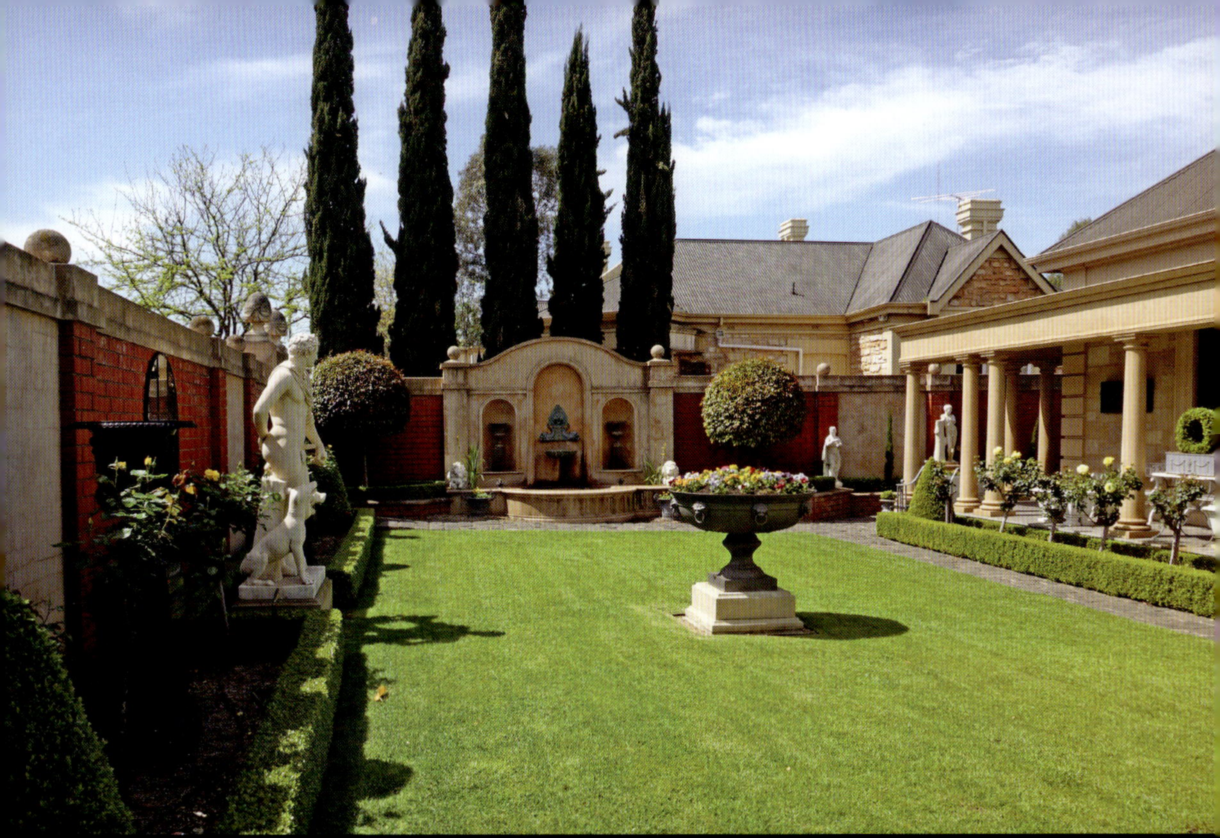

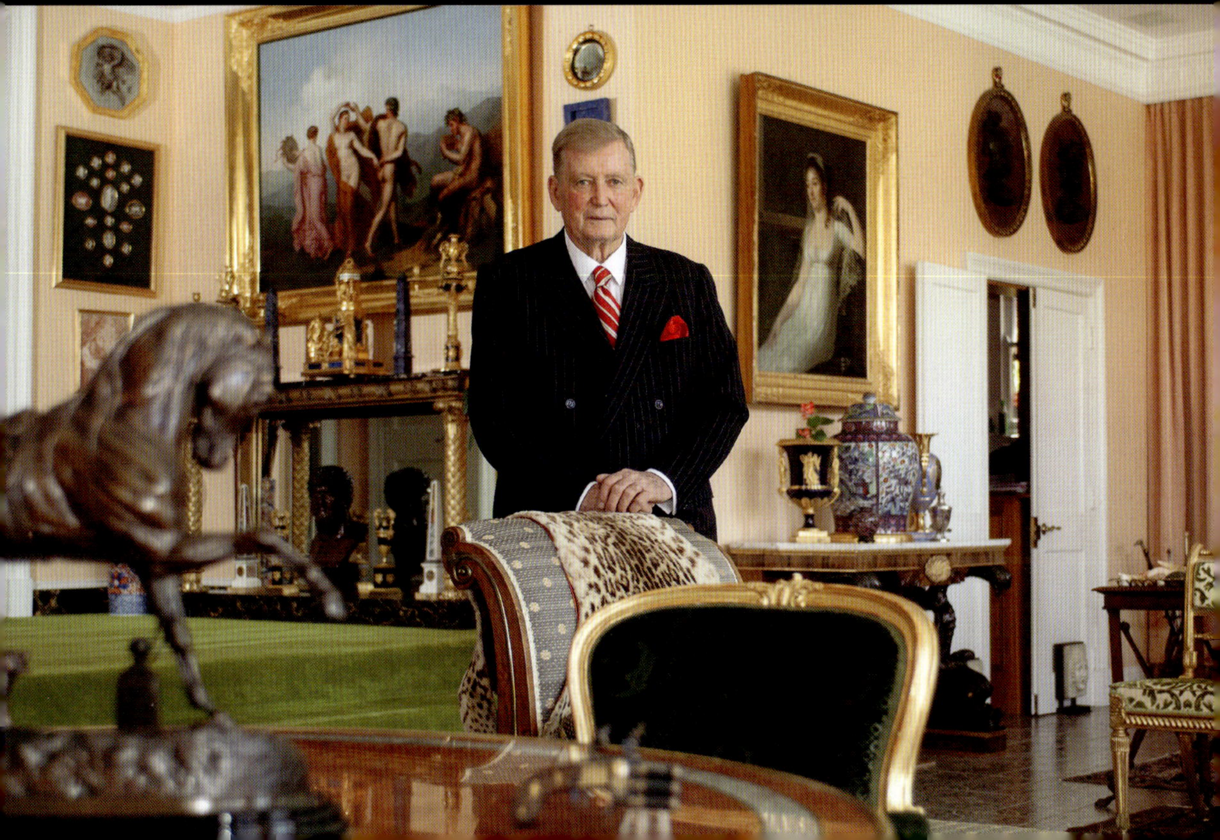

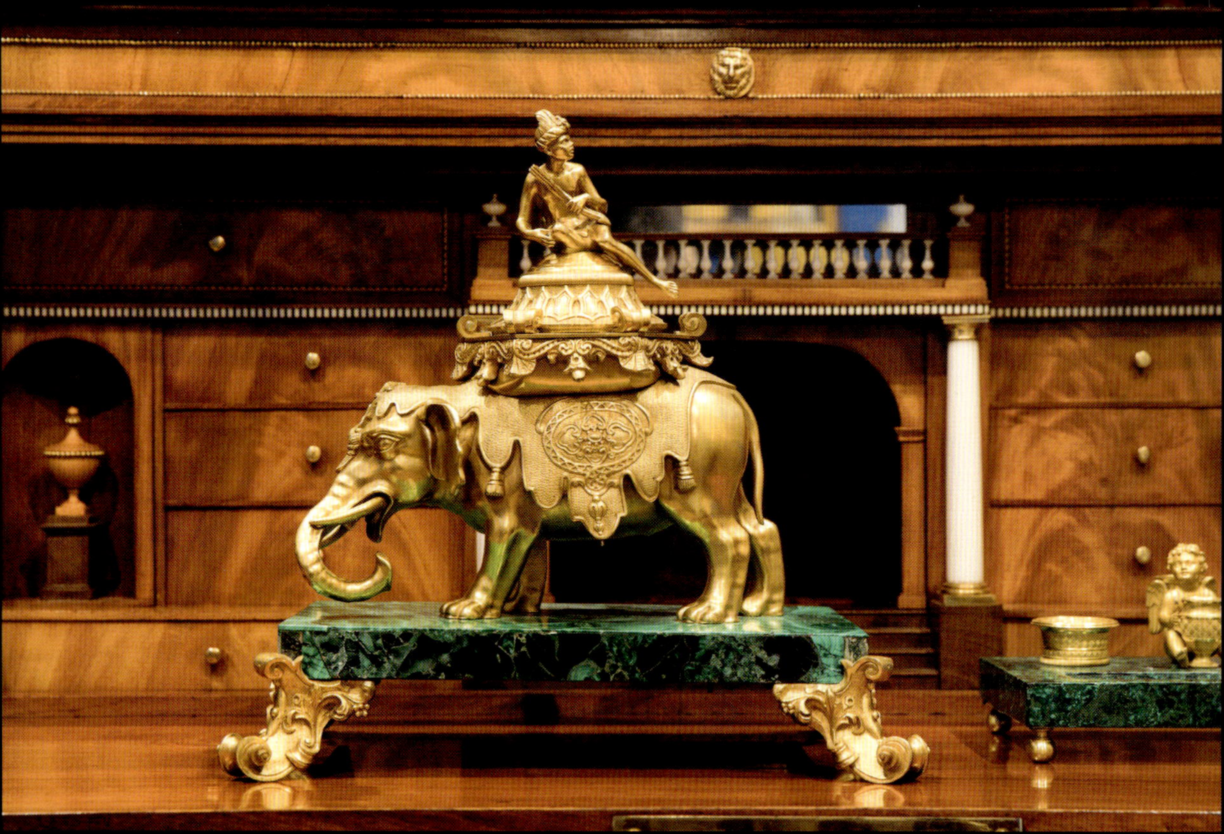

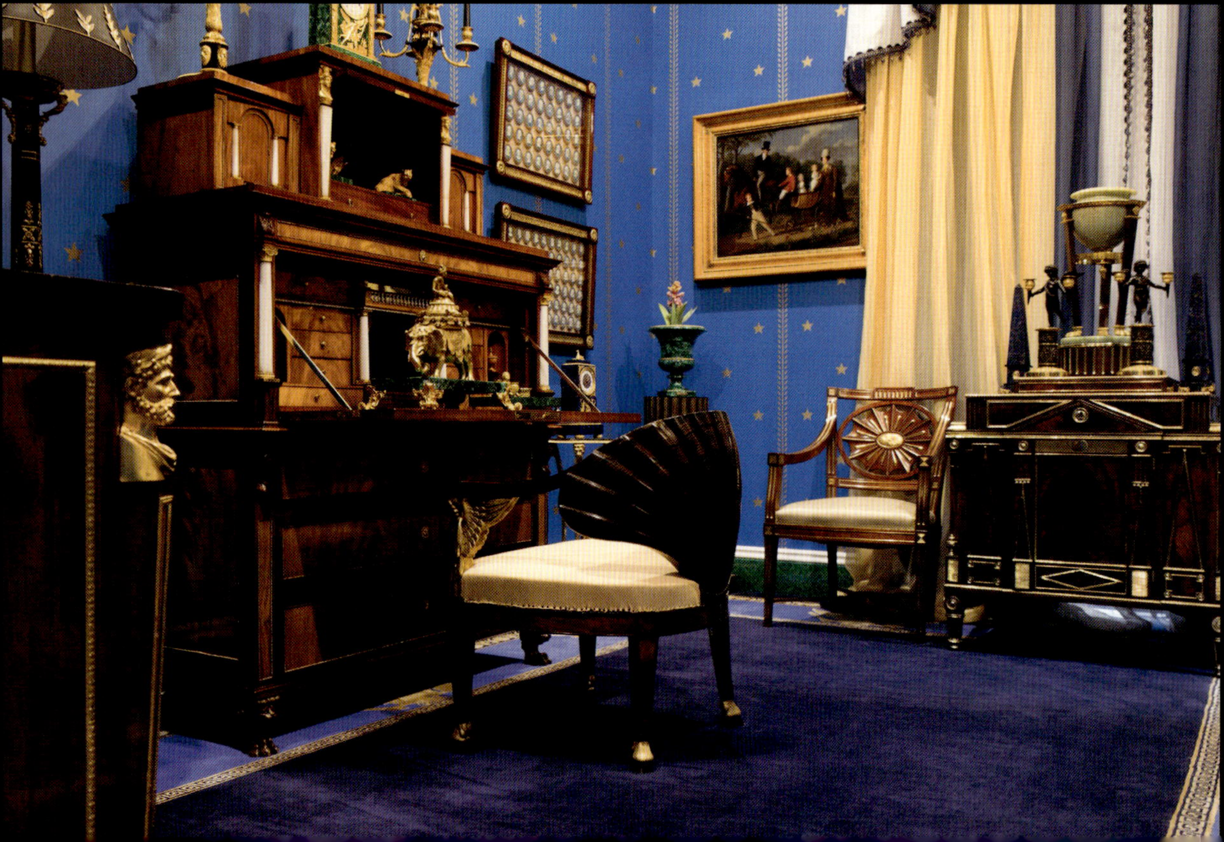

THE RUSSIAN ROOM

Following a theme from Pavlovsk Palace, St Petersburg, and Maria Feodorovna, wife of Paul I, in 2010, David commissioned a reproduction of wallpaper found in Pavlovsk and a bespoke carpet (2011) adorned with the crest of the Empress. Following his wishes, these remained in storage until after his death and replaced what was the Green bedroom in early 2016. The French Empire marble *Fireplace*, c. 1820, with inset Wedgwood medallions, was installed in 2009 and the *Swan head pelmet*, c. 1830, and drapes in 2016. For David, this was the main guest bedroom used on occasion by visiting dog judges and friends. David also upgraded the bed for this room to a Russian Empire *Sleigh bed*, c. 1810, in the manner of Andrei Voronikhin (Russia 1759–1814) with carved eagle heads to the top rail.

Opposite page:
Top: *Elephant inkwell*, France, 1829.

Bottom: The Russian room, featuring a Noach Sorman *Secretaire*, 1814, a Russian *Shellback armchair*, c. 1805, with wallpaper and carpet commissioned by David Roche.

This page:
Top: *Eagle tazza*, Russia, c. 1840.

Bottom: *Cigar humidor*, Russia, c. 1890.

Furniture

The room is centred on an important mahogany, ormolu-mounted, *Secretaire*, 1814, by Noach Sorman (Sweden 1789–1822). Sweden had close ties to Russia and Sorman regularly exported furniture like this for the Russian market. The secretaire contains a number of levers that when activated reveal hidden compartments. The smaller, mahogany *Secretaire*, c. 1795, is widely published in books on Russian furniture; interestingly, during a restoration in 2010 it was found to be German-made in Munich, again for the Russian market. The *Pair of armchairs,* 1790–1800, are attributed to the Russian architect and designer Andrei Voronikhin, who worked on Pavlovsk Palace and supplied similar chairs for the Lantern room. The *Shellback armchair*, c. 1805, and substantial *Commode*, c. 1785, are both fine examples of Russian neoclassical furniture.

Lighting

The room is lit by an attractive Russian *Gustavian-style chandelier*, c. 1790, of delicate form with a stem of cobalt blue blown glass. Acquired in Sweden, it was hung in the Russian room in 2008. David acquired many pairs of candelabra, and this room features three sets, all Russian, dating from 1800 to 1820.

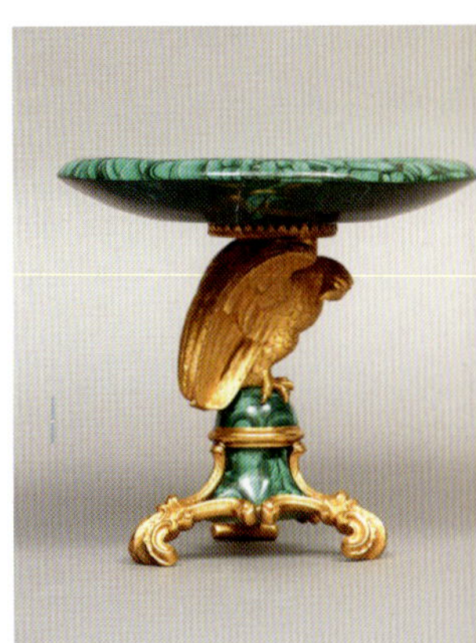

Principal Objects

The main feature of the room are the many malachite objects that David collected such as the French ormolu *Elephant inkwell*, 1829, and the fine Russian *Eagle tazza*, c. 1840. The large *Cigar humidor*, c. 1890, was inherited from his mother and was likely a Russian icon box, before being altered in London to its current form. The use of semi-precious stones in objects and as polished specimens fascinated David. The Ivan Hallberg (designer, Russia

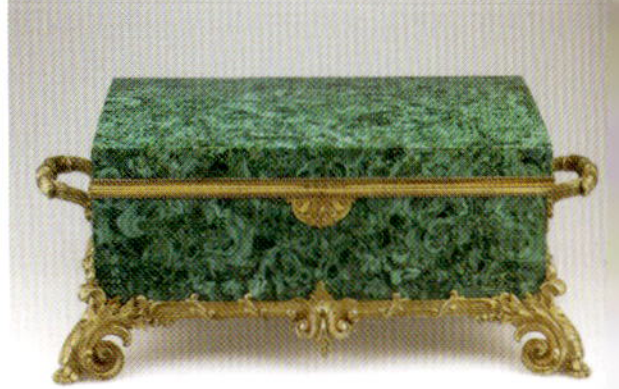

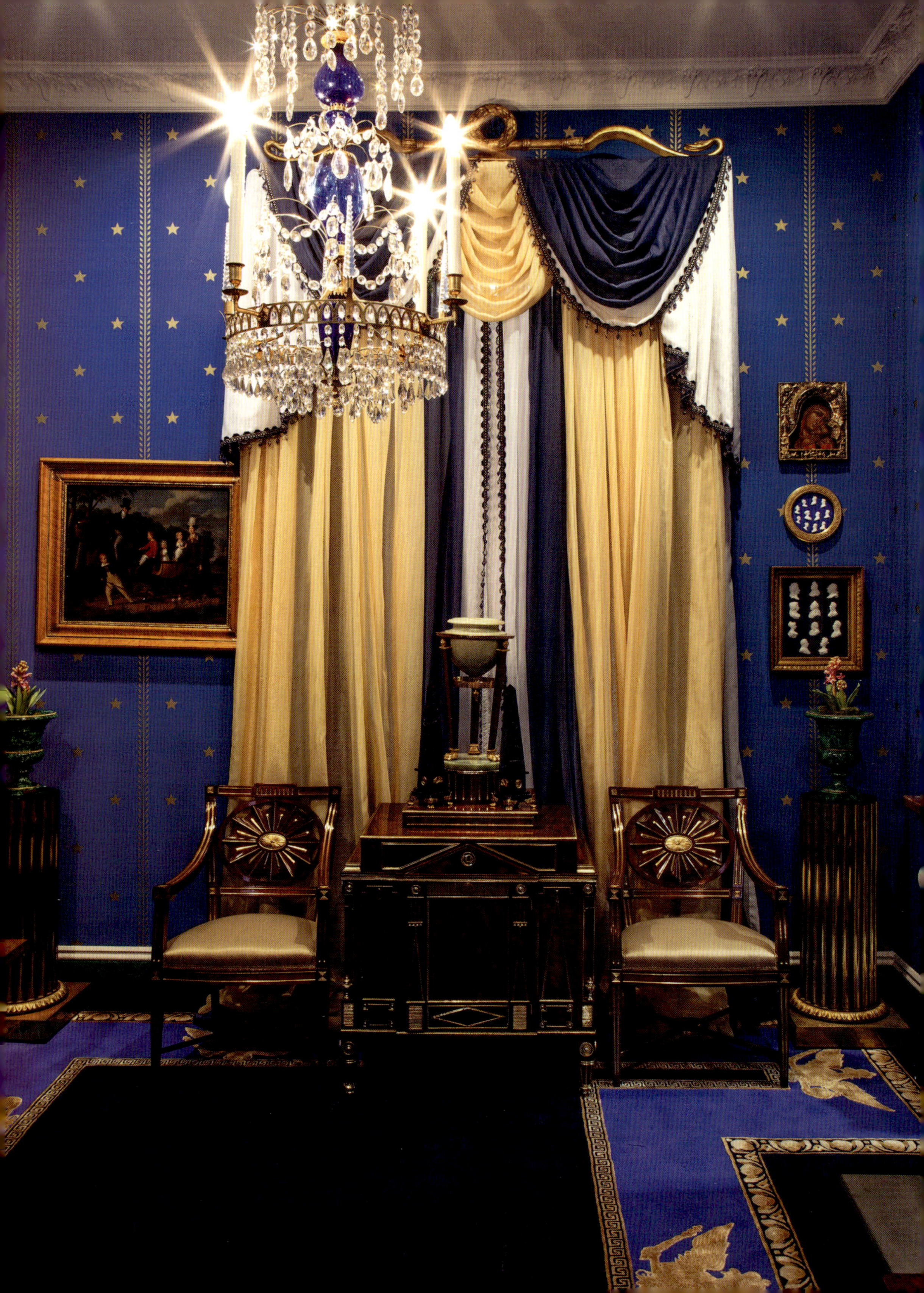

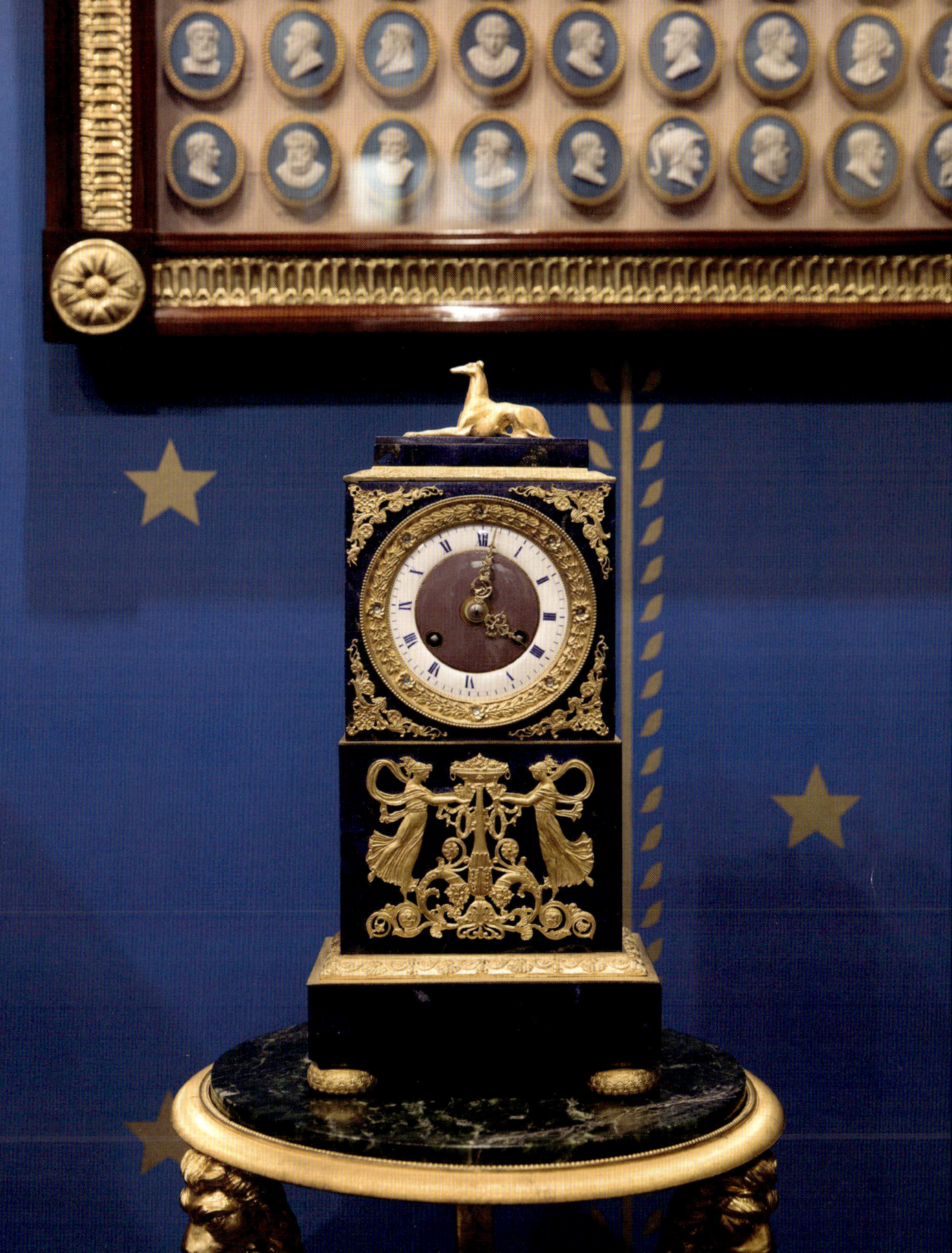

Previous spread:
Left: The Russian room, featuring a German *Secretaire*, c. 1795, *a Pair of armchairs*, attributed to Andrei Voronikhin, 1790–1800, a Russian *Tazza*, c. 1840, and a *Gustavian-style chandelier*, c. 1790.

Right: The Russian room (detail) with a French lapis lazuli *Clock*, c. 1810, sitting on a French *Gueridon* table, c. 1795. On the wall, a framed set of Russian *Intaglios*, c. 1800.

1778–1863) Russian *Tazza*, c. 1840, is a fine example, combining antigorite and porphyry with ormolu mounts. The lapis lazuli *Pair of obelisks*, c. 1922, were bought in London in 2007, with a Maria Callas (1923–1977) provenance.

Principal Pictures

No Russian room would be complete without images of the Russian imperial family and David's collecting focussed on the reign of Catherine the Great (1729–1796), her son Paul I (1754–1801), and his children. The two paintings David acquired are both formal court images of the ruler in full regalia (including the blue sash of St Andrew the Apostle) of the type used to furnish diplomatic embassies or the like. The image of *Catherine the Great, Empress of Russia*, c. 1791, is attributed to Johann Baptist Lampi the Elder (Austria

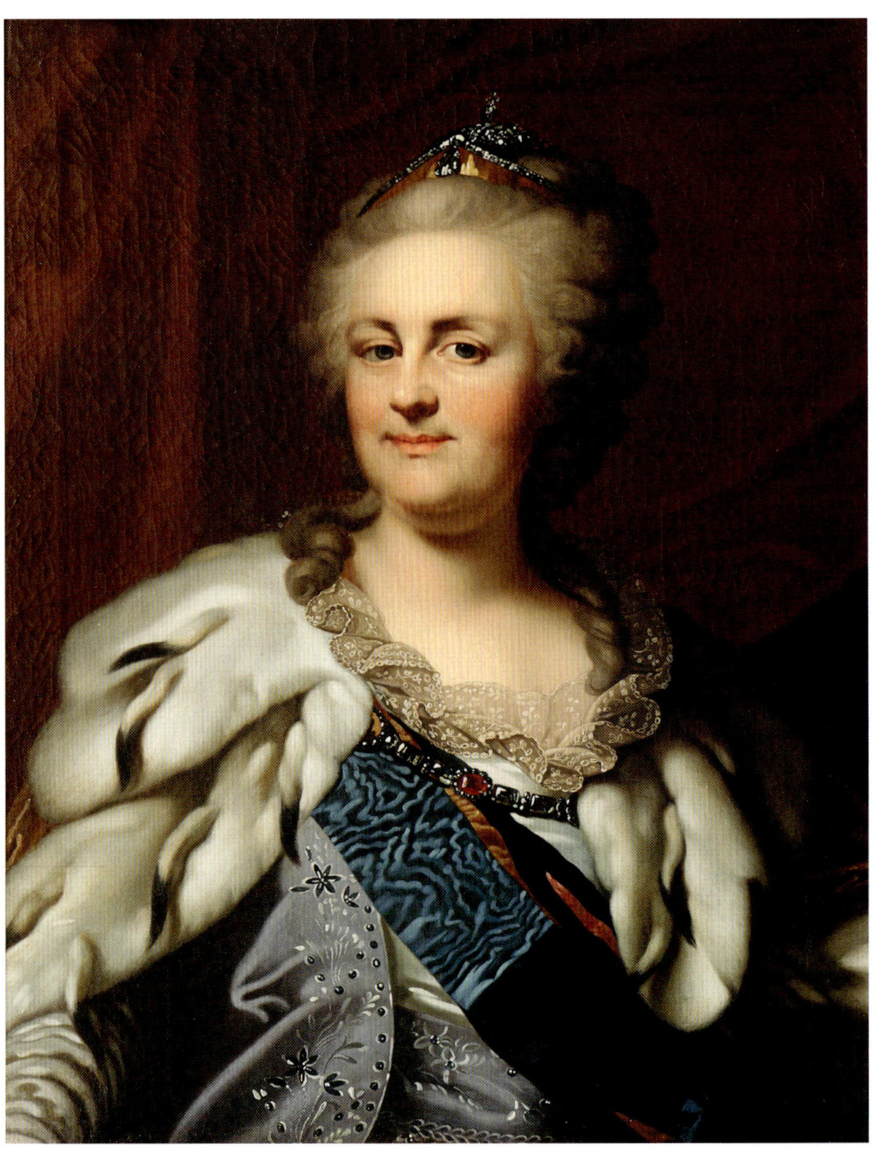

Right: *Catherine the Great, Empress of Russia*, attributed to Johann Baptist Lampi the Elder, c. 1791.

1751–1830) and was later owned by the 7th Count of Villagonzalo (1851–1901), Spanish Ambassador in St Petersburg (1893–1897). The second is by Franz Krüger (Germany 1797–1857), who visited Russia in 1832 and likely painted *Nicholas I, Tsar of Russia*, during his stay. Krüger also painted a larger portrait of the Tsar, which now hangs at the Museum of Tsarskoye Selo. An intriguing painting by Anthelme-François Lagrenée (France 1774–1832) of *A gentleman (probably Andrei Voronikhin) on horseback with family*, c. 1810, appealed to David immensely, the charming scene loosely based on the park at Pavlovsk Palace. Voronikhin was an accomplished architect and designer, who worked on the Palace – a residence David adored – after a disastrous fire in 1803, which led to David purchasing Voronikhin-designed pieces.

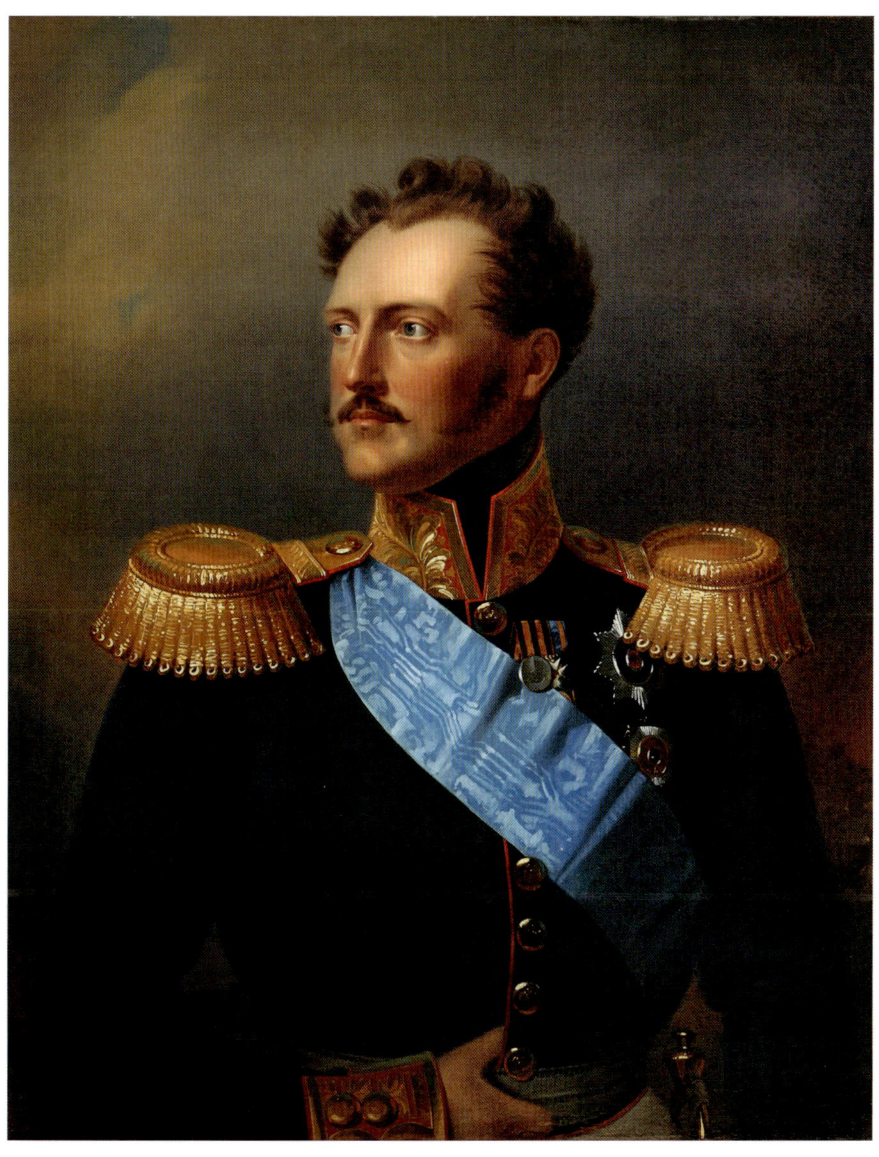

Left: *Nicholas I, Tsar of Russia*, Franz Krüger, c. 1832.

THE RED HALLWAY

Running the full length of the house is a dark green carpet with black stars, which David had started to design after seeing a similar carpet at the White House in Washington DC. Following David's wishes in 2011, Chicago-based interior designer Lewis Wallack had the carpet woven in 2014 and laid in 2016. The walls are covered with raspberry-coloured, French silk damask wallpaper hung in 2000. The two pairs of pillars supporting archways have a faux-painted malachite finish and gilding by Steve Baliga, dating from 1999. Previously, the hallway had three Blades of Piccadilly Regency chandeliers and a large Sheraton-style mahogany bookcase, all of which now reside in the new museum wing.

Furniture

A handsome pair of Regency *Games tables*, c. 1805, after designs by Thomas Hope (Britain 1769–1831) and Thomas Chippendale the Younger (Britain 1749–1822) line the hallway. They feature distinctive ebonised and gilded hocked monopodia supports terminating in winged Egyptian masks and a 'D' form rosewood top. Acquired separately in 1995 and 2008, they bring together a pair that almost certainly belonged to London dealer Temple Williams, as well as the acclaimed British collector, Wilfrid Evill. The French Empire *Cabinet*, c. 1820, is stamped for Georges-Alphonse Jacob-Desmalter (France 1799–1870), from the family of cabinetmakers to nobility and royalty. This was David's telephone cabinet, next to which is his large, comfortable 'O'Connor Don' Irish Regency *Armchair*, c. 1810. The mahogany *Longcase clock*, c. 1815, is by Benjamin Lewis Vulliamy (Britain 1780–1854), clock-maker to George III and the Prince Regent (later George IV).

This page: Pair of Regency *Games tables*, after Thomas Hope and Thomas Chippendale the Younger, c. 1805.

Opposite page: The Red hallway looking toward the den. Topmost, a Russian *Chandelier*, c. 1810, below, the *Longcase clock*, c. 1815, by Benjamin Lewis Vulliamy.

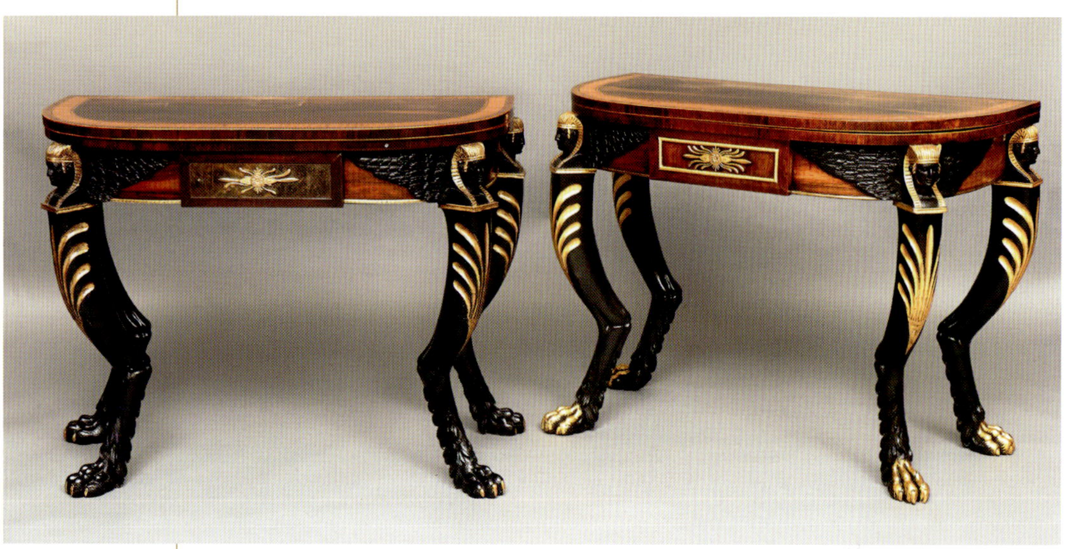

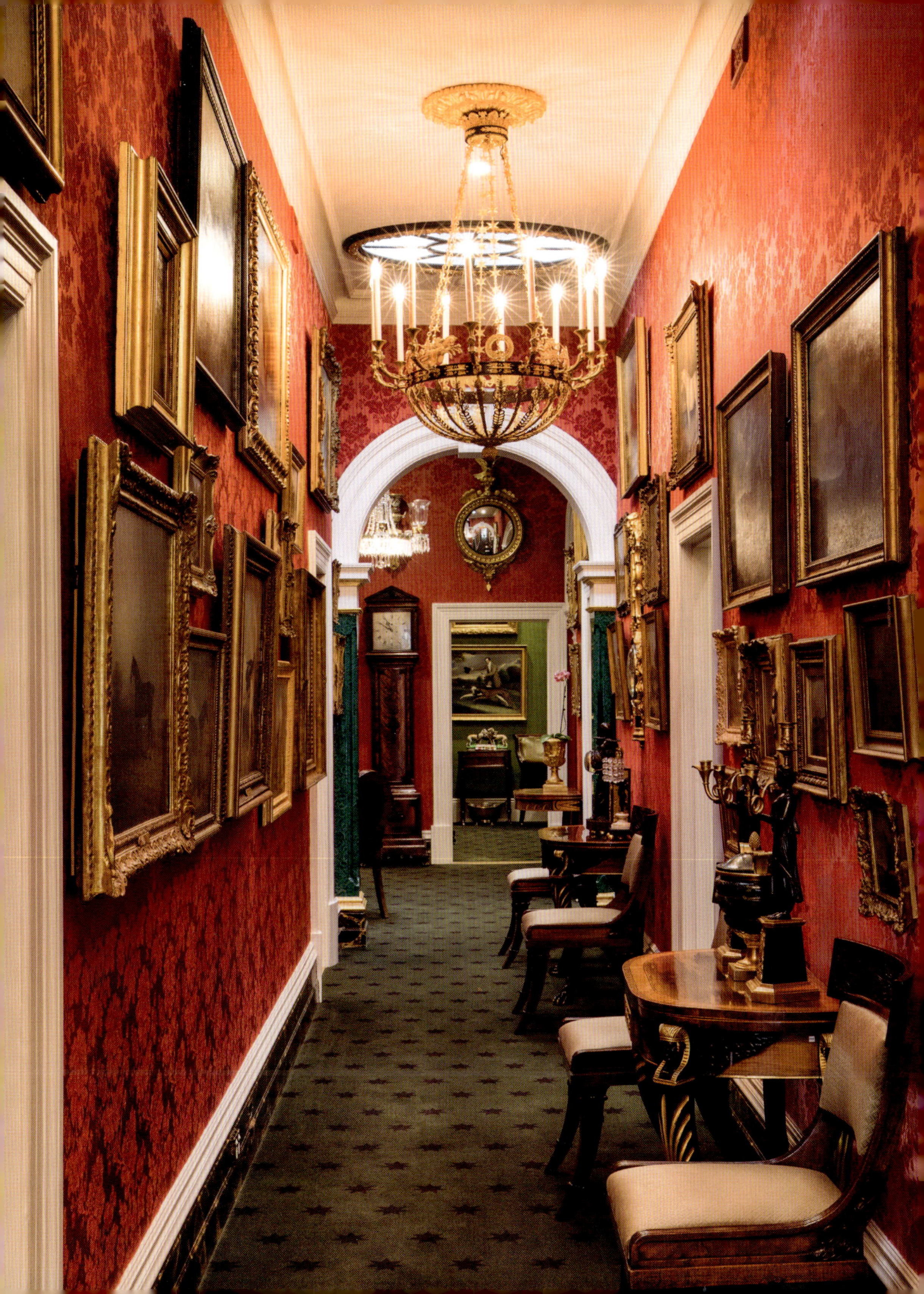

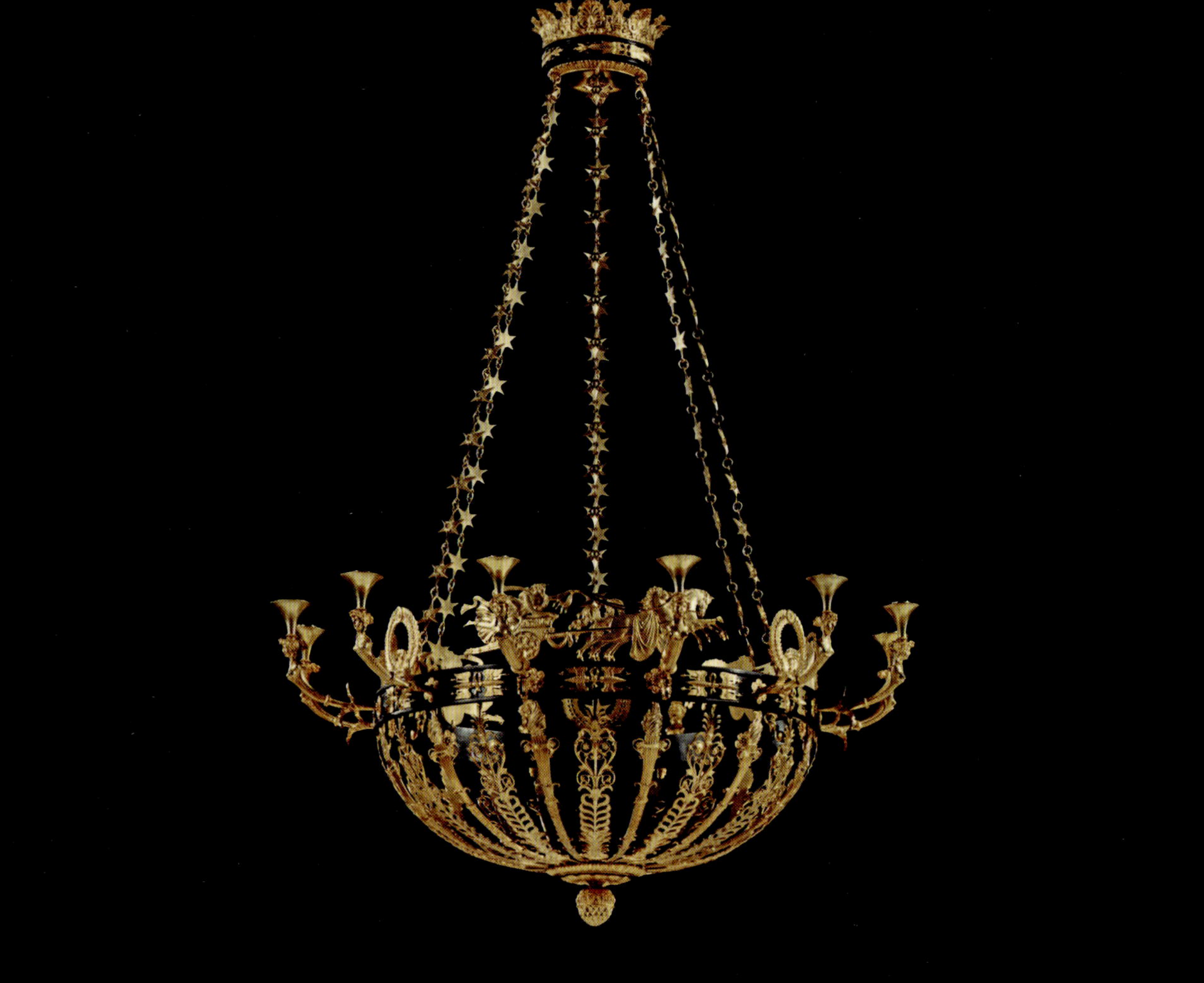

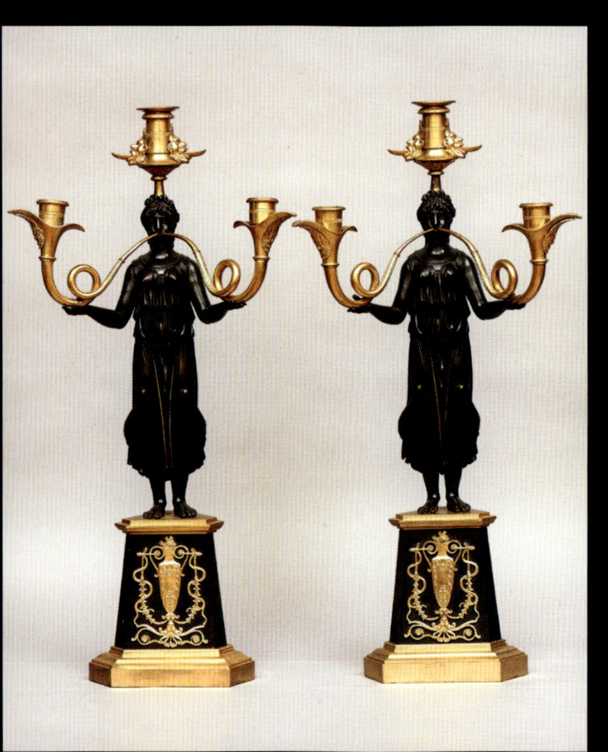

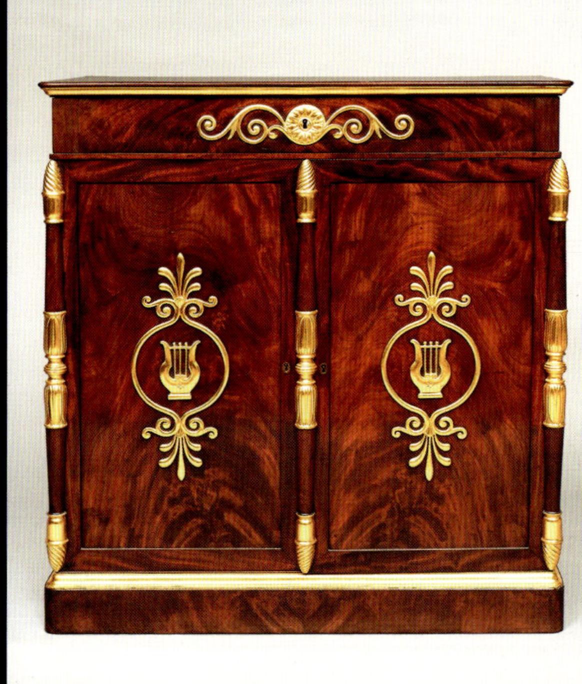

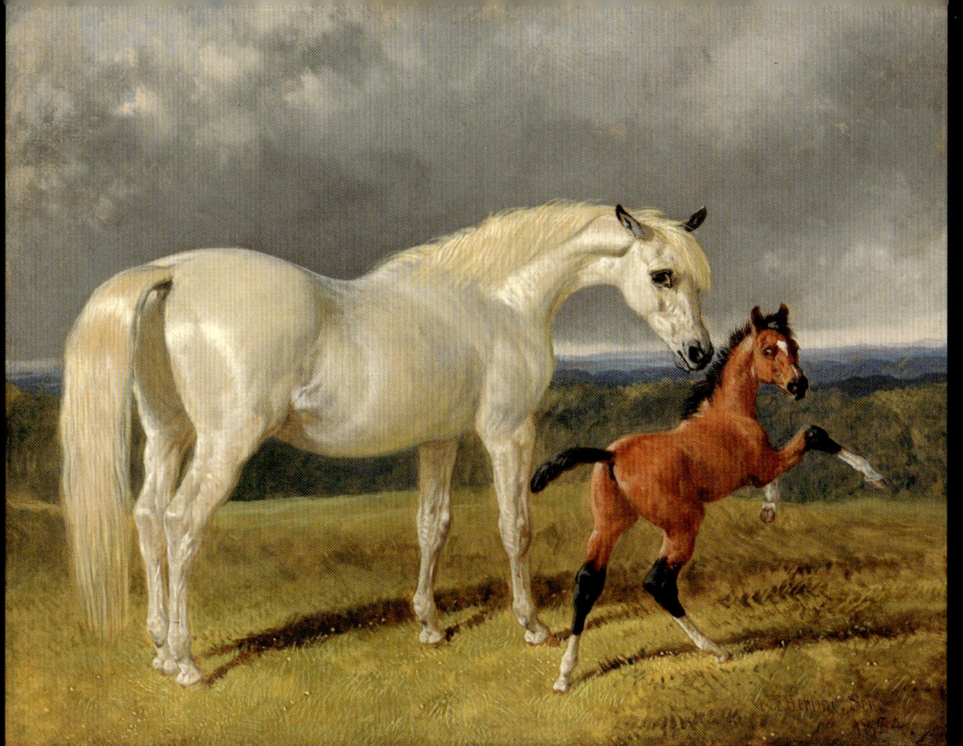

Opposite page:
Clockwise from top:
Chandelier, Russia, c. 1810.

Cabinet, Jacob-Desmalter, c. 1820.

Pair of three-light candelabra, attributed to Pierre-Philippe Thomire, c. 1805.

This page:
Top: *White mare and foal*, Frederick Herring Snr, 1854.

Bottom: *Bay hunter with a black pony and a hound*, Charles Towne, 1812.

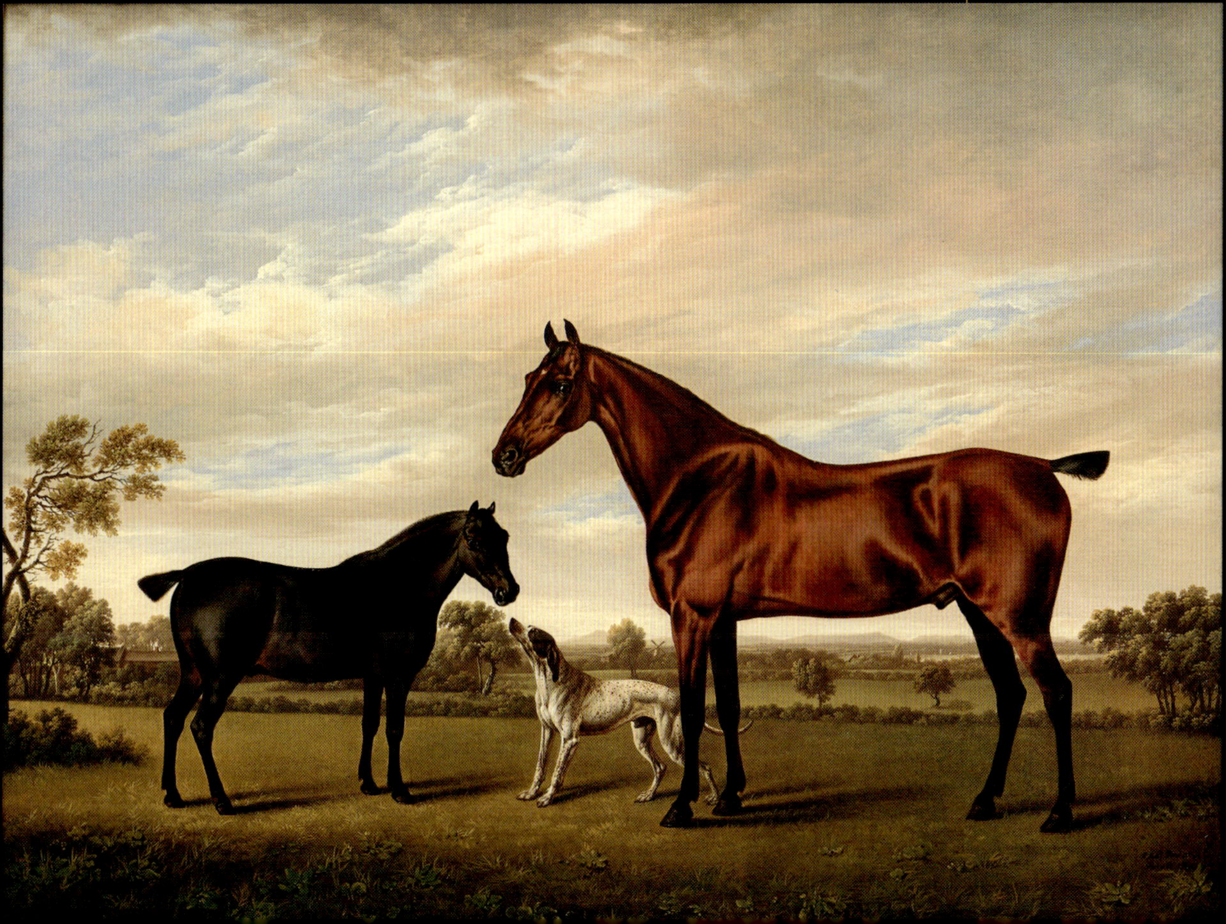

Lighting

A superb pair of gilt-bronze Russian Empire *Chandeliers*, c. 1810, hang in the hallway, bought originally for the Roman room. In the neoclassic Greek Revival-style, they hang from six star suspension chains supporting large basket-shaped dishes issuing 12 candle branches, the ring surmounted by horse drawn chariots symbolising victory. The *Pair of three-light candelabra*, c. 1805, on the games table are attributed to Pierre-Philippe Thomire (France 1751–1843), after a Pierre-Louis-Arnulphe Duguers de Montrosier (France 1758–1806) design of trumpeting neoclassic maidens.

Principal Objects

The English Regency vitrine displays two significant French Empire services that were acquired by David because they contain early depictions of Australian flora and fauna. The Pierre Neppel Manufactory *Part dessert service*, 1805–1810, includes a plate illustrating the *Vue Du Jardin Des Plantes* menagerie with kangaroos in Paris. This service with views of France was reputedly owned by Pauline Borghese (née Bonaparte) in Italy. The Paris Porcelain *Part zoological coffee and tea service*, c. 1805, similarly depicts a kangaroo and more unusually, a Tasmanian devil or spotted quoll. Situated on the games tables are a French *Covered vase* in porfido verde and ormolu, c. 1825, and the famous Thomas Hope model *Isis clock (Pendule à L'Égyptienne)*, 1805–1810, manufactured in France and attributed to Andre-Antoine Ravrio (France 1759–1814).

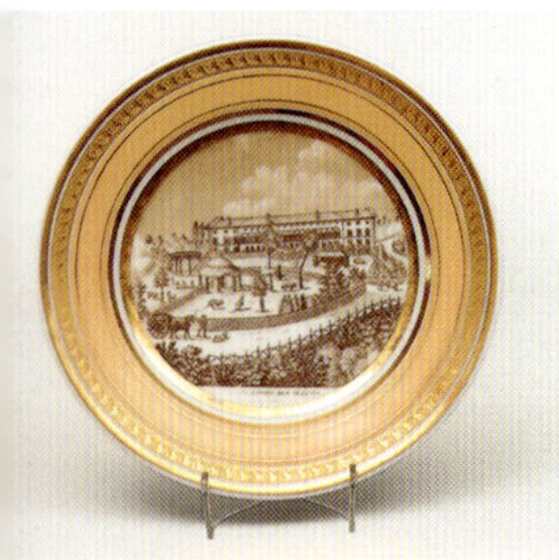

Above: Part dessert service (plate illustrating the *Vue Du Jardin Des Plantes*), Pierre Neppel Manufactory, 1805–1810.

Right: Part zoological coffee and tea service (cup and saucer with kangaroo), Paris Porcelain, c. 1805.

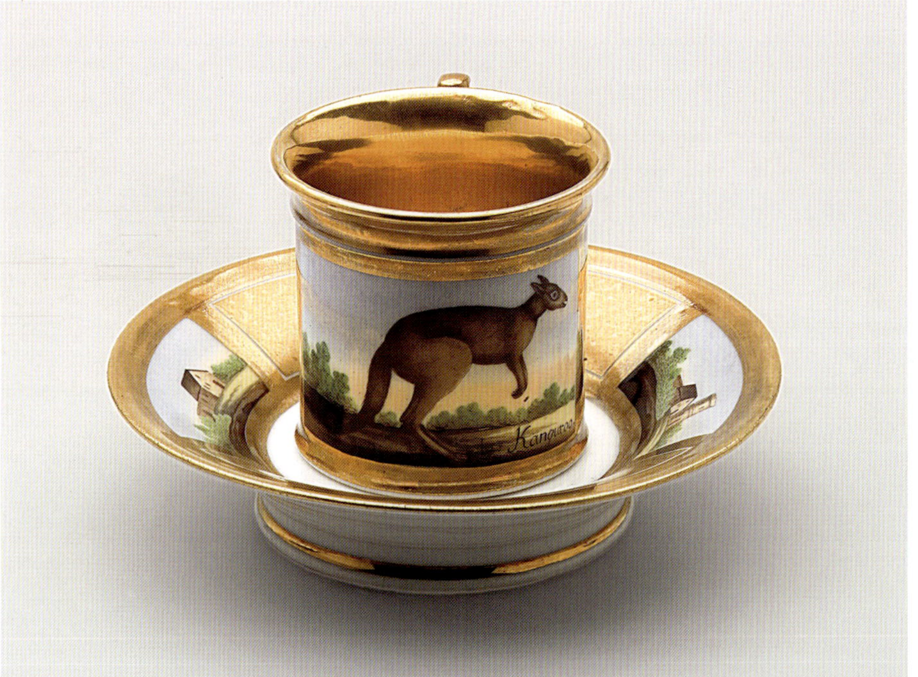

Principal Pictures

The hallway was a favourite space that David used to display his 19th century English sporting paintings, a genre also collected by his father. David would later inherit some pictures, which added to his own significant collection. The work of John Frederick Herring Snr (Britain 1795–1865) was a particular favourite of David's as the artist convincingly captured the 'spirit', energy and anatomy of the horse. *White mare and foal*, 1854, and *Mr. H.M. Greaves's liver chestnut hunter, tethered to a gate at Page Hall, Yorkshire*, 1840, are two excellent examples by this talented painter. Other paintings of note include Charles Towne's (Britain 1763–1840) *Bay hunter with a black pony and a hound*, 1812, and Abraham Cooper's, RA (Britain 1787–1868) spirited *Grey stallion* (Millennium), 1820. For the horse racing enthusiast, the pair of paintings *Roxanna* and *Scham*, 1845, by Frank Calcroft Turner (Britain 1782–1846), illustrate the Godolphin Arabian stallion and its mate; their bloodline remaining famous. The delightful painting by Edmund Havell Jnr (Britain 1785–1864) of *Mr R. Hanbury's favourite foxhound*, 1844, was purchased in London in the early 1950s and gifted to David by his mother. A brewery family, Sampson Hanbury, Robert's uncle, was a renowned Master of Hounds at Puckeridge kennels, Hertfordshire from 1801–1832. Slightly offbeat paintings of poultry were frequently acquired by David, mainly in naïve-style for the kitchen. The one exception is the grand-scaled Ernst Hasse (Germany 1819–1860), *The fowl run (Geflügelhof)*, 1854.

Below: *Mr R. Hanbury's favourite foxhound*, Edmund Havell Jnr, 1844.

Left: *The fowl run (Geflügelhof)*, Ernst Hasse, 1854.

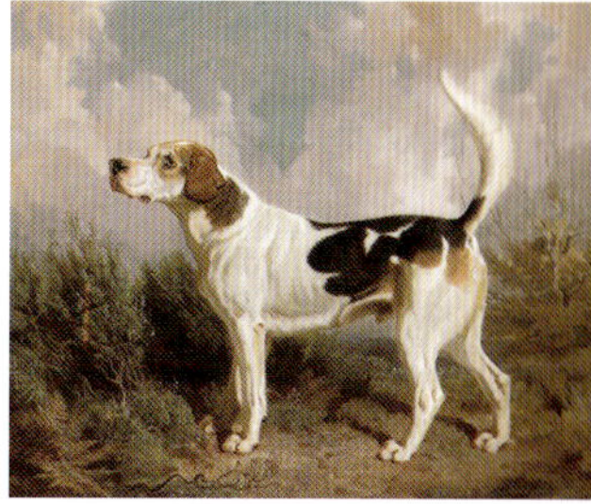

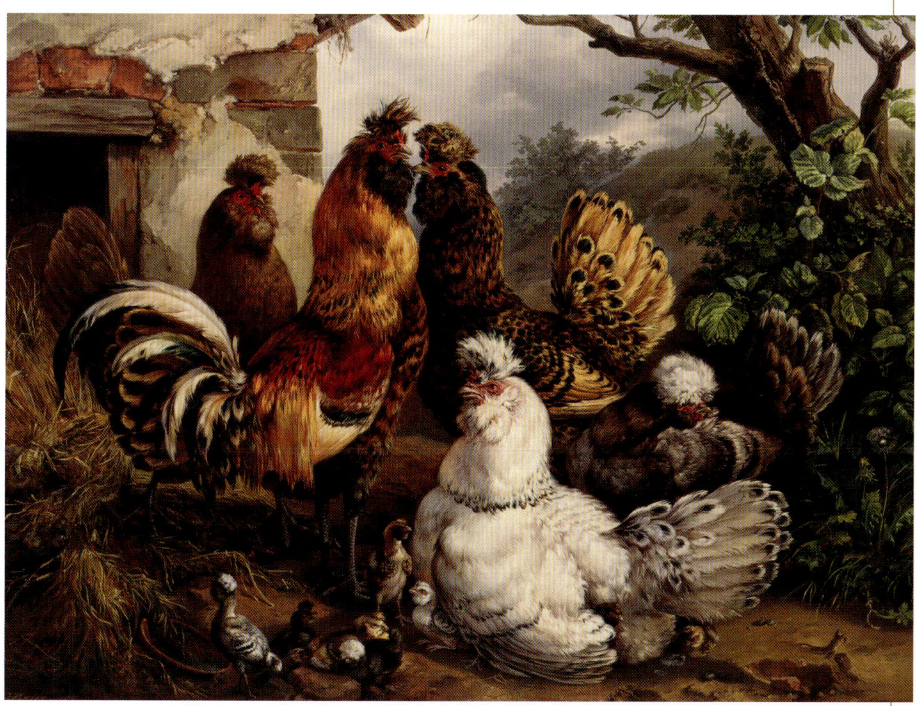

THE DRESSING ROOM AND ENSUITE

A spacious area for a dressing room and ensuite was created off the main bedroom, from what would have been a smaller bedroom. The timber cupboards were repurposed and glazed in early 2016 to display David's considerable collection of winning canine ribbons, rosettes, trophies and memorabilia, including photographs and pedigree certificates. A *Pair of George IV argand lights*, c. 1830, illuminates the room. The bathroom is painted trompe-l'oeil to resemble Hadrian's villa at Tivoli outside Rome – statues, gardens and ponds feature by Adelaide artist Robert Stirling. David employed Robert in 1993 and also had him paint two pieces of Wedgwood black basalt ware in faux niches. Small bronzes and ormolu statuettes are displayed on a high windowsill and on the basin cabinet sit a *Pair of glass obelisks*, c. 1810, attributed to Baccarat (France established 1764), which David purchased in London in 1982. The marble Grand Tour copy of *Capitoline Antinous* is by Domenico Castellani (Italy d. 1821) and dated 1781.

Left: *Pair of glass obelisks*, attributed to Baccarat, c. 1810.

Right: The trompe-l'oeil ensuite featuring an Italian 19th century *Statue of a Bacchant*.

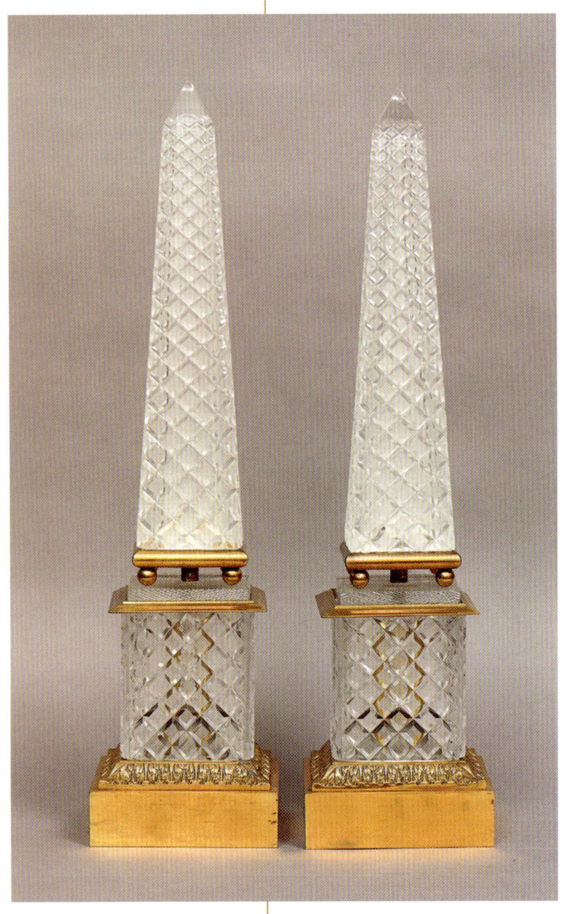

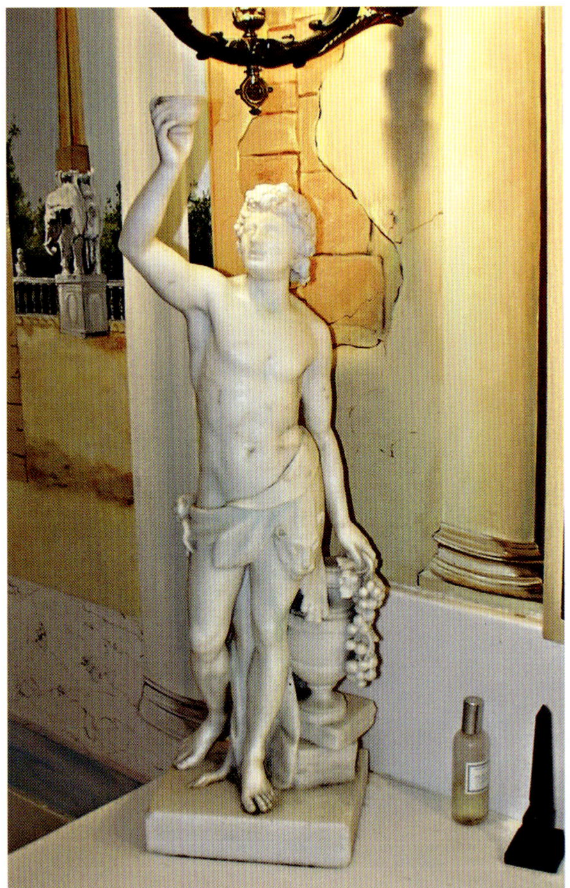

THE MAIN BEDROOM

The bedroom was David's most treasured room, filled with English Regency and French Empire period furniture, paintings, sculptures, and objets d'art. New purchases and favourite objects found a place in this room so that David could enjoy them every night and when he woke in the morning. The bespoke Zoffany 'oak-garland' wallpaper was ordered in Britain in 2000, replacing one selected by designer Marion Hall Best (1905–1988), possibly by Florence Broadhurst (1899–1977). David's mother was friends with Best, and they likely chose the paper for Fermoy House in the 1960s. David's favourite faux-leopard fur velvet for his bedspread and upholstery came from Lelièvre, Paris, designers and manufacturers of fine fabrics. The addition of an exquisite set of curtains in the High-Regency style, made by Chrissie Jeffery of Stitches Soft Furnishings Sydney, c. 2001, completed a sumptuous room that David adored. Chrissie and David referred to James Arrowsmith's *Analysis of Drapery* for inspiration. The silk fabric is Taffeta Faille du Barry by Veraseta, Paris, selected to match the colour of the

Below: The main bedroom featuring a French Empire-style bed, Hopilliart and Leroy, c. 1900; faux-leopard fur velvet bedspread from Lelièvre in Paris; *Dish light chandelier*, c. 1800; and bedside *Pedestal cabinets*, c. 1810, Spanish. The Oak-garland wallpaper is by Zoffany.

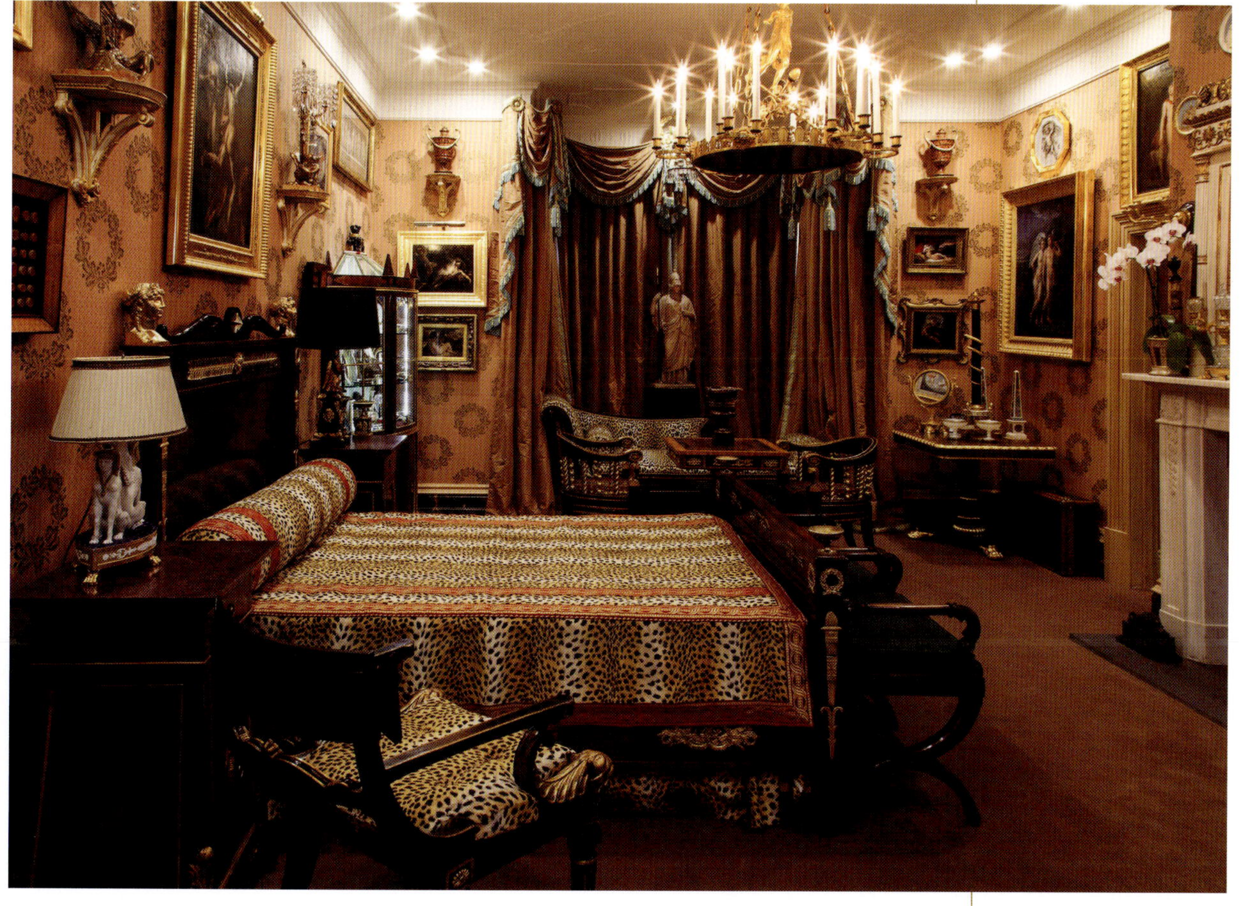

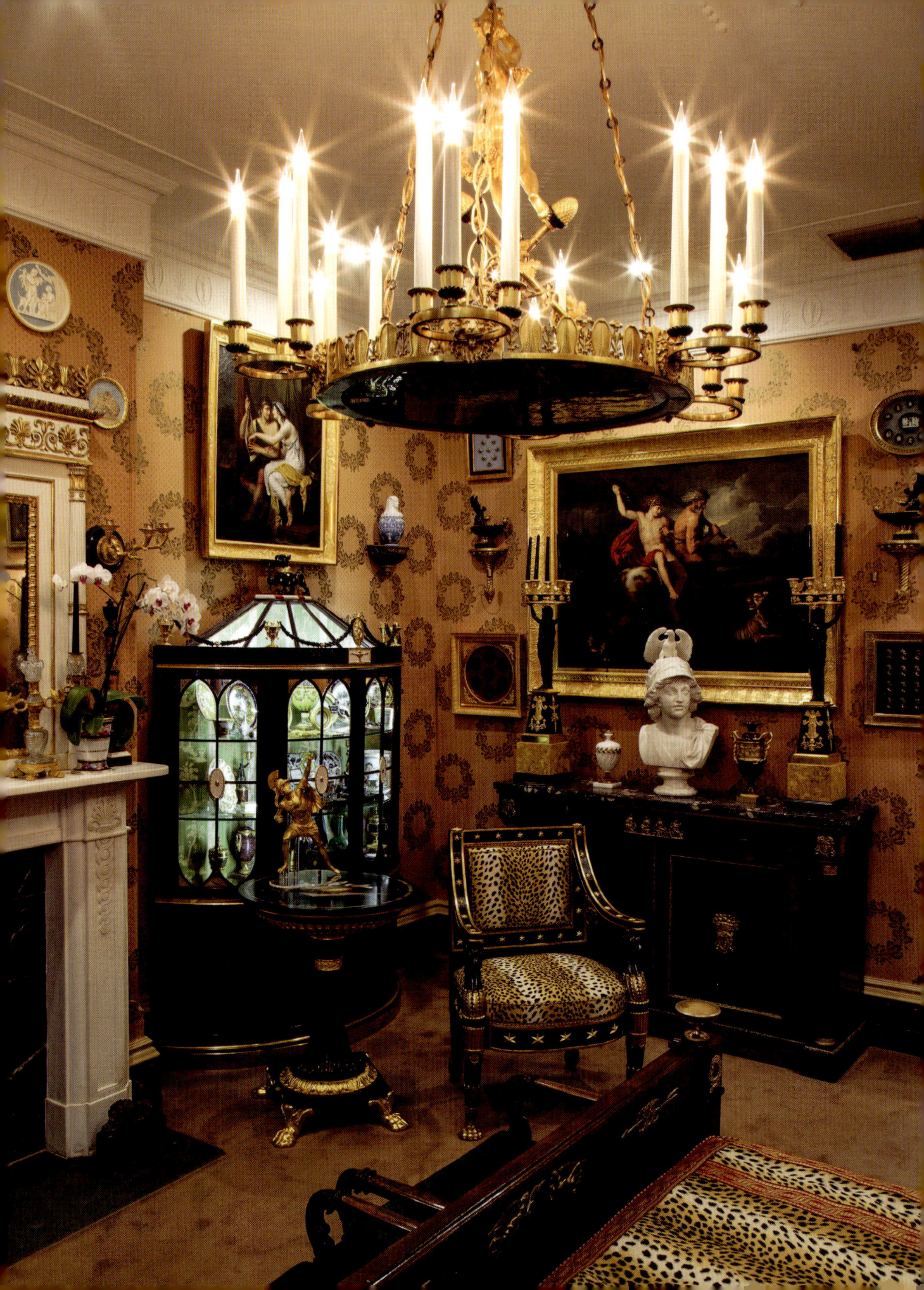

underside of an evergreen magnolia leaf. The ceiling was lowered to create a more intimate ambience, and is decorated with simple neoclassic mouldings. The room always contained two demi-lune display vitrines and items would find their way to his bedside cabinets so that they could be held, examined for all their minute details, and enjoyed. Although often no longer in this room, David kept his Ciuli, Percier & Fontaine *Bacchus table,* c. 1810, and substantial Jean-Baptiste Santerre (France 1651–1717) painting of *Adam & Eve*, c. 1716, here.

Furniture

The bedroom has a range of fine quality English Regency furniture, including a Gillows of Lancaster (Britain 1730–1814) *Chaise longue,* c. 1810, with carved lion masks; a *Pair of Regency stools*, c. 1810, carved from rosewood and inlaid with brass; a painted *Regency leopard armchair*, c. 1810, in the manner of the designer George Smith (Britain c. 1786–1826); a *Lion head klismos chair*, c. 1815, after the designer Thomas Hope; and attributed to Thomas Chippendale the Younger, a *Pair of Egyptian revival arm-chairs*, c. 1805. The three *Ickworth vitrines*, c. 1810 and later, owe their origin to the Hervey family, specifically the Hervey Earls (later Marquesses) of Bristol at Ickworth, in Suffolk, identifiable by the distinct leopard crest. One was later included in the furnishings of Chequers at Buckinghamshire, the country residence for British prime ministers. The other two were owned by an American, Clinton Ledyard Blair, and furnished Blairsden, his magnificent mansion in Peapack, New Jersey. A fine Irish table with an Italian micromosaic top of *Doves of Pliny*, 1820, and a superb *Games table*, 1835, from the Carl Christian Inhulsen (Germany 1800–1858) workshop furnish the room. The latter table was also manufactured to furnish Charlottenhof Palace in Sanssouci Park, Germany. Finally, the *French Empire-style bed*, c. 1900, is by Hopilliart and Leroy (France established 1781), which David acquired in England from a film studio sale with a provenance to an old Dirk Bogarde (1921–1999) movie.

Lighting

An impressive central *Dish light chandelier*, c. 1800, that David acquired in Paris in 2004 lights the room. Initially believed to be French, it is now thought to be Russian. The main feature of the chandelier is the dancing Bacchanalian nymph above the circular coronet with its deep amethyst-coloured glass dish. On the wall behind the bed are an English Regency *'Sister Parish' pair of girandoles*, c. 1810, once owned by the legendary interior decorator to the Kennedy White House. On the mantelpiece are a *Pair of coronation candelabra*, c. 1820, attributed to Blades of Piccadilly (Britain active 1783–1829), a rare example celebrating George IV's ascension to the

Opposite page: The main bedroom featuring English Regency *Ickworth vitrines*, c. 1810. The *Regency leopard armchair*, in the manner of George Smith, c. 1810, is next to an Irish table with an Italian micromosaic top of *Doves of Pliny*, 1820. The large painting is *The education of Achilles by Chiron*, Bénigne Gagneraux, 1785, which hangs behind a pair of Russian Imperial *Eagle candelabra*, c. 1800.

Below: Lion head *Klismos chair*, after Thomas Hope, c. 1815.

Games table, Carl Christian Inhulsen Workshop, 1835.

'Sister Parish' girandole (one of a pair), Britain, c. 1810.

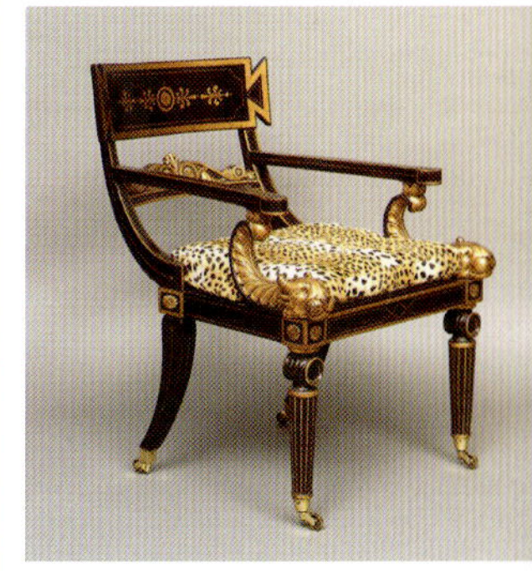

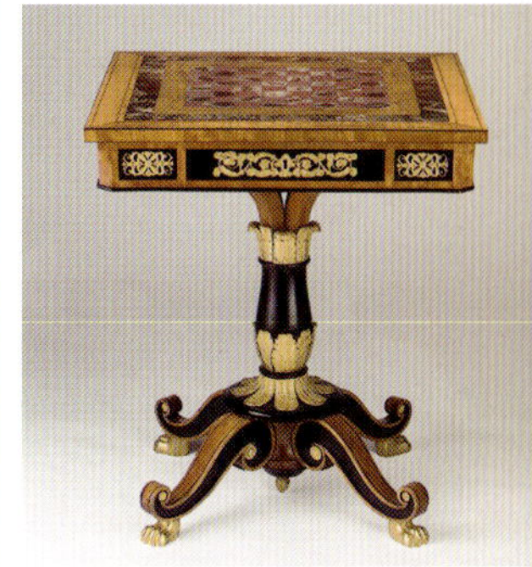

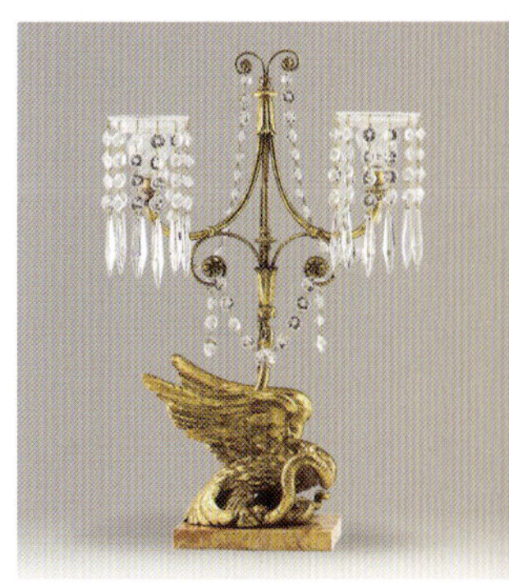

Top: *Cameo of Empress Catherine the Great as Minerva*, James Tassie after Empress Maria Feodorovna, c. 1789.

Middle and Bottom: *Private hand seal of Tsar Alexander I*, Russia, c. 1820, including its carved amethyst matrix.

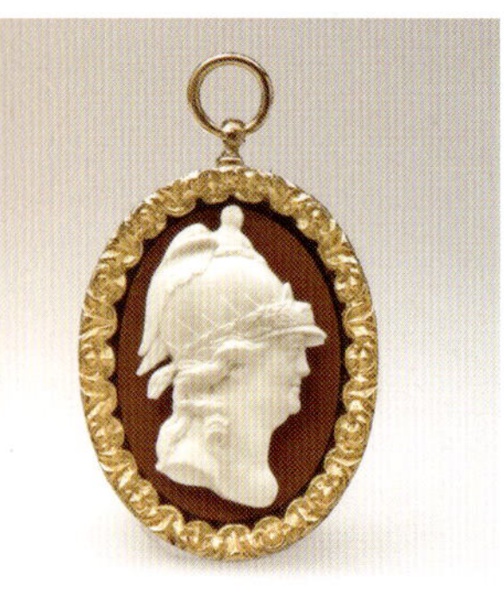

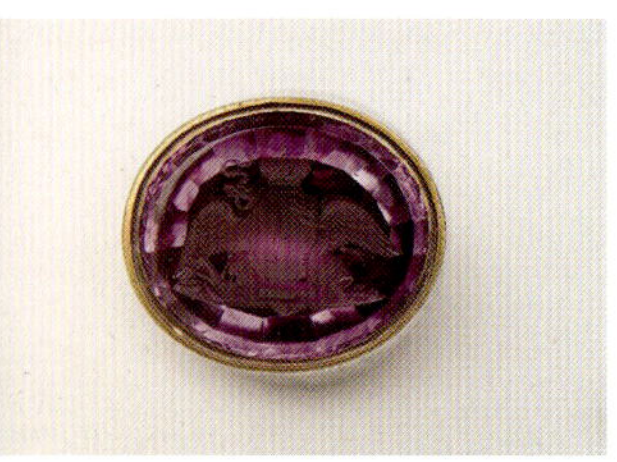

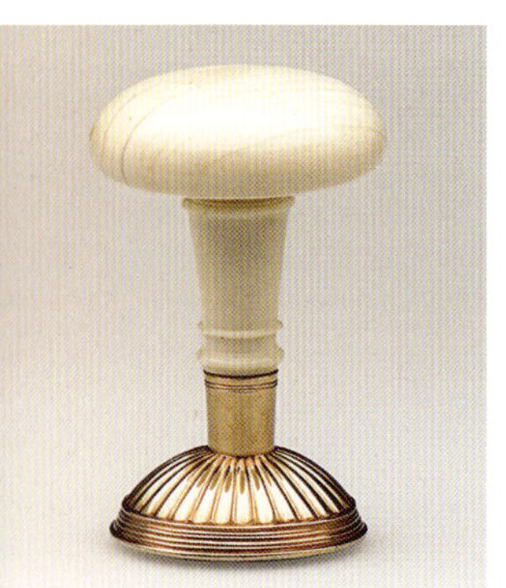

Following spread:
Left, top: A selection of small boxes including a *Parrot bonbonniere*, Birmingham/South Staffordshire, c. 1760, and *Meissen Bonbonniere* in the form of a white rat c. 1745.

Left, bottom: David's collection of 70 stick pins, ranging in date from the 19th to 20th centuries.

throne. On the sideboard sit a Russian *Pair of Imperial eagle candelabra*, c. 1800, of an Egyptian form found at Pavlovsk Palace, St Petersburg.

Principal Objects

The bedroom is a treasure trove of objets d'art, porcelain, mounted hardstone objects, and 'favourites' which he wished to see, handle and enjoy each day. A purchase that caused some stress due to its cost, but gave immense pleasure, is the *Column centrepiece*, c. 1800, attributed to the Imperial Glass Factory (Russia 1777–1917). Probably made as part of an elaborate table setting for Russian aristocracy, the centrepiece effortlessly combines a deep ruby-coloured glass column with ormolu mounts and snake, as well as a porcelain base and ormolu plinth. Equal in stature is the Joseph Coteau (France 1740–1812) *Mantel clock*, 1796, a rare Directoire period clock by arguably the finest French enamellist of the 18th century. David first saw this clock on temporary loan to the Frick Museum in New York and was able to buy it from the Dalva Brothers many years later. The room also houses one of the most unusual items in the collection, a Durs Egg (Switzerland/Britain 1748–1831) *Flintlock pistol*, c. 1800, presented in 1802 by Lieutenant-Colonel Thomas Thornton to Napoléon Bonaparte, then First Consul of France. The stock is inlaid in gold with Thornton's coat-of-arms and the battle honour 'Marengo' against a martial trophy to commemorate this significant victory by Napoléon. Once a pair of duelling pistols, David always hoped to find the other after buying the first in London in 2006.

A number of Russian items are housed in the bedroom vitrines, including a *Cameo of Empress Catherine the Great as Minerva*, c. 1789, after an original by Empress Maria Feodorovna (Russia 1759–1828). A *Private hand seal of Tsar Alexander I* (Russia 1777–1825), c. 1820, and a selection of pieces from the Workshop of Fabergé, including a superb *Parasol handle*, 1903–1917, by Workmaster Henrik Wigström (Russia 1862–1923), are also on display.

Also in the vitrines are a selection of precious metal boxes by Pierre-François Mathis de Beaulieu (France active 1768–1791) *Snuff box (with hair panel)*, 1775; and Joseph-Étienne Blerzy (France active 1768–1806) / Jean Petitot (France 1607–1691), *Snuff box (with miniature portrait)*, 1775–1776; as well as a superb gold and enamel rococo *Etui*, c. 1750, made in Britain. Similarly plentiful are an array of 18th century British enamelled copper boxes ranging from souvenir pieces through to exquisitely painted examples such as the *Hawk's head bonbonniere*, c. 1765, and *Parrot bonbonniere*, c. 1760.

The bedroom vitrines have some of David's porcelain, although the majority is displayed in the drawing room and dining room. Of note are the Bow China Works (Britain c. 1748–1774), *Tea bowl and saucer*, c. 1750, in a rare 'Trellis pattern', and a Chelsea Porcelain Factory (Britain c. 1745–1770),

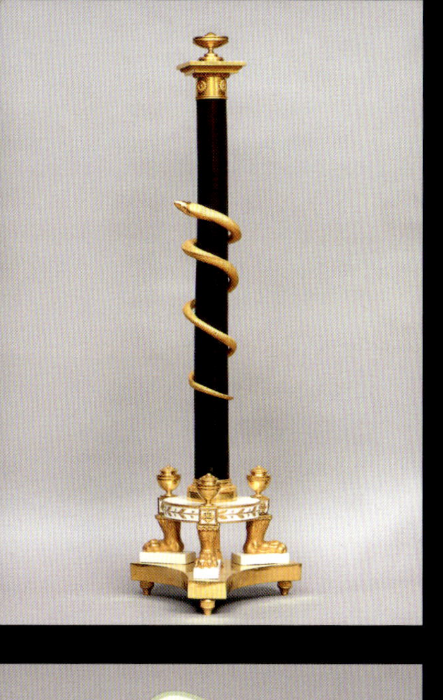

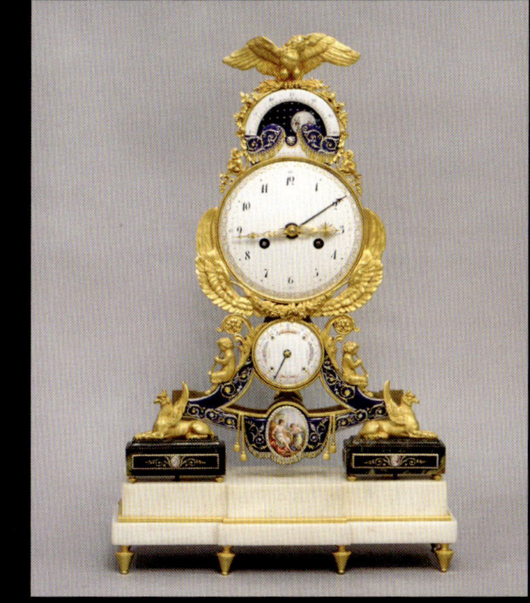

Clockwise from top left:
Column centrepiece, attributed to the Russian Imperial Glass Factory, c. 1800.

Mantel clock, Joseph Coteau, 1796.

Flintlock pistol, Durs Egg, c. 1800.

Snuff box with miniature portrait, Joseph-Étienne Blerzy and Jean Petitot 1775–1776.

Etui, Britain, c. 1750.

Parasol handle, Fabergé Workmaster Henrik Wigström, 1903–1917.

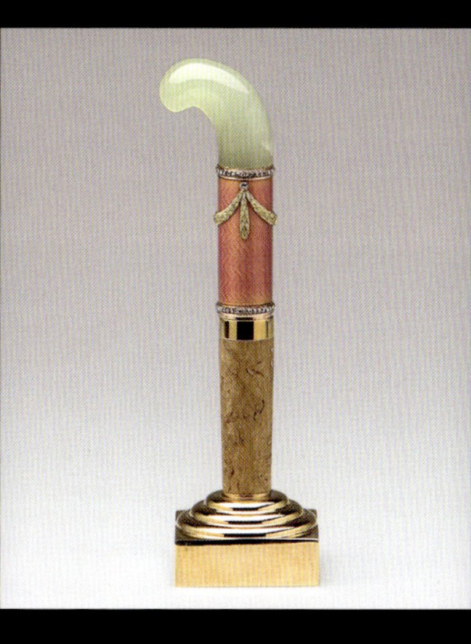

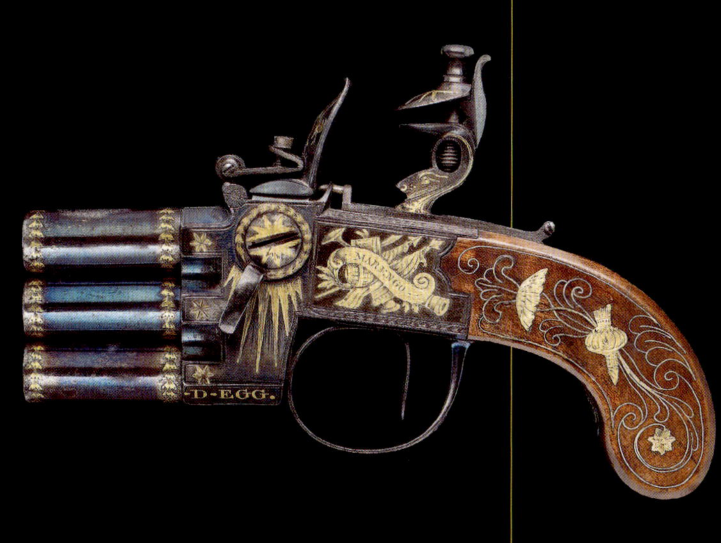

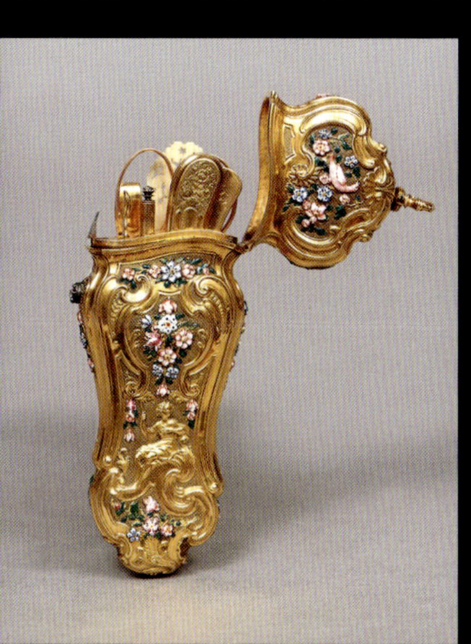

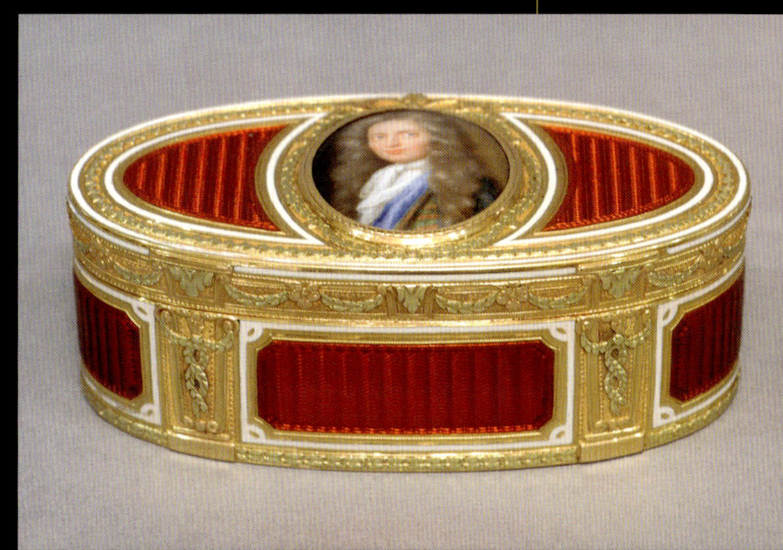

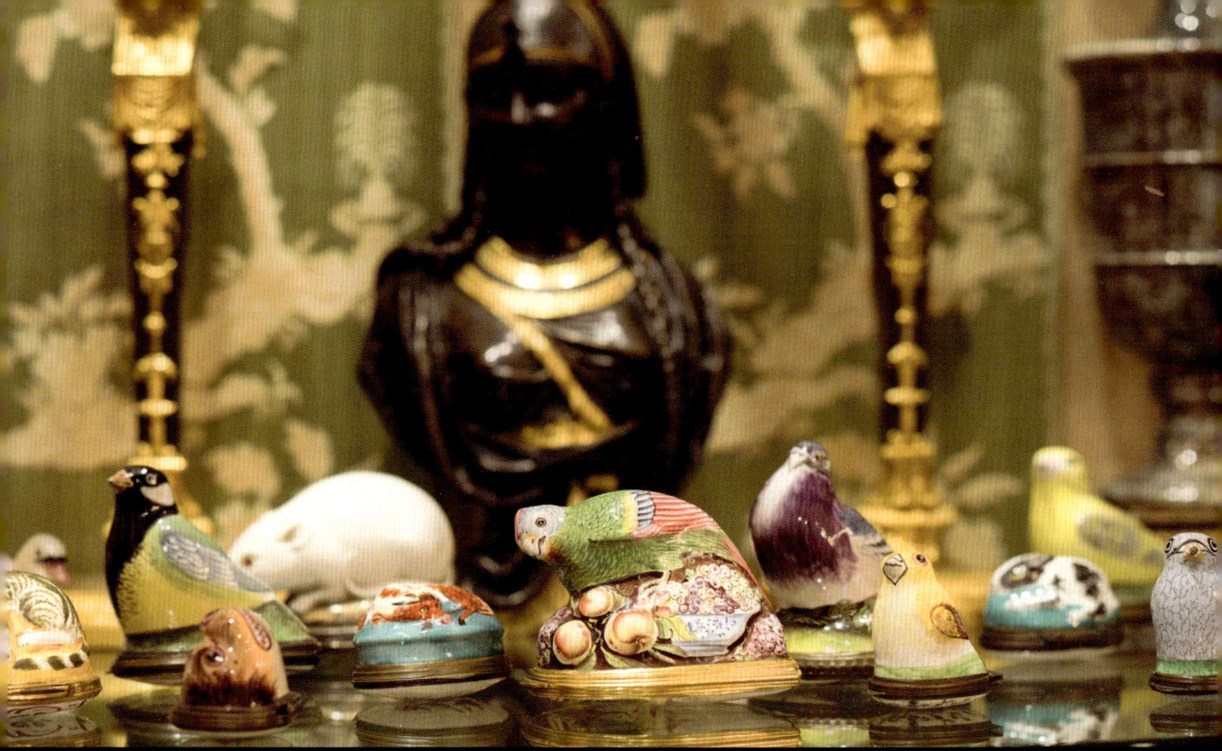

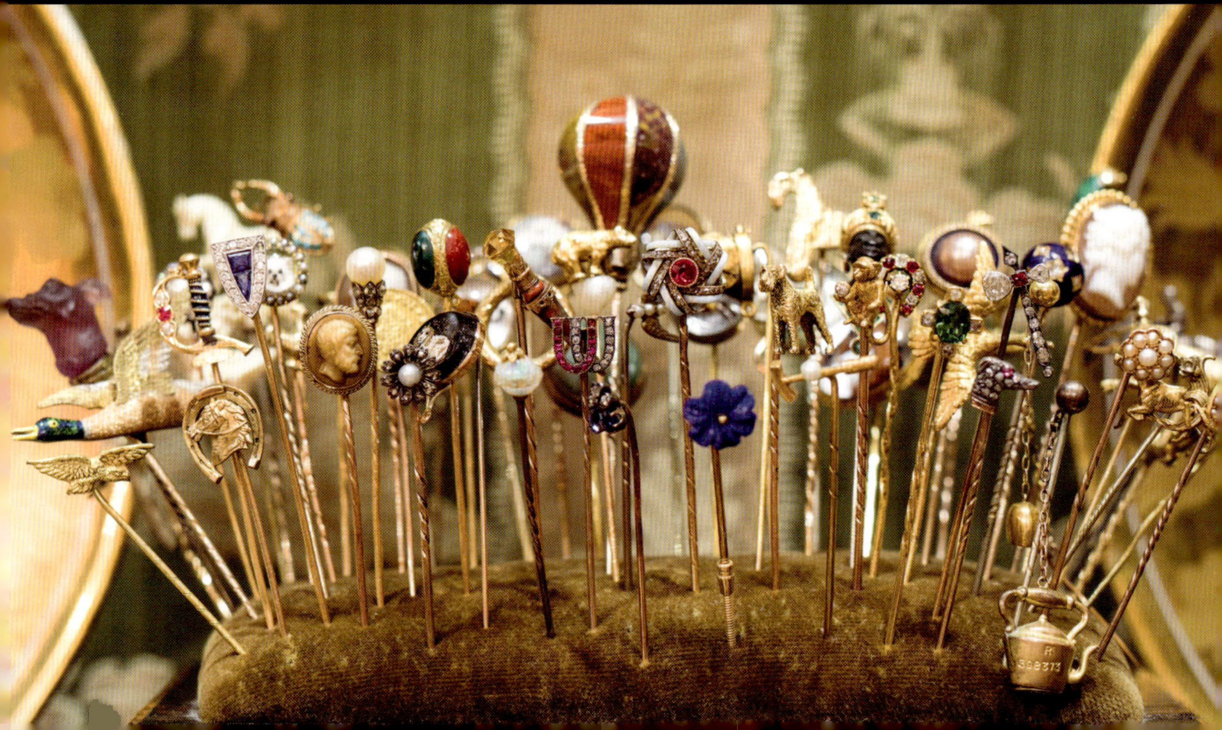

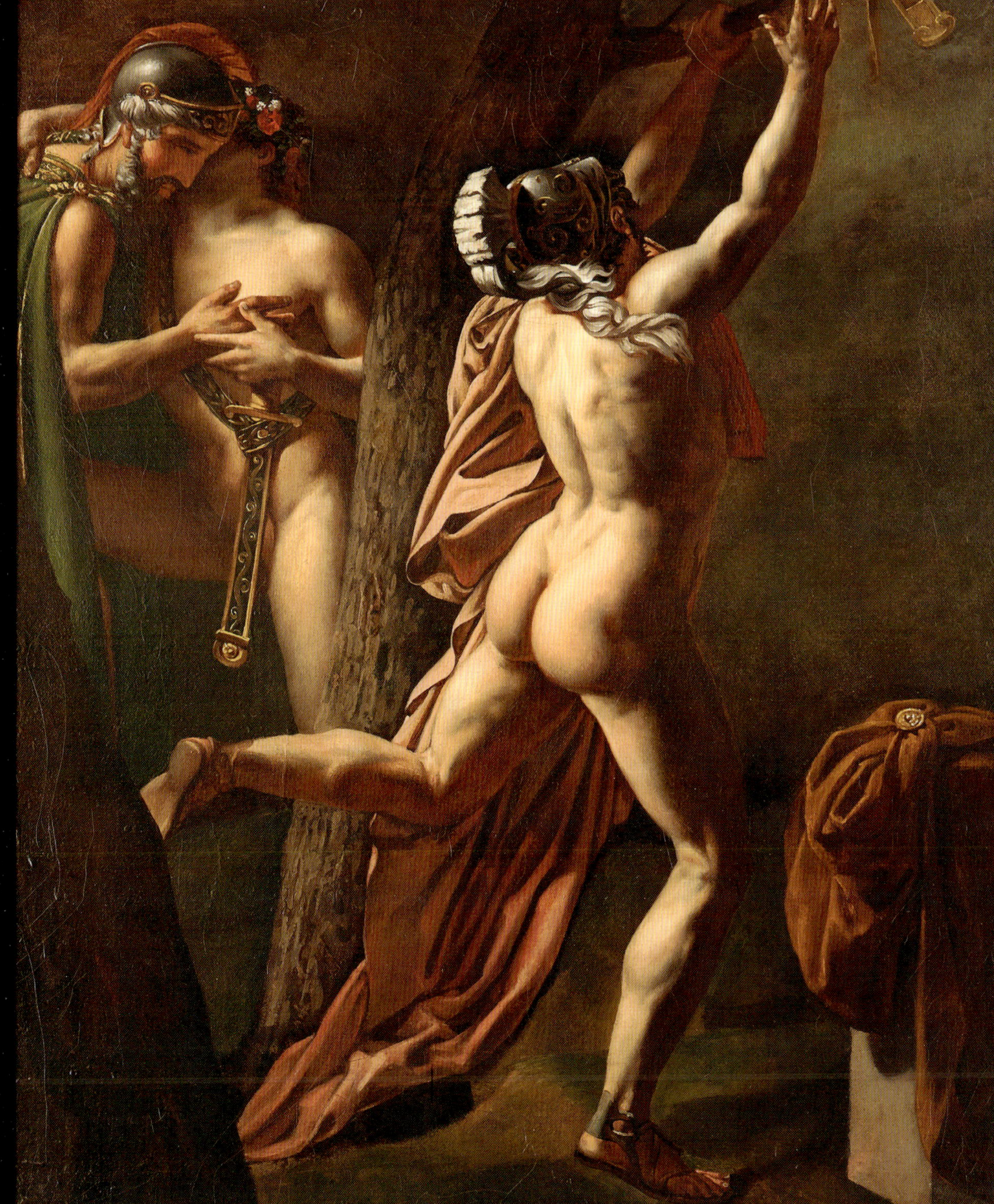

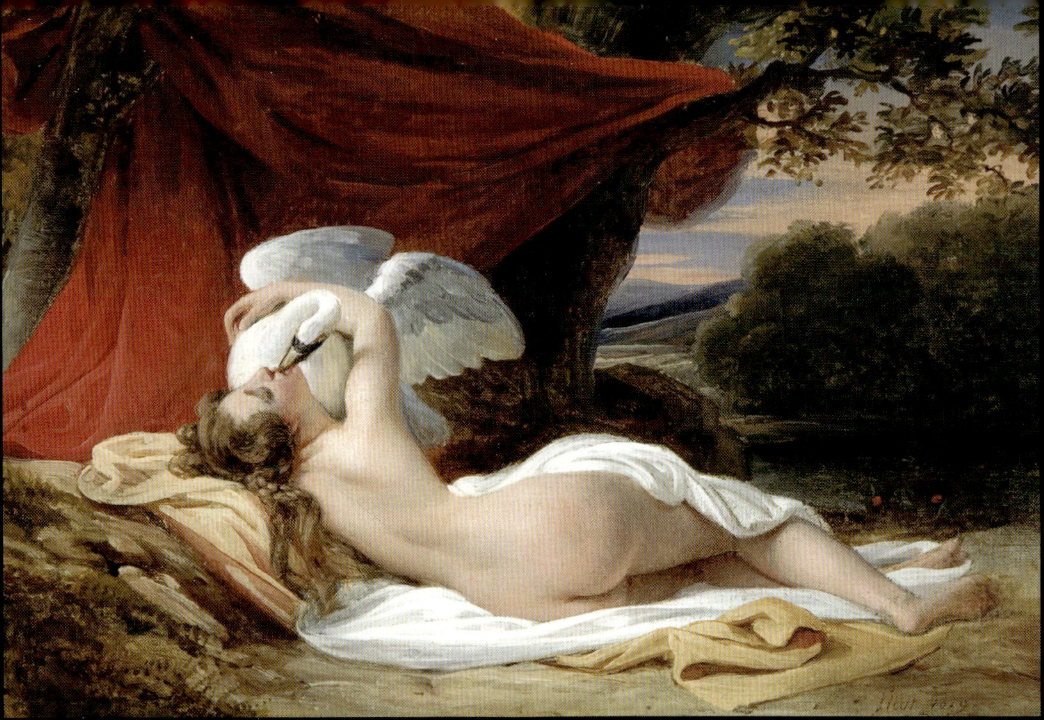

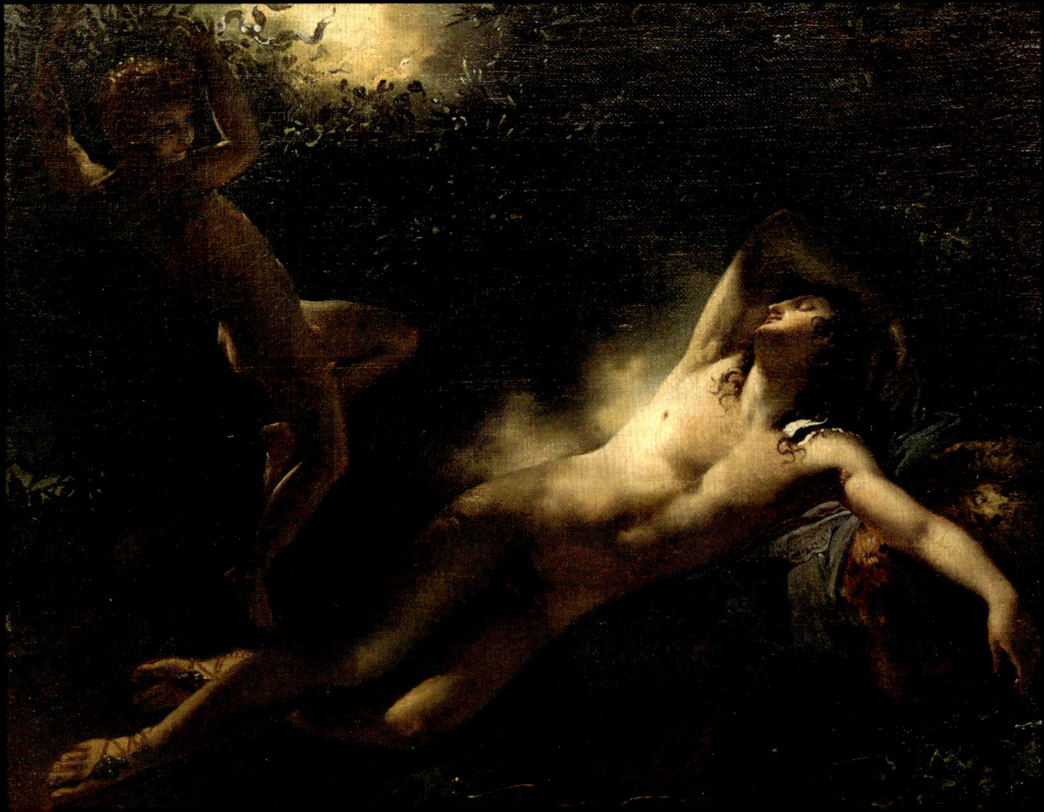

Botanical moulded plate, c. 1755, with painted flowers, insects and vegetables; the mould pattern the same as the celebrated Warren-Hastings service. Regency porcelain also features with a series of painted feather and shell pattern pieces, including a Worcester Porcelain Factory (Britain established 1751) Barr, Flight & Barr Period, *Pair of square scalloped dishes*, 1805–1820.

Passionate about semi-precious stones, David was a great admirer of English Blue John, even visiting one of the old mines in Derbyshire. He acquired several Blue John pieces, but the most captivating is the large *Vase*, c. 1800, with superb amethyst-coloured bands. Fortunately for David, the neoclassic period favoured the decorative use of many types of stones and was widespread in influence allowing the purchase of many pieces, including a Swedish *Pair of porphyry vases and covers*, c. 1780, and an unusual French *Vase of ormolu and petrified wood*, c. 1790.

Principal Pictures

For David, the bedroom was a space to display his neoclassical paintings illustrating themes from mythology, with preponderance for the idealised human form. Two beautiful cabinet pictures were acquired for the room: Anne-Louis Girodet's (France 1767–1824), *Sleep of Endymion*, c. 1810, and François Édouard Picot (France 1786–1868) *Leda and the swan*, 1829. The Girodet is a smaller version of what many consider to be his masterpiece, the *Sleep of Endymion*, 1791, at the Louvre in Paris, which was originally acquired by Louis XVIII (1755–1824) of France. Above the bed is a fascinating *Vignette of Leonidas at Thermopylae*, c. 1805, created by a studio assistant of Jacques-Louis David (France 1748–1825) during the extended period that David worked on his monumental historical painting of Leonidas. Another fine French painting is Bénigne Gagneraux's (France 1756–1795) *The education of Achilles by Chiron*, 1785, commissioned by art collector Cardinal François-Joachim de Pierre de Bernis (France/Italy 1715–1794), whilst French ambassador to Rome. Although of a later date, Frederic, Lord Leighton's (Britain 1830–1896) *Study for Perseus on Pegasus (hastening to the rescue of Andromeda)*, c. 1895, is a handsome addition to the bedroom and continues the mythological theme established by David.

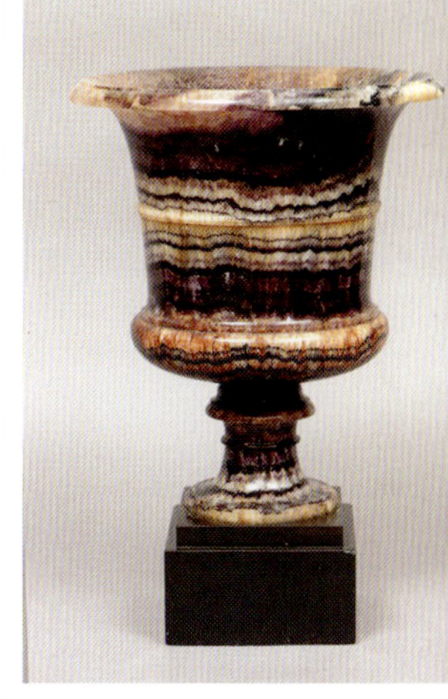

Previous spread:
Right: *Vignette of Leonidas at Thermopylae*, Studio of Jacques-Louis David, c. 1805.

Opposite page:
Top: *Leda and the swan*, François Édouard Picot, 1829.

Bottom: *Sleep of Endymion*, Anne-Louis Girodet, c. 1810.

This page: *Blue John Vase*, c. 1800.

THE ENTRANCE LOBBY

With the addition of a marble floor, the entrance lobby continues the same décor as the hallway with raspberry-coloured, French-silk-damask wallpaper and faux-painted malachite pillars. Of note are the Werner & Mieth Workshop (Germany 1792–1819) *Pair of wall lights*, c. 1800, to a Karl Schinkel (Germany 1781–1841) design. This model was commissioned by King Friedrich Wilhelm II and once graced the Winterkammer and the Summer apartments in Schloss Charlottenburg, Berlin. Furniture includes a William IV rosewood *Breakfront cabinet*, c. 1835, and an unusual, sophisticated, American *Convex mirror*, c. 1810, in the English Regency style.

Below: *Wall light* (one of a pair), Werner & Mieth Workshop, c. 1800.

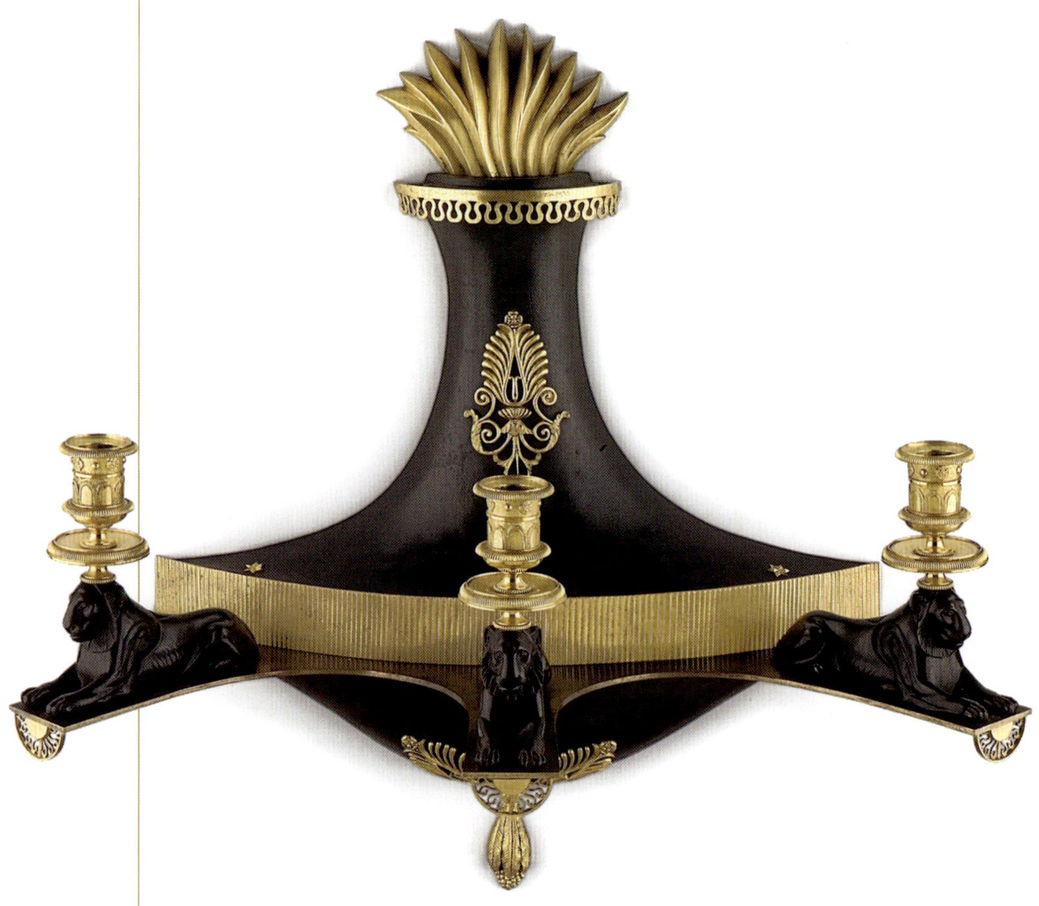

THE DEN

His everyday and evening room, David themed the den as an Englishman's study. The walls are upholstered in Jim Thompson green-lined silk fabric while the woollen verdure curtains came from his mother's house in North Adelaide. The Forwood Down & Co. (Australia 1873–1955) *Fireplace surround and grate*, c. 1900, is one of the few surrounds original to the home. From the window, David could look into his front garden and keep an eye on the comings and goings of his staff, or wait for visitors to come through the gate from Melbourne Street. As the den was nearest to the front door, it was often used by David as a reception room, and it was from here that the highly anticipated Melbourne Cup was watched annually. It was also where he studied both art and dog breed catalogues and watched television. Favourite shows were on BBC and ABC, such as the Antiques Road Show, Air Crash Investigations and murder mysteries. Devoted to pottery, English mahogany and rosewood furniture as well as racing, hunting, coursing and canine portraits, the den is the perfect male retreat.

Below: The den, featuring English Regency furniture and the painting *A gentleman coursing for hares*, James Ramsay, c. 1820.

Following spread: The den, featuring a *Pair of bergere chairs*, c. 1830, attributed to Gillows of Lancaster; an English Regency, Greek revival settee, c. 1815; and the *Breakfront library bookcase*, c. 1825.

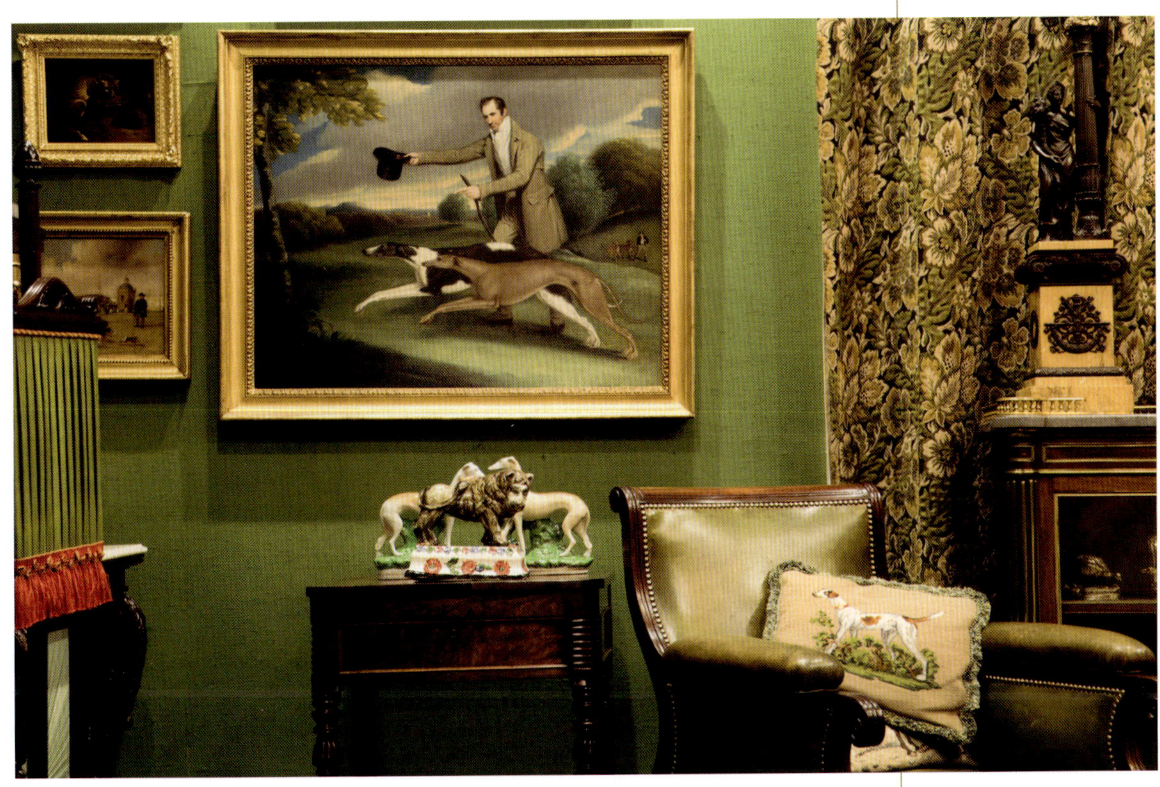

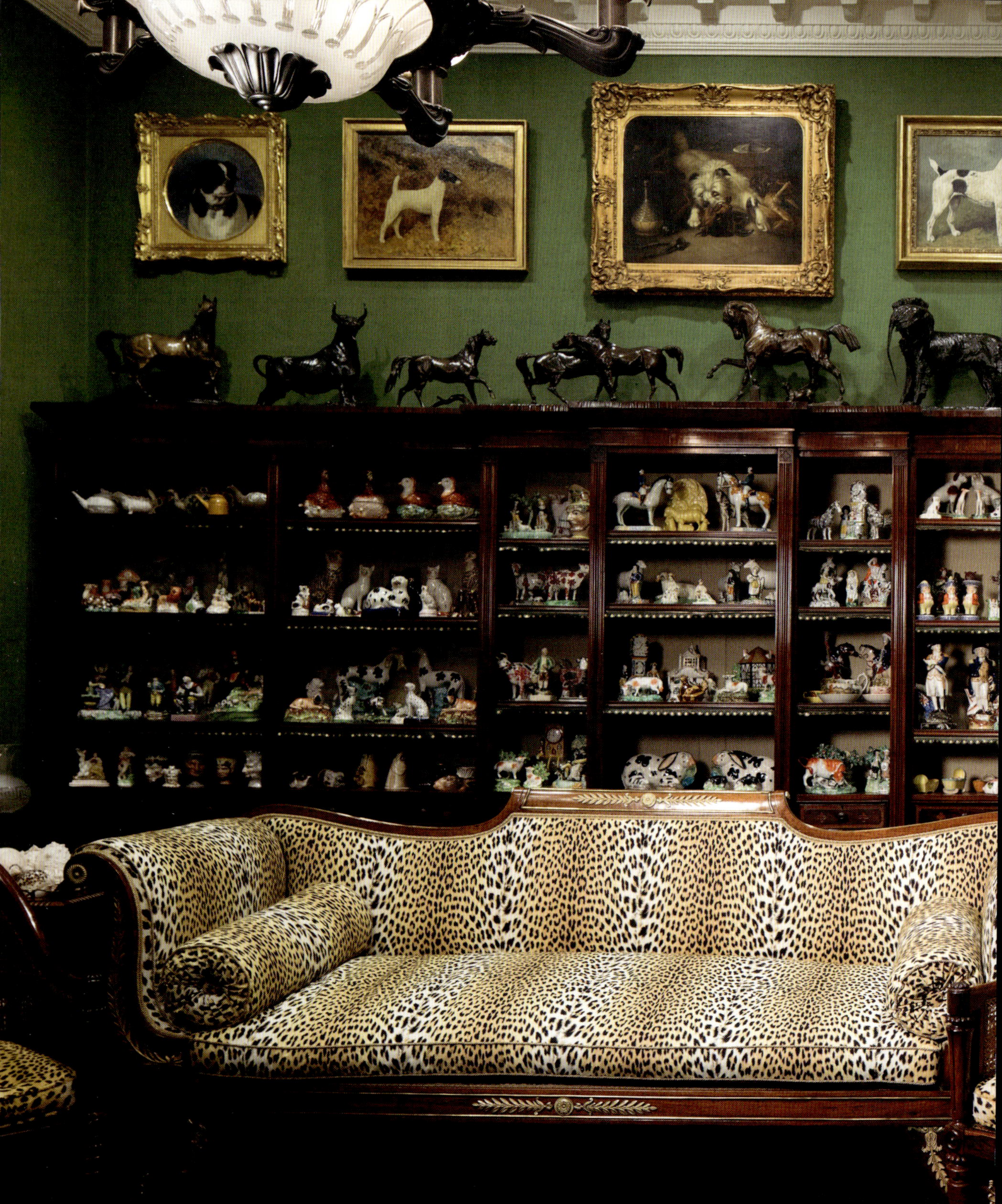

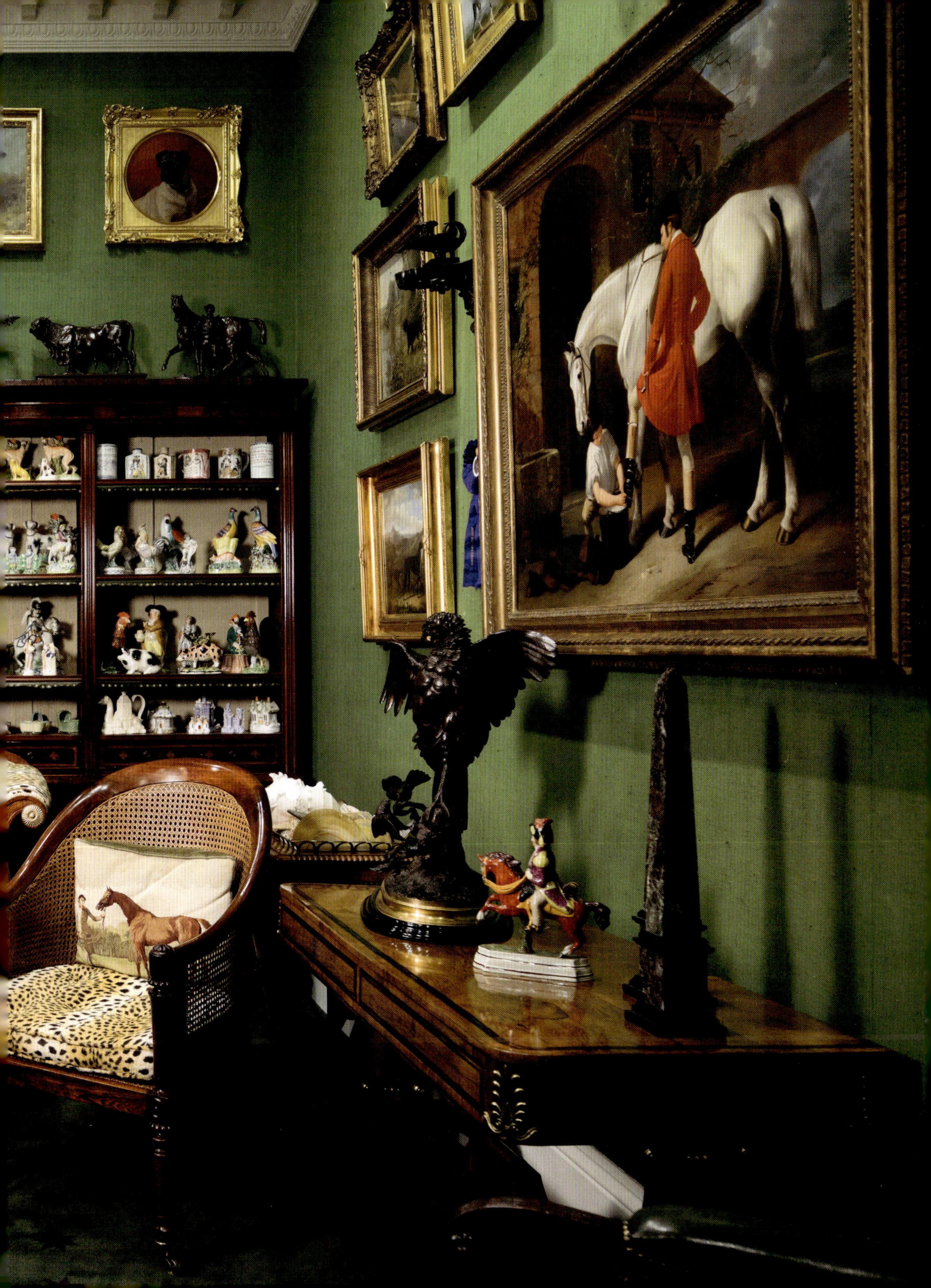

Furniture

The furniture in the den is English Regency in high-quality rosewood and mahogany; the seating furniture is neoclassic in taste and influenced by French examples. The *Pair of bergere chairs*, c. 1830, are attributed to Gillows of Lancaster and London, while the pollard oak *Pair of Regency jardinières*, c. 1810, were acquired at the Rene Rivkin sale in Sydney in 2001. The pretty *Pair of pole screens*, 1805–1810, in the Grecian style came from Harewood House in Yorkshire and are attributed to Thomas Chippendale the Younger. Lord Harewood commissioned Thomas Chippendale (Britain 1718–1779) and his son to supply much of its furniture. The dominant feature of the room, however, is the large gothic-style *Breakfront library bookcase*, c. 1825, filled with English Staffordshire ware and salt-glazed pottery. David bought the bookcase in 1981 from an Adelaide Hills property and much to his delight, it fitted the eastern wall of the den perfectly.

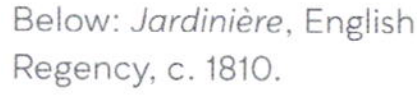

Below: *Jardinière*, English Regency, c. 1810.

Right: An English Cabinet bookcase in the Louis XVI style, c. 1880.

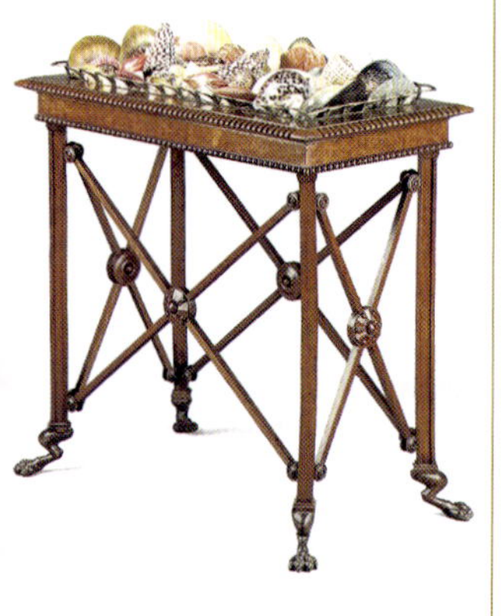

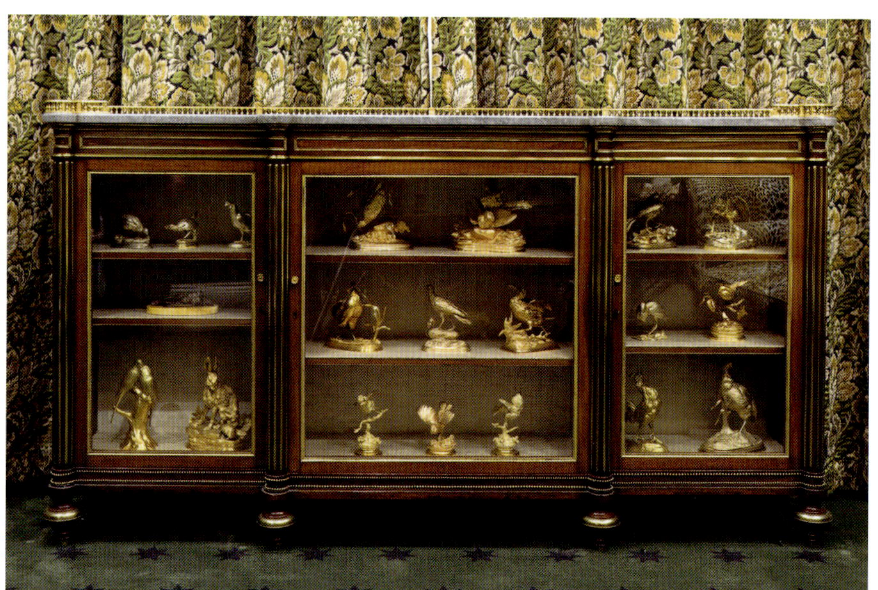

Lighting

The den is centred by an impressive scaled *Six-arm colza oil dish light*, c. 1835, attributed to Thomas Messenger & Sons (Britain 1797–1860s) or possibly William Collins, both of Birmingham and known for their high-quality chandeliers. Originally, the urns were filled with rapeseed oil (canola), following an invention by the Frenchman, François-Pierre-Ami Argand (France 1750–1803) in 1784. Gravity fed, the oil burned in rings, generating a much greater light and transforming the interiors of grand apartments in the evenings. The chandelier was later converted to gas and, in turn, to electricity.

Principal Objects

The den was the principal room that David used to display his Staffordshire pottery, and the large bookcase was a perfect setting for this impressive collection. Unsurprisingly, animals feature prominently – dogs, cats, fowl, rabbits, pigs, sheep, cows, lions, horses, deer, bears, elephants and more! Some were collected for rarity, others for their perfect condition, and a few for their colouring, such as the rare yellow Staffordshire *Bucolic group*, c. 1820. While many are purely decorative figurines, others have a range of purposes, such as the Staffordshire Pottery *Pair of foxhounds*, c. 1850, which double as spill vases, or a cow that doubles as a creamer. Actors, performers, cradles with babies, mythical and real figures from history are also represented, including a rare Staffordshire *Cavalry Officer*, c. 1790; a Pearlware *Equestrian model of a general*, c. 1815; a *Military figure, possibly the Duke of Wellington*, c. 1810; and a Prattware *St George and the dragon*, c. 1810. Bacchic jugs, stirrup cups and teapots in earthenware, some with salt-glazes like the *Camel teapot*, 1745, were all collected by David and sourced from local to international antique shops, and from car-boot sales to fancy London fairs.

Left: *Cavalry Officer*, Staffordshire, c. 1790.

Below: *Admiral Lord Nelson*, Staffordshire, c. 1805.

Bottom: *St George and the dragon*, Prattware, c. 1810.

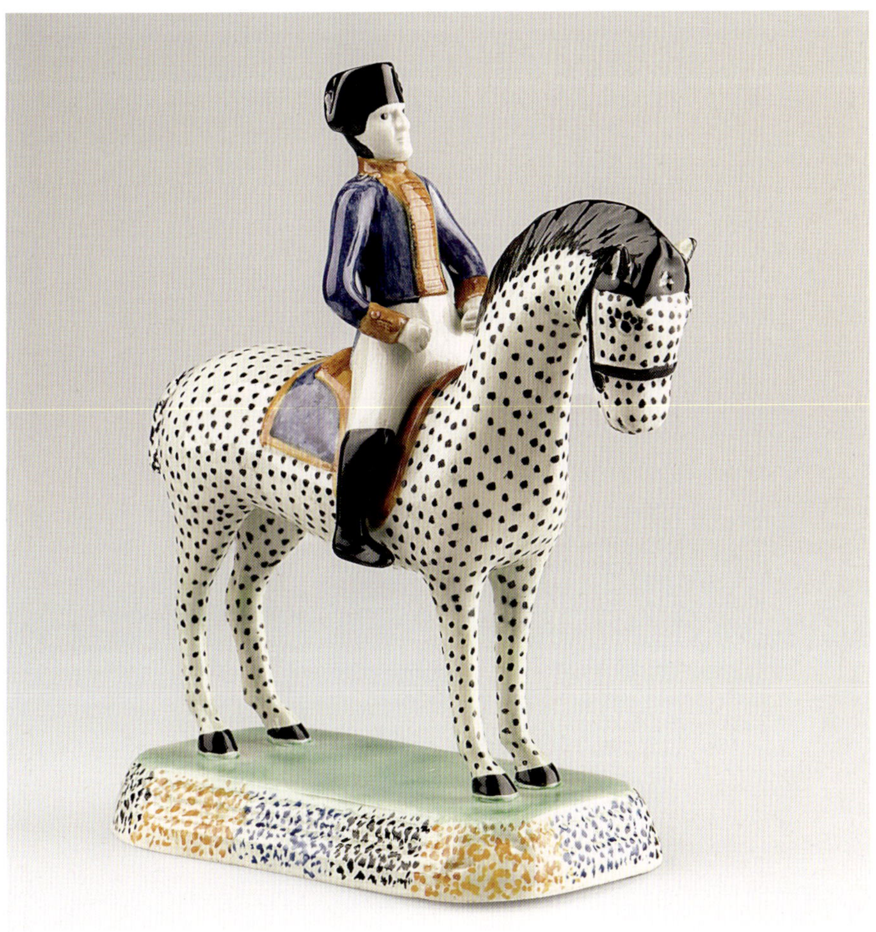

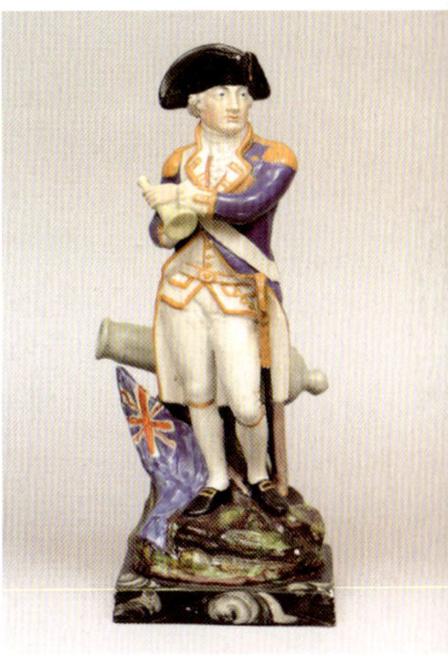

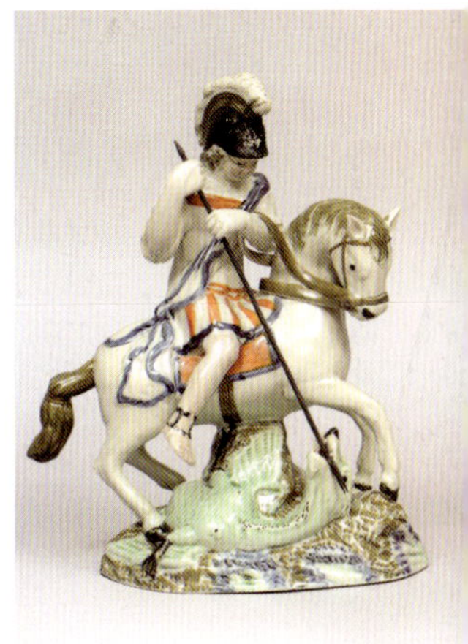

Below: *The stallion 'Angelo'*, Pierre Lenordez, c. 1850.

Opposite page: Clockwise from top: *Border terrier with a rabbit*, Edwin Landseer, c. 1825.

A Pointer in a landscape at sunset, Maud Earl, c. 1900.

Fox terriers 'Wait and see', Arthur Wardle, 1913.

Hunting party with setters on the moors, George Earl, 1867.

Principal Pictures

With its green-lined walls and multitude of holes that testify to crowded and frequently changing picture hangs, the den houses an array of 19th century British canine art that is unique in Australia. Pivotal to the room is Maud Earl's (Britain/United States 1863–1943) *A Pointer in a landscape at sunset*, c. 1900, which David knew well from the London Kennel Club where it hung for many decades on long-term loan. A member of the club, David was thrilled to acquire the painting as he had already developed a small collection of her work. A talented painter of dogs, Earl exhibited widely in Britain and Europe and later America after she moved there in 1915. She came from a family of animal portrait artists: her father George Earl (Britain 1824–1908), is represented in the collection with *Hunting party with setters on the moors*, 1867, and *Drake – a pointer*, c. 1875, a famous canine of the day.

The collection also contains an Edwin Henry Landseer, RA, RI (Britain 1802–1873) *Border terrier with a rabbit*, c. 1825. One of Britain's most celebrated animaliers, Landseer has placed the terrier in a natural setting, capturing the quality of its coat and attentive expression. Other canine paintings of note include John Frederick Herring Snr's *Staffordshire bull terriers*, c. 1840; Arthur Wardle's, RI, RBC (Britain 1864–1949) *Fox terriers 'Wait and see'*, 1913; and Gustav Muss-Arnolt's (United States 1858–1927) *Pointing and backing – pointer and a setter in the field*, 1895. A favourite painting of David's was Frederick Thomas Daws' (Britain 1878–1956) *Champions All*, 1927. The sentimental subject appealed, especially as David knew in reality that such a group of dogs would never live peacefully together!

Sculpture

One of the delights of this room is the large number of bronzes and gilt-bronzes of horses, dogs, bulls, birds and waterfowl by a range of 19th century French artists, including well-known French sculptors Pierre-Jules Mêne (France 1810–1879) and Jules Moigniez (France 1835–1894). Other artists represented are Alfred Dubucand (France 1828–1894), Ferdinand Pautrot (France 1832–1874), François Michel Pascal (France 1810–1882), Pierre Lenordez (France 1815–1892), Georges Gardet (France 1863–1939), Paul-Édouard Delabrièrre (France 1829–1912) and Charles Valton (France 1851–1918). Many of the smaller birds were bronze and gilded by David; he displayed them on his Hume *Bureau plat* in the drawing room. Lenordez's *The stallion 'Angelo'*, c. 1850, was bought in the United States in 2004, as it was a model his father once owned.

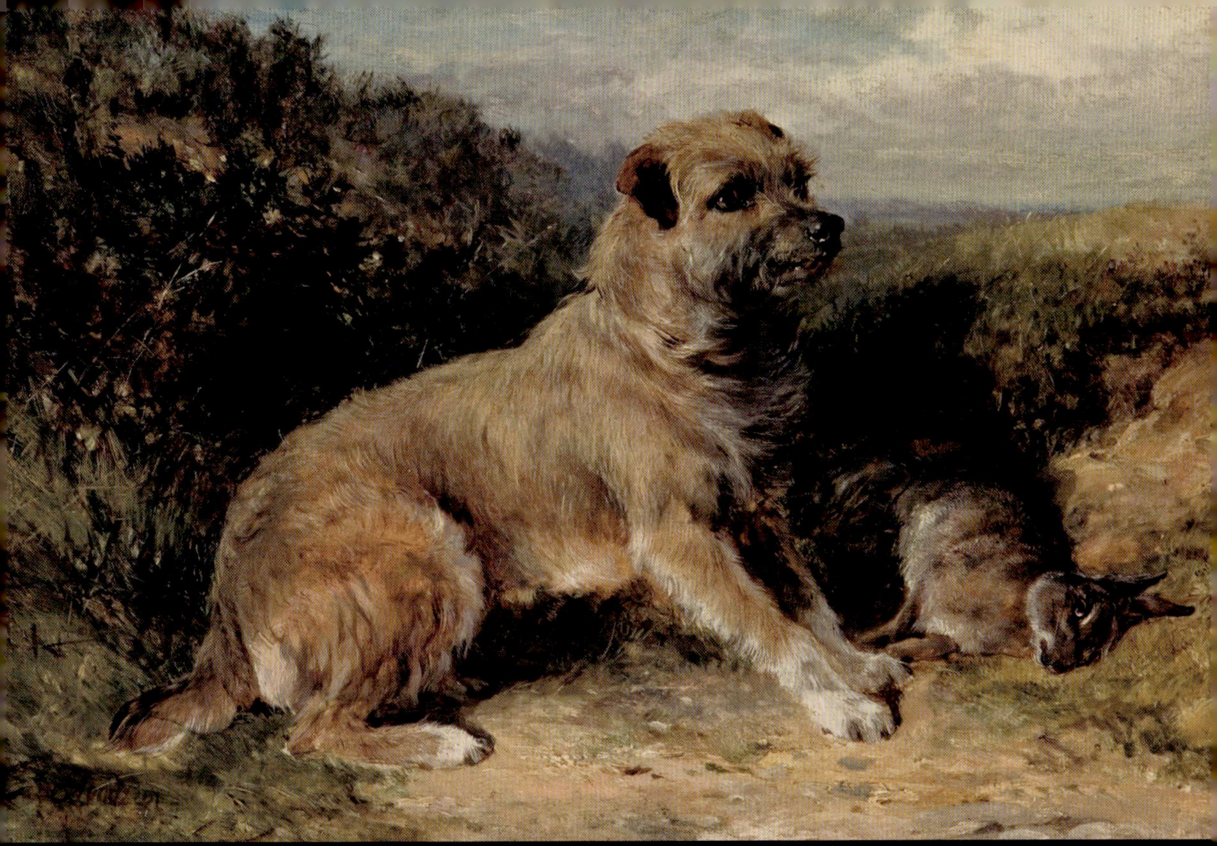

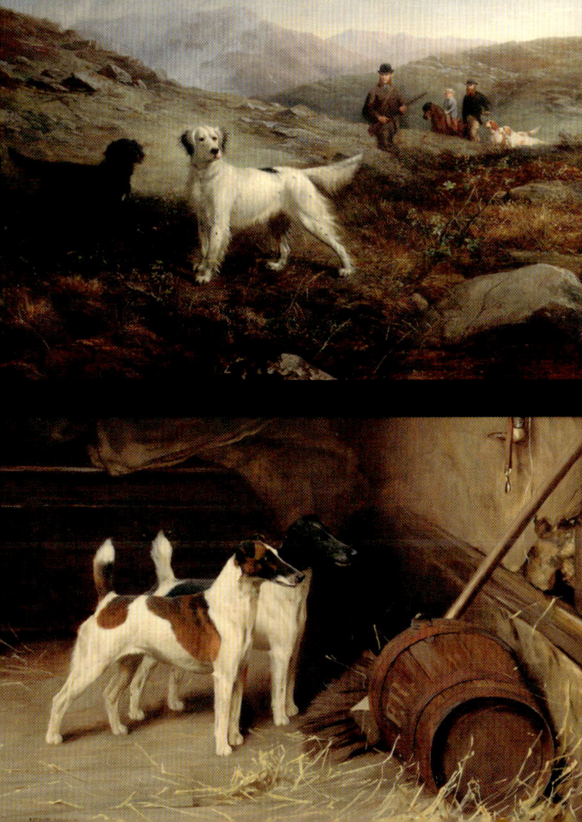

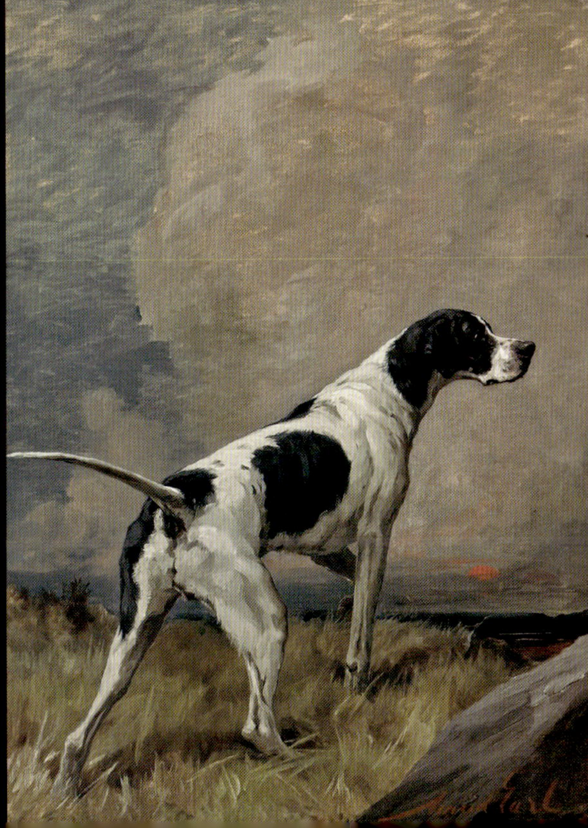

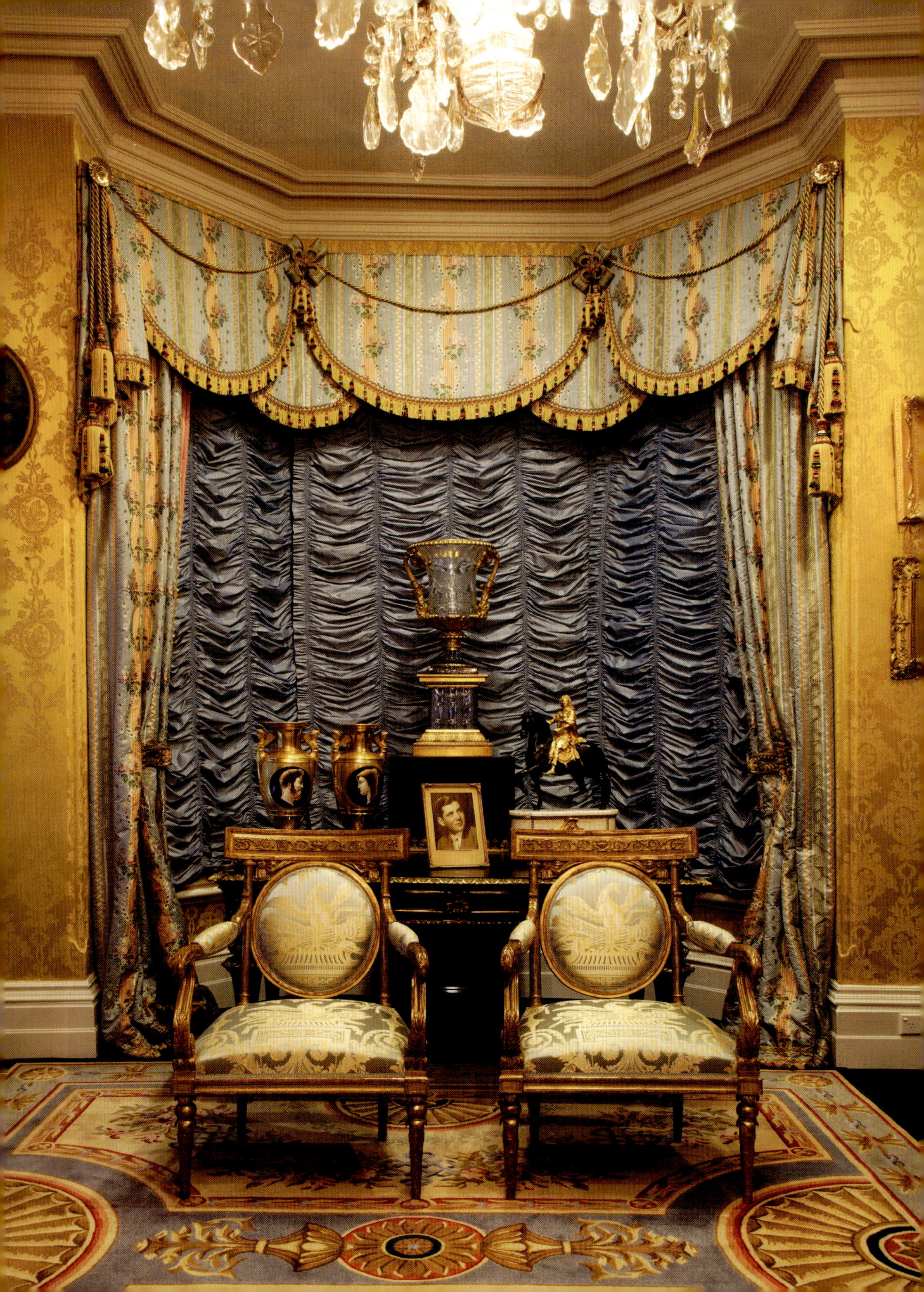

THE DRAWING ROOM

This semi French-themed drawing room was beautifully decorated in yellow silk by interior designer, Angus Foulds (1929–2016) in the mid 1970s and was intended for formal gatherings. David later replaced the matching silk curtains with sumptuous curtains created by Stitches Soft Furnishings in 2006. Made of French silk in Verel Favorite and colour 'Egee' on traditional looms at Lyon and with hand-dyed *passementerie* by De Clerc, these curtains and their arrangement are influenced by the bed-chamber and state bed of Queen Marie Antoinette at Versailles Palace. The modern Savonnerie-style carpet was commissioned by David in c. 2004 to fit the room. The French marble *Louis XV-style chimney-piece* was added and dates from c. 1875. The drawing room features a painted ceiling of cherubs, the only one in the house, which David commissioned in 2004 from the Australian artist Ian Pollok. The cherubs were loosely based from decorated objects owned by David and art books belonging to Pollok.

Opposite page: The drawing room with yellow silk walls and French silk curtains in the bay window. A pair of *'Hercules' armchairs*, attributed to Giacomo Quarenghi, c. 1795, sit in front of a *Writing table*, attributed to Robert Hume, c. 1815, and a *Vase on pedestal*, Russian Imperial Glass Factory, 1830.

Furniture

The room contains some very fine examples of French, English and Italian furniture in both the chinoiserie and neoclassic styles. Oriental lacquer was frequently admired by David and for many years he wished to purchase a fine commode. In 2005, he acquired the *Lacquer commode*, 1765, attributed to Pierre-Antoine Foullet (France Master 1765), with its extravagant ormolu mounts, superb French-made lacquer in the Chinese-style and original Breche d'Alep marble top. From the same period, but transitioning to neoclassic, is the signed Nicolas-Jean Marchand (France 1697–after 1775) *Secretaire abattant*, 1770–1775. Here the French lacquer is flat with stylised flowers and birds; the form angular and plain, and the mounts smaller and more subdued.

A rare pair of Italian vitrines *Mars & Minerva* and *Neptune & Juno*, c. 1790, feature painted maritime motifs and heraldic shields. Believed to be from Naples, a rich and cosmopolitan centre, they date from the rule of Ferdinand IV (Italy 1751–1825). From the same city, but during French occupation, are the pair of French Empire-style *Armchairs*, c. 1810, in the manner of Jacob Frères (France active 1796–1803). The chair clearly reflects the taste set by Caroline (née Bonaparte) and Joachim Murat, King of Naples 1808–1815. The Italian connection also encompasses Russia, with a *Pair of 'Hercules' armchairs*, c. 1795, attributed to Giacomo Quarenghi (Italy 1744–1817). A prolific architect and designer under Catherine the Great, Quarenghi's chair and other existing variants seem associated directly with the Empress.

David's love for English Regency furniture is not forgotten in the room

This page:

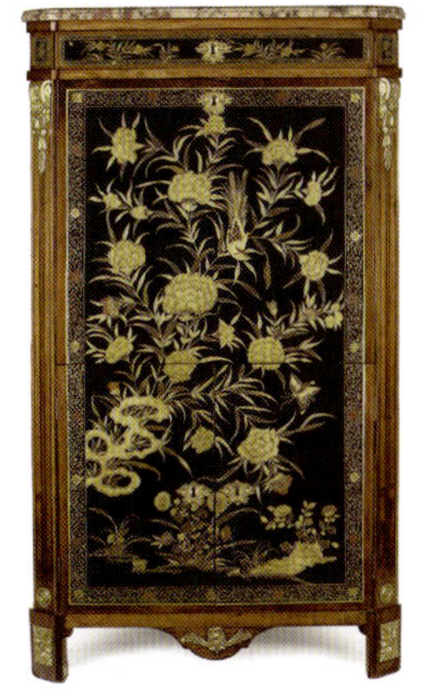

Top: *Secretaire abattant*, Nicolas-Jean Marchand, 1770–1775.

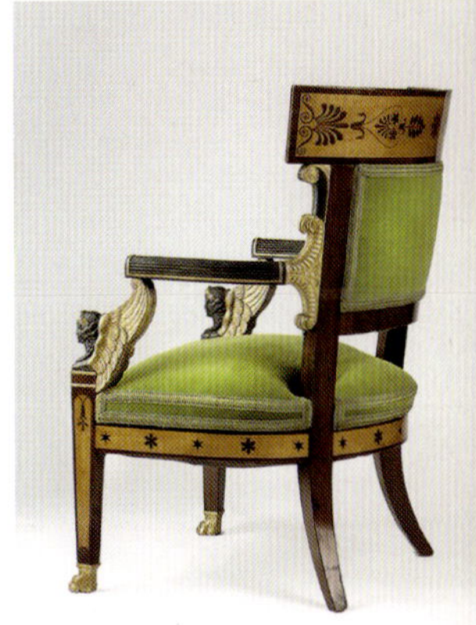

Bottom: French Empire-style *Armchair* (one of a pair), Italy, c. 1810.

with two contrasting pieces – a gilded *Console table*, c. 1815, and a *Writing table*, c. 1815, attributed to Robert Hume (Britain active 1808–1840). The *Console table*, with its palm trunk columns, has an exotic flavour favoured by the Prince Regent as expressed in the Royal Pavilion, Brighton. The ebony and gilt-brass *Writing table*, solid and masculine, is undoubtedly important, but currently something of an enigma.

Top: *Pair of candelabra*, Pierre-Philippe Thomire, c. 1810.

Bottom: *Vase on pedestal*, Russian Imperial Glass Factory, 1830.

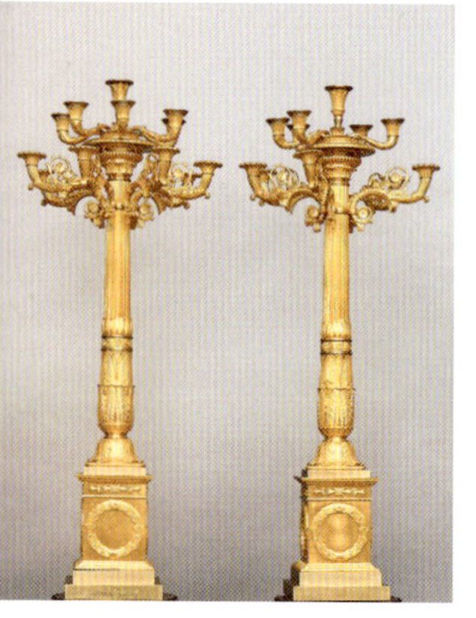

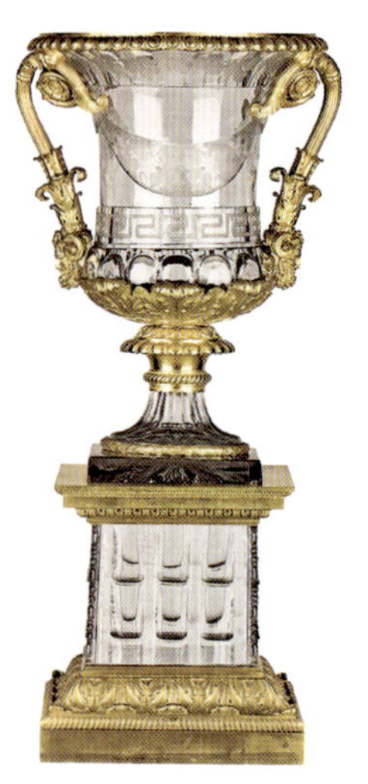

Lighting

The room is centred by a large, early 19th century *Glass chandelier*, probably of German origin. With six arms and two internal levels of lights, the chandelier is unusual for its range of solid glass balls, beads, flowers, blown elements and cut drops. Of note are the Russian *Pair of candelabra* (two of four), c. 1800, to a design found in Pavlovsk Palace, St Petersburg. David acquired a pair in 1995 and a further pair of the same design in 2011. In the bay window sit David's finest Pierre-Philippe Thomire *Pair of candelabra*, c. 1810. A renowned bronzier, Thomire supplied French royalty and at the time of these neoclassic Empire candelabra, Napoléon and his entourage.

Principal Objects

When David first travelled to Russia in 1994, he was staggered at the scale and opulence of Russian Empire interiors and their furnishings. Determined to acquire more Russian objects, his proudest acquisition was the *Vase on pedestal*, 1830, attributed to the Imperial Glass Factory. Standing at 89 centimetres, this superb cut and engraved vase with sumptuous ormolu mounts had pride of place in the Roman room originally, with the backdrop of David's swimming pool and Grecian temple folly. Other rarities include a large *Pair of Venetian terracotta painted jars*, c. 1800, and French *Lidded urns*, 1820, made from purple and green agate with ormolu mounts.

European and English porcelain is an important feature of the drawing room and has been displayed in a variety of vitrines over many decades. David was happy buying rococo and neoclassic porcelain from a range of factories. He wasn't particular about collecting only this 'factory' or that 'period'. Similarly, it didn't matter to him whether items were tablewares or figurines, as long as they fulfilled his criteria of beauty, quality and provenance. These criteria became increasingly important as David got older and the collection was constantly reviewed and upgraded. This included David flying in experts John and Henry Sandon from England to assess his collection in 2008. A somewhat terrifying experience for David as pieces were deemed good, bad or indifferent, he nevertheless came around to their advice over time.

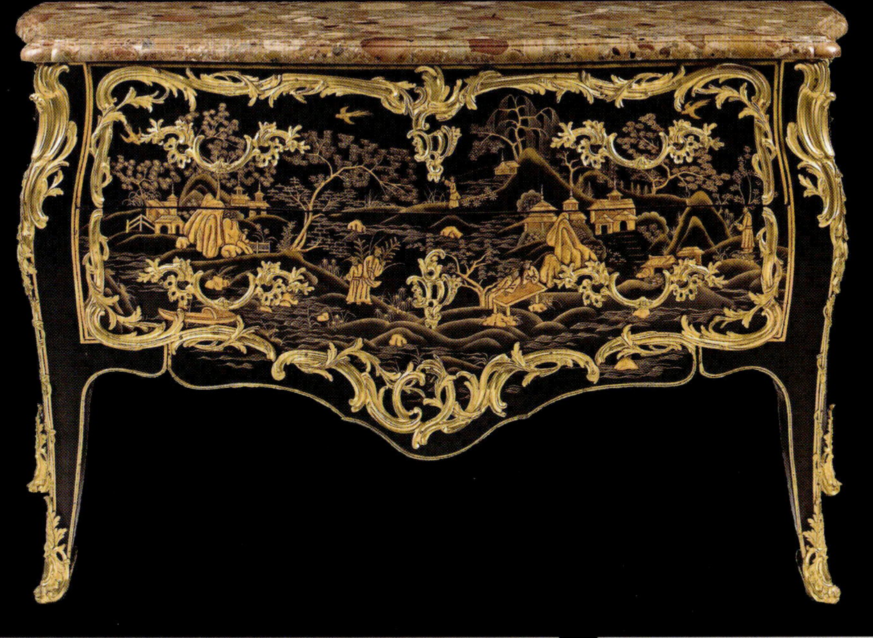

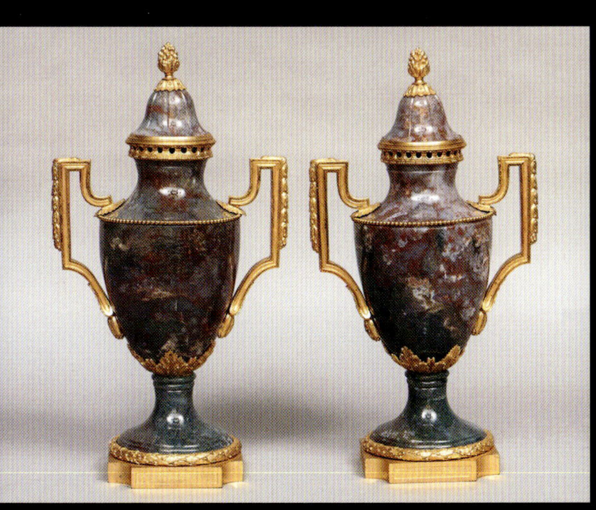

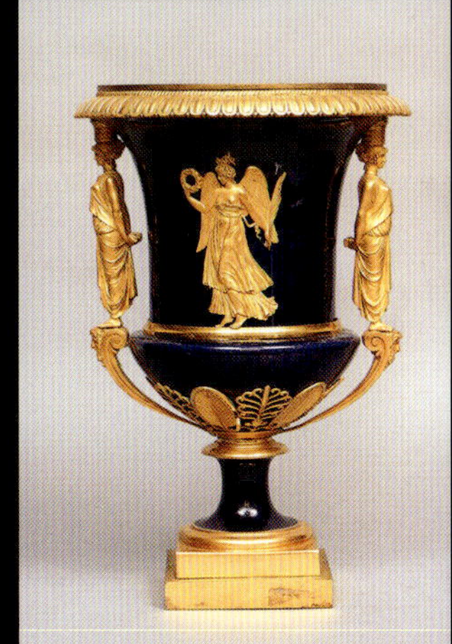

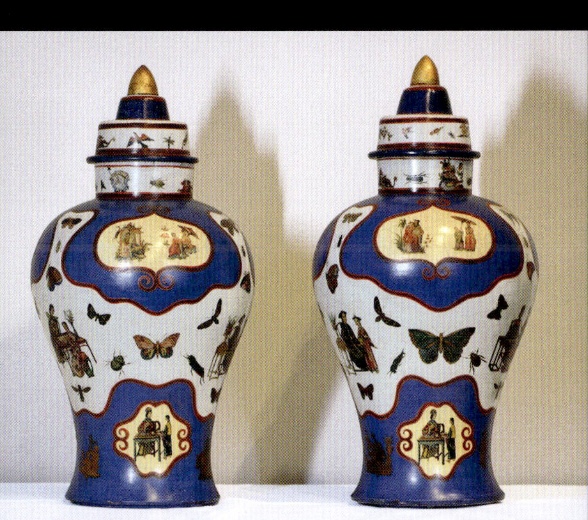

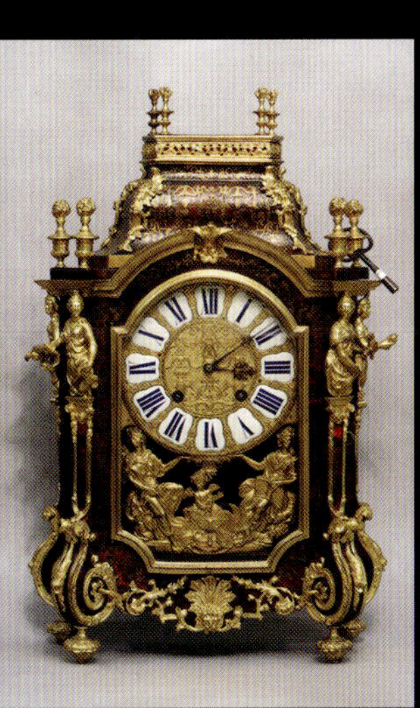

Lacquer commode, attributed to Pierre-Antoin[e] Foullet, 1765.

Ormolu mounted vase, Sevres Porcelain Manufactory, c. 1810.

Boulle striking table clock, Balthazar Martinot II (movement), c. 1690.

Pair of Venetian terracotta painted jars, Italy, c. 1800.

Lidded urns, France, 1820.

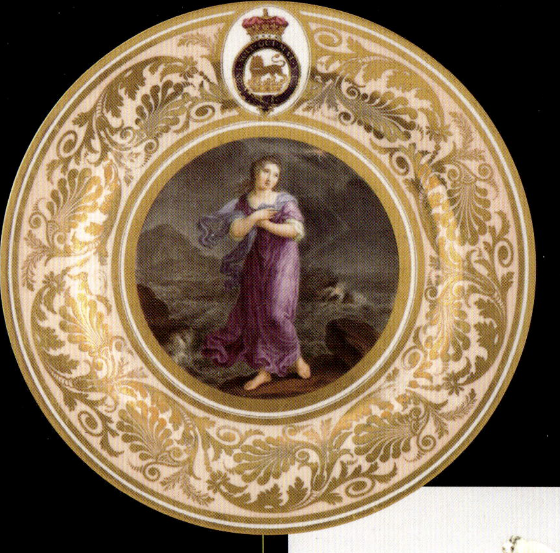

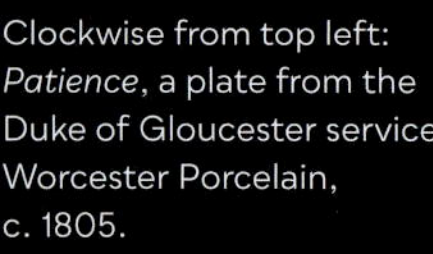

Clockwise from top left:
Patience, a plate from the Duke of Gloucester service, Worcester Porcelain, c. 1805.

Madonna and child, Chelsea Porcelain, c. 1755.

Ostrich, Fürstenberg Factory, c. 1758–1759.

Billing doves bonbonniere, Chelsea Porcelain, c. 1760.

The gardener and his companion, Worcester Porcelain, c. 1770.

Three coffee pots and covers, Meissen Porcelain, c. 1735–1740.

Commedia dell'Arte figure of Harlequin, Chelsea Porcelain, c. 1755.

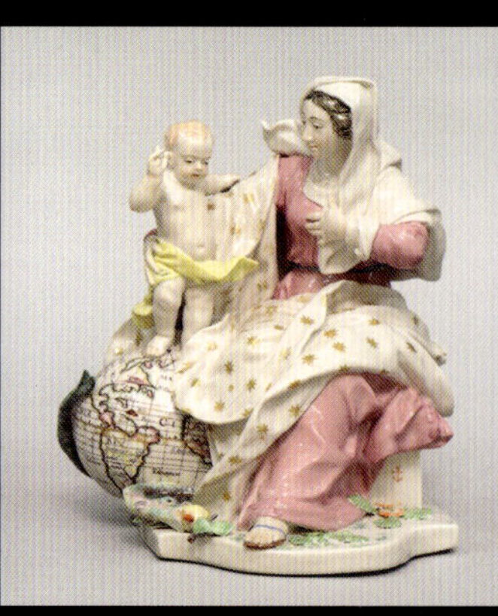

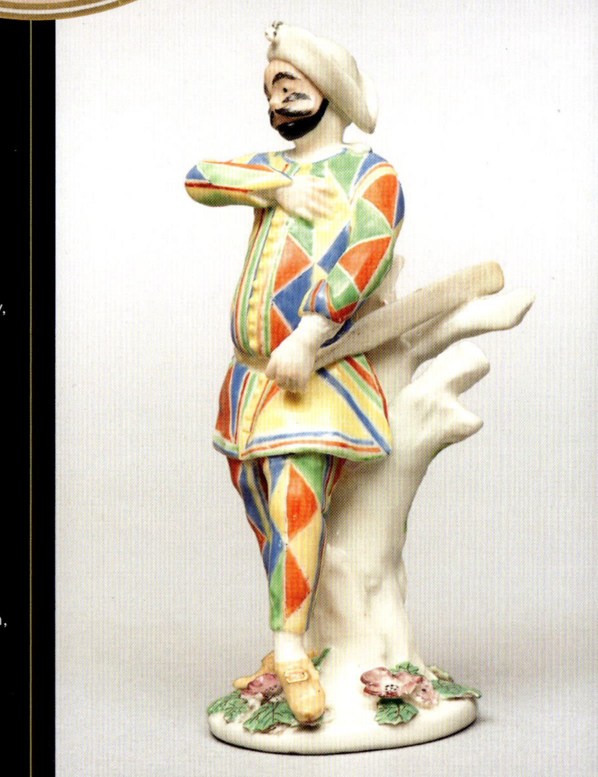

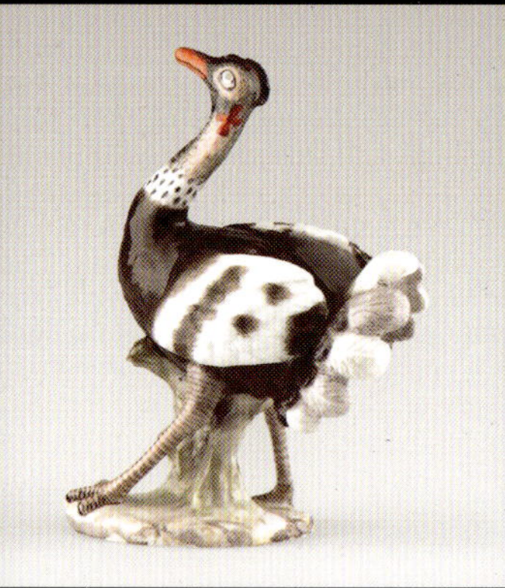

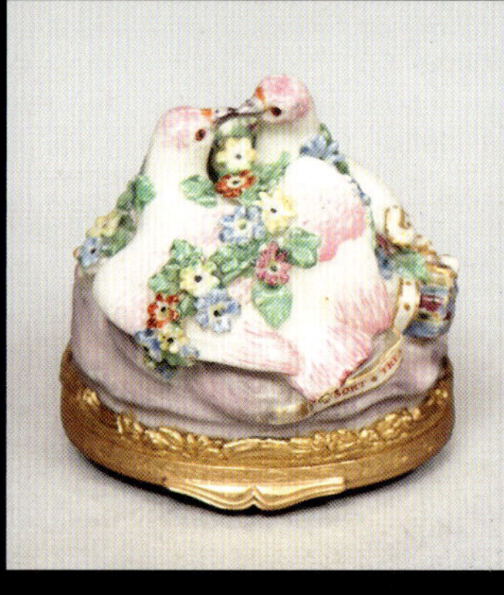

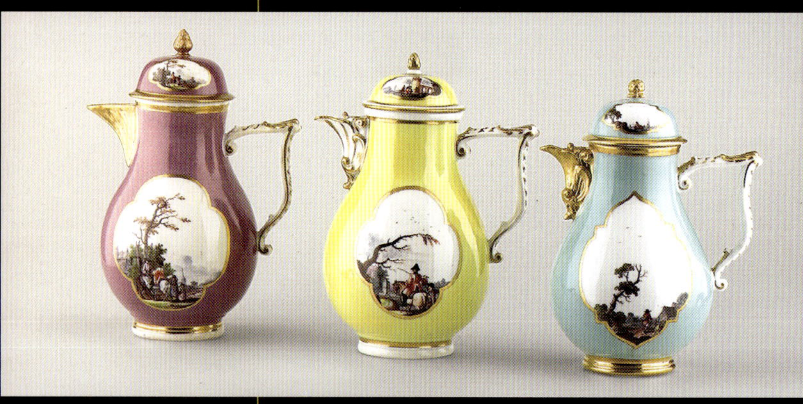

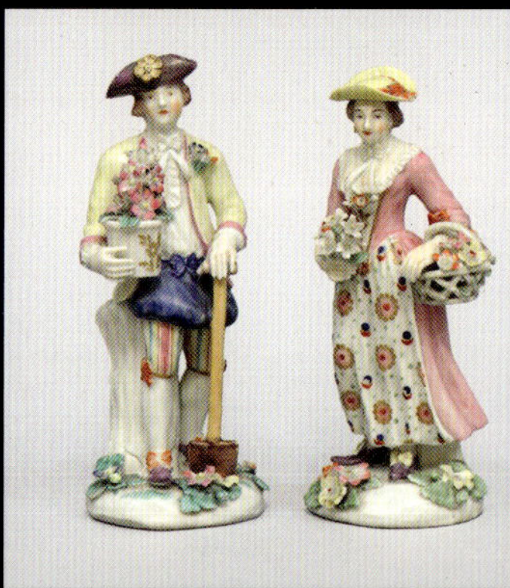

Single plates from important dining services particularly caught David's imagination and on view are Worcester Porcelain plates from *The Duke of Gloucester service*, c. 1765, the *Stowe service*, c. 1813, the *Duke of Clarence 'Hope' service*, 1790–1791, and *'Patience'* from the *Duke of Gloucester service*, c. 1805. Meissen Porcelain (Germany established 1710) plates from the *St Andrew service*, 1744–1745, the *Prince Orlov service*, 1770, the *Swan service*, c. 1738, and the so-called *Christie-Miller service*, 1740–1744, as well as Imperial Porcelain (Russia established 1744) plates from the *Tsar Paul I service*, c. 1790, and the *Grand Duke Mikhail Pavlovich service*, 1825–1855. Gardner Porcelain (Russia 1766–1892) plates from the *Order of St Vladimir service*, 1783–1785, and *Order of St George service*, 1778, are also on display.

Some of David's most interesting figurines are by the English manufacturer Chelsea Porcelain and include the *Madonna and child*, c. 1755, *The carpenter*, c. 1755, a *Commedia dell'Arte figure of Harlequin*, c. 1755, and the superb *The music lesson*, c. 1760. Other English examples include Worcester *The gardener and his companion*, c. 1770, and Derby Porcelain (Britain c. 1750–1848) *The singing lesson*, c. 1765. Of the many European pieces, for rarity, the standouts are a Zurich Porcelain Factory (Switzerland 1763–1790) *Hungarian soldier with a Turkish prisoner*, 1770–1775, and a Fürstenberg Factory *Ostrich*, c. 1758–1759. In more general terms, flower sellers, the occupations and figurines that include dogs singing and dancing feature prominently. While outside the vitrine, large campagna-style urns, hexagonal lidded vases and cache pots were bought to decorate the tops and bottoms of furniture.

Principal Pictures

The drawing room has come to be an elegant location for portraiture, featuring mainly feminine aristocratic subjects from France, Britain and Germany. The official portrait of *Therese Queen Consort of Bavaria* (1792–1854), 1827–1830, after Joseph Karl Stieler (Germany 1781–1858), was acquired from the extraordinary House of Hanover auction at Schloss Marienburg, Germany, in 2005. It depicts Therese wearing her double-sided coronation tiara by Marie-Étienne Nitot (Paris 1750–1809) and sumptuous Empire gown with gold thread. She normally hangs over the mirror above the fireplace. In France, Louis Michel van Loo (France 1707–1771) was a frequent painter of French royalty and the court, and was a sought after portraitist. *Portrait of an aristocratic lady*, c. 1768, captures an attractive, bright-eyed young woman in fine fur-trimmed clothes. At this time van Loo was Director of the special school of the French academy known as the *École Royale des Élèves Protégés.*

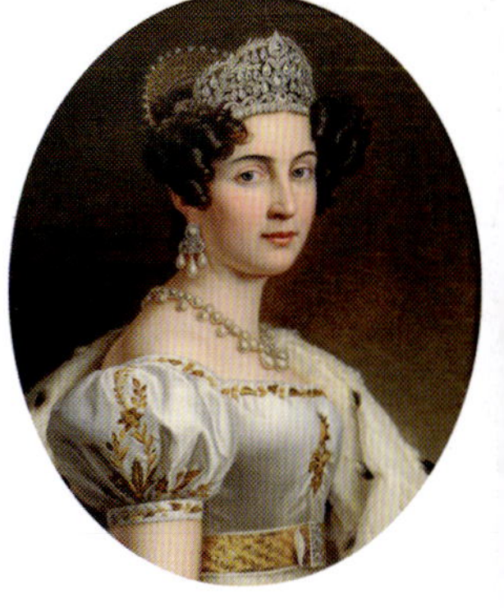

Above: *Therese Queen Consort of Bavaria*, after Joseph Karl Stieler, 1827–1830.

Of the British portraits in the room, the Thomas Phillips (Britain 1770–1845) was purchased in London in 1992. David liked her pose and white dress. Only in 2016 was the sitter confirmed as *Frances Thomasine, Countess Talbot* (Britain 1782–1819), wife of the 2nd Earl Talbot (Britain 1777–1849), c. 1800. Phillips painted the family on several occasions at Ingestre Hall and this image dates to her marriage. The second portrait is by the highly fashionable London artist Francis Cotes, RA (Britain 1726–1770) of *Mrs George Rogers* (Britain 1724–1786), 1768. In fine drapery, set outdoors, Mrs Rogers waters an exotic lily, alluding to her family enterprise. The daughter of Jonathon Tyers, impresario, patron of the arts and owner of the New Spring (Vauxhall) Gardens, she inherited a share of this famous centre of public entertainment in London.

Sculpture

David's interest in French royalty and equine subjects led him to acquire a handsome bronze after Martin van den Bogaert, called Desjardins (France 1637–1694) of *The Sun King, Louis XIV, on horseback*, c. 1710. A life-size monument was erected in Lyon in 1691, and a range of reductions and variations of the monument exist by a number of French foundries. It would seem this is one such example from the 18th century.

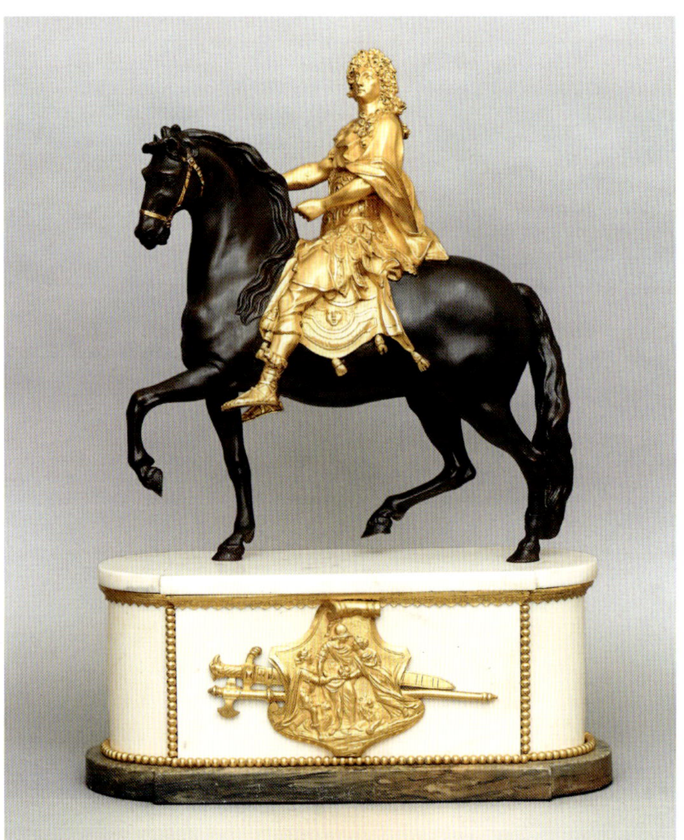

Right: *The Sun King, Louis XIV, on horseback*, after Martin van den Bogaert, called Desjardins, c. 1710.

Opposite page: *Mrs George Rogers*, Francis Cotes, 1768.

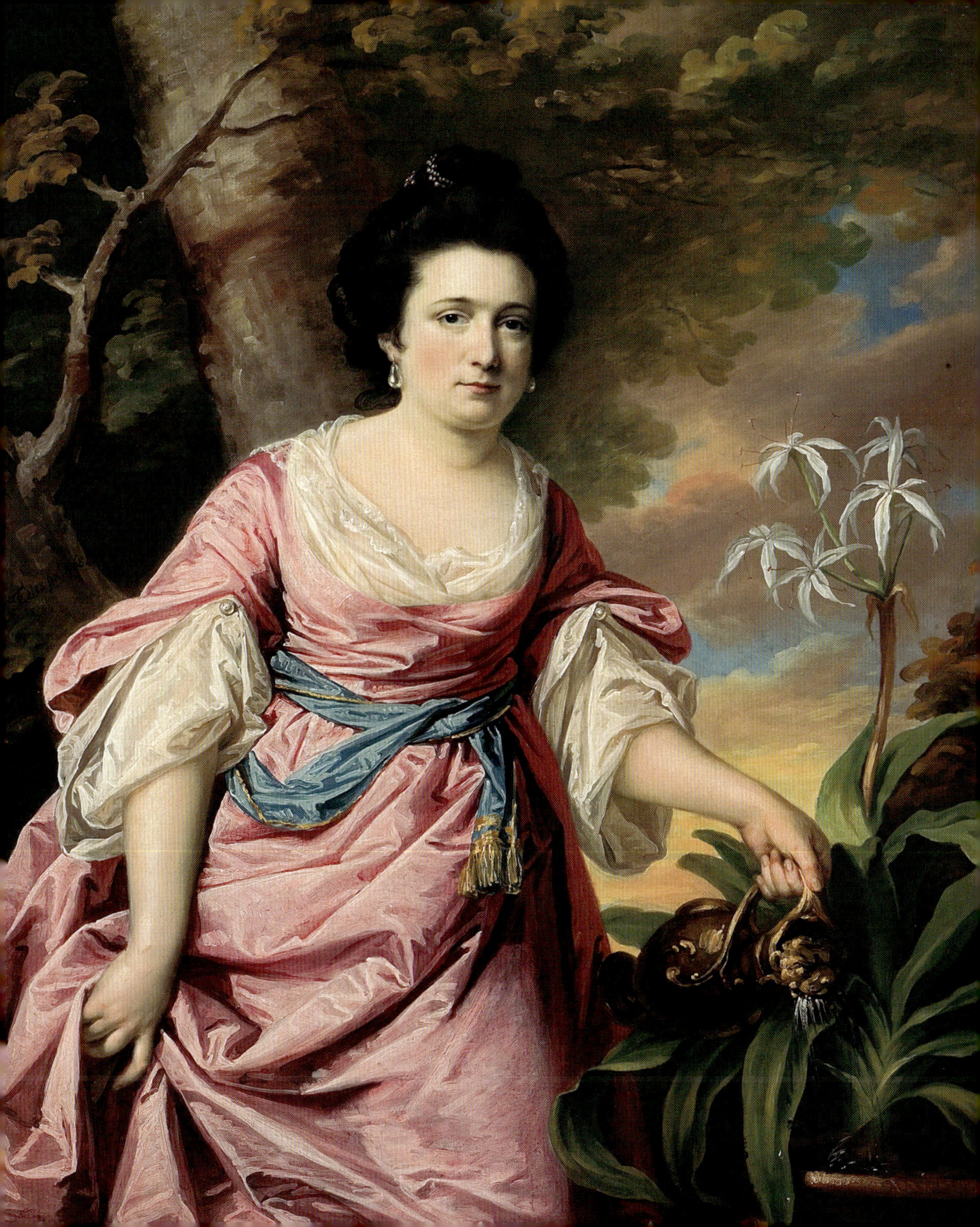

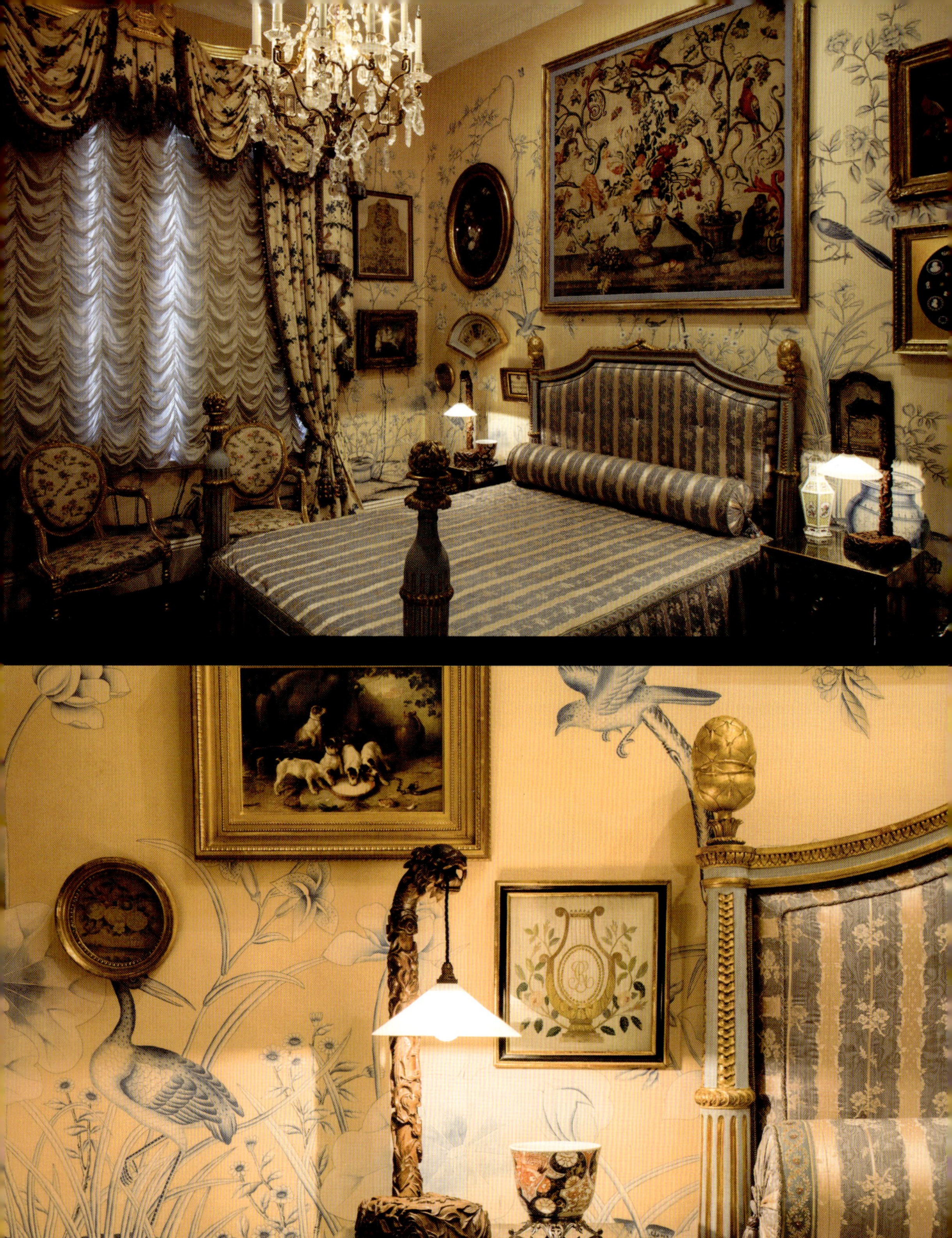

THE CHINOISERIE BEDROOM

The spare bedroom has had a number of incarnations over the decades and was previously pink. It was used on occasion for visiting international dog judges and as a room for David's mother when she came to visit. Some of the smaller paintings in the room are gifts from her to David. The walls are covered in de Gournay's bespoke 'Askew' chinoiserie patterned wallpaper installed in 2001. The sumptuous curtains in moire 'Penelope' from George Le Manach (France established 1829), Paris, are in corresponding tones, and supplied by Stitches Soft Furnishings. Although no chimney flue exists, David added the French marble *Demi lune fireplace surround*, c. 1800, to help anchor the room visually. The chinoiserie theme extends throughout and includes a number of important Japanese and Chinese items collected by David over his lifetime.

Opposite page:
Top: Chinoiserie bedroom featuring the *Double bed*, attributed to Giuseppe Maria Bonzanigo, 1790–1810, and a framed Grotesques tapestry, attributed to the workshop of John Vanderbank, 1700–1725.

Bottom: Chinoiserie bedroom (detail) with Dragon table lamp and a framed Regency *Needlework lyre*, c. 1810.

Furniture

The room is dominated by the *Double bed*, 1790–1810, which stylistically relates to other known examples created by Turin-based, Giuseppe Maria Bonzanigo (Italy 1745–1820). Bonzanigo was one of Italy's leading neoclassic cabinetmakers and wood sculptors. David acquired the bed through Sotheby's in 2003. The bedcover is a lampas moiré from Luigi Bevilacqua of Venice. Regilded and reupholstered, the *Pair of cabriolet armchairs*, c. 1775, are a pretty, French-style design in the manner of English furniture maker, John Linnell (Britain 1729–1796). Not always on display, but acquired for the room, is a French *Commode*, c. 1820, which David bought primarily for its provenance. It came from the bedroom of Arthur Wellesley, 1st Duke of Wellington (Britain 1769–1852), at Stratfield Saye House, Hampshire.

Lighting

The room is centred with an attractive French Louis XV-style *Rock crystal chandelier*, c. 1780, with polished and faceted rosette, diamond, lozenge and pear drops. The central shaft is amethyst-clad and the square hammered metal mounts, with additional acanthus and tendril elements are gilded.

Principal Objects

The fireplace mantel, hearth and chinoiserie Chippendale-style vitrine display a range of Japanese and Chinese porcelain, cloisonné and objets d'art. Like many collectors of European art, David happily strayed into some Asian art when it complemented his collection and rooms. From the Japanese Edo Period (1615–1868) is a rare 18th century novelty folding *Lantern (Te-shoku),*

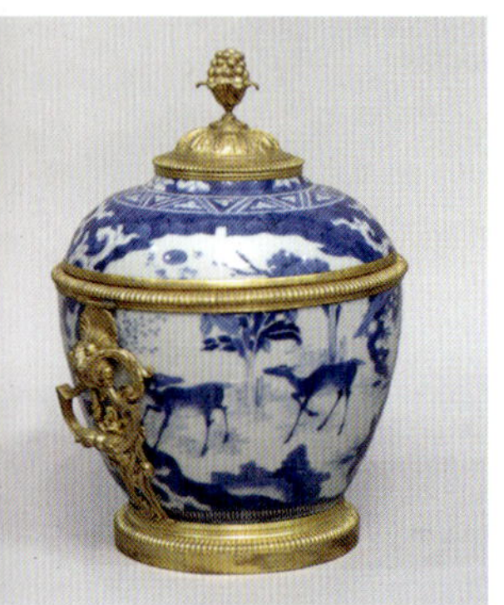

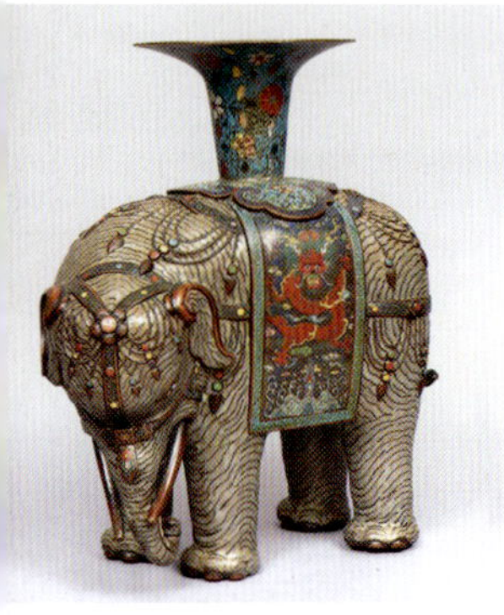

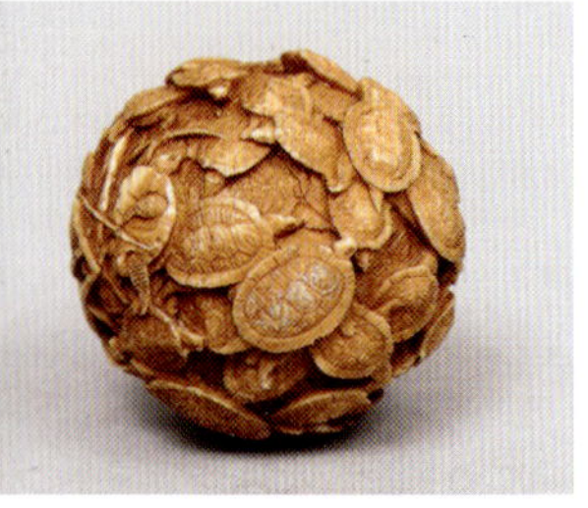

Top: *Covered jar*, China, c. 1625, with French mounts, c. 1715.

Middle: *Cloisonné elephant*, China, 1830–1860.

Bottom: *Okimono puzzle ball*, a bale of Terrapins, Japan, 1868–1900.

Right: *Tobacco leaf pattern wares*, Chinese Export Porcelain, 1775–1785.

Opposite page: *Chinese court ladies bearing gifts*, c. 1780. Attributed to the Imperial Palace Workshop, Forbidden City, Qianlong Period (1736–1795).

a Shokasai *Four-case inro (Horse racing at Kamo shrine)* with *Ojime (bead)*, c. 1850; and a lacquered *Incense box (Kogo)*, c. 1860. More plentiful are objects from the Meiji Period (1868–1912), including Okimono of a *Puzzle ball*, *White elephant* and a *Monkey trainer (Sarumawashi)*; and a carved wood, metal inlaid, *Fujin, God of wind box* c. 1870. Amongst David's Chinese porcelain are two handsome examples mounted in ormolu, illustrating the prestige with which they were held in Europe. A blue and white decorated *Covered jar*, c. 1625, with French mounts, c. 1715; and blue crackle glaze *Vase with dragons*, c. 1640, with French mounts, c. 1880, are both displayed on the mantelpiece. In the vitrine is a selection of Chinese Export Porcelain *Tobacco leaf pattern wares*, 1775–1785, which David loved, and purchased frequently. The large *Cloisonné elephant*, 1830–1860, originally bought in 1992 for the drawing room, is now in the hearth. Near the door as you leave the room is a panel of superb quality and beauty attributed to the Imperial Palace Workshop, Forbidden City, Qianlong Period (1736–1795) of *Chinese court ladies bearing gifts*, c. 1780.

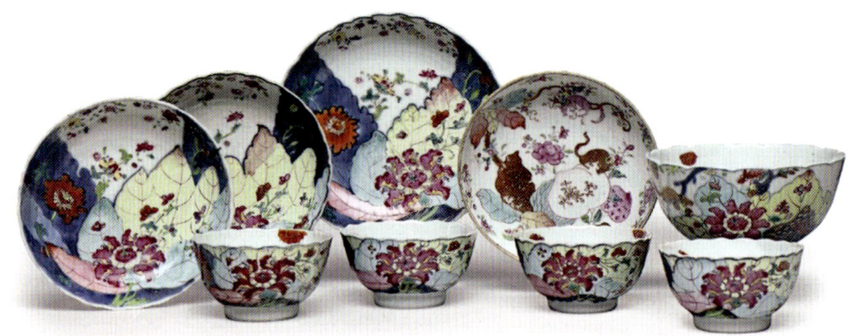

Principal Pictures

Appropriate for a bedroom are the range of smaller, more intimate paintings depicting children, still lives of flowers, European pastoral and city scenes, and orientalist-inspired pictures. There are a number of painted porcelain wall plaques and framed embroideries, the latter of a religious nature. David acquired the framed *Fan (Nymphs awakening Cupid)*, c. 1780, from the estate auction of Princess Margaret, Countess of Snowdon, in 2006. David had a long wishlist but on this occasion was outbid by Queen Elizabeth's representatives on the other lots of interest.

A highlight of the room is the rare *Grotesques tapestry*, 1700–1725, attributed to the workshop of John Vanderbank (Flanders/Britain 1683–1725), displayed above the bedhead. While reduced in size, it maintains good colour and is charming in its depiction of exotic birds and animals set amongst potted trees and a central vase filled with flowers. Vanderbank was Yeoman Arras-maker to the Great Wardrobe, supplying the British royal family with

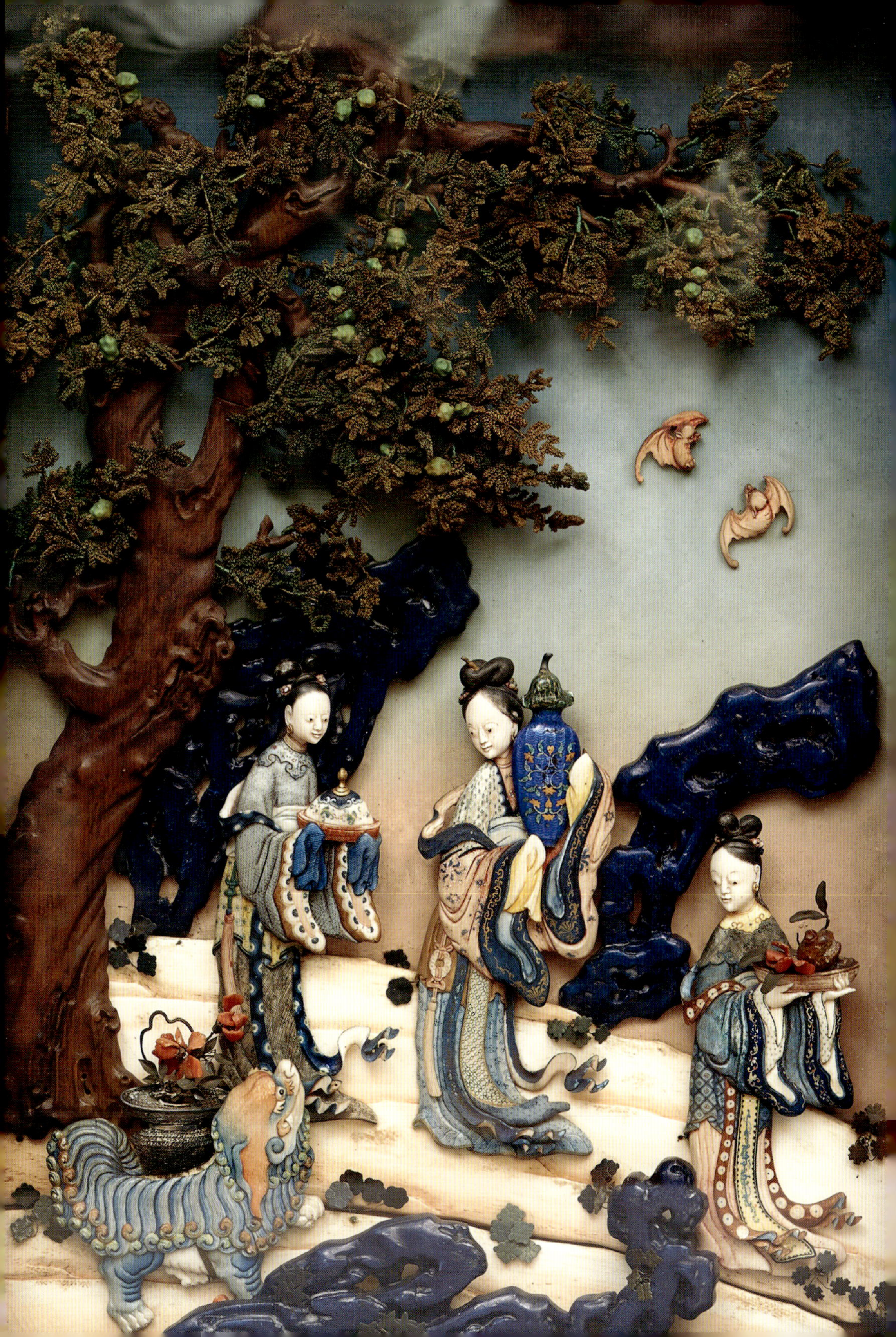

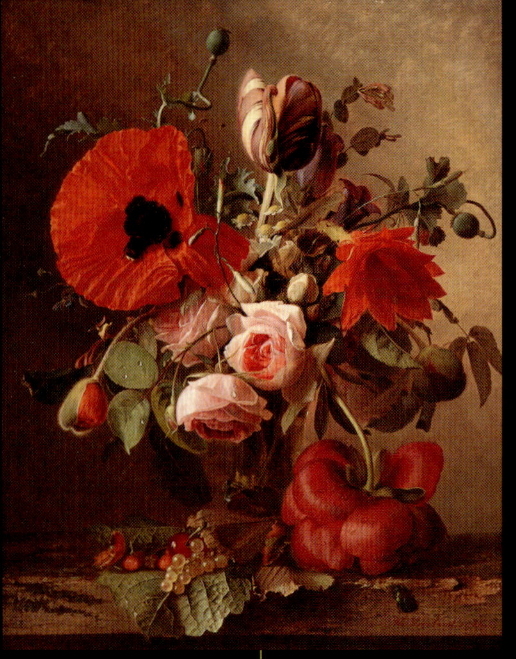

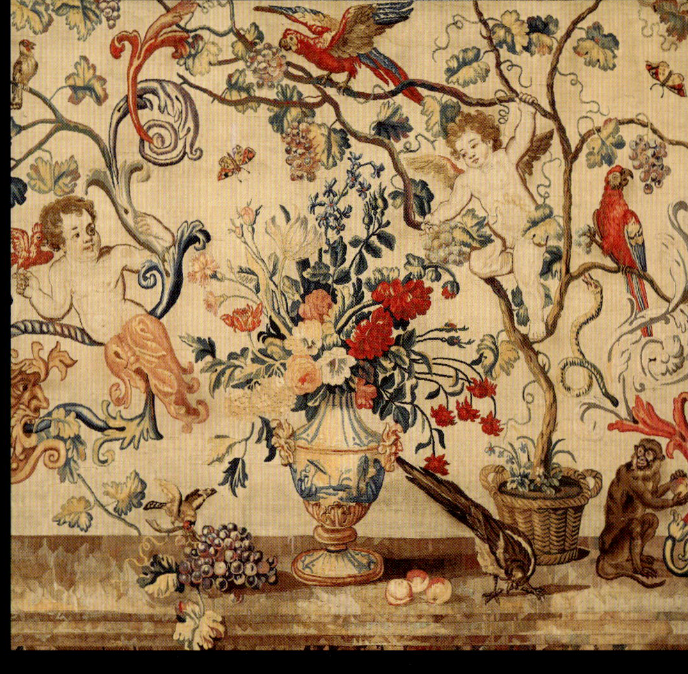

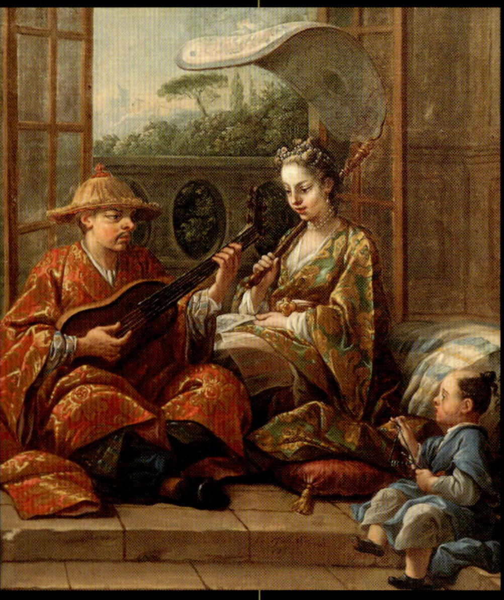

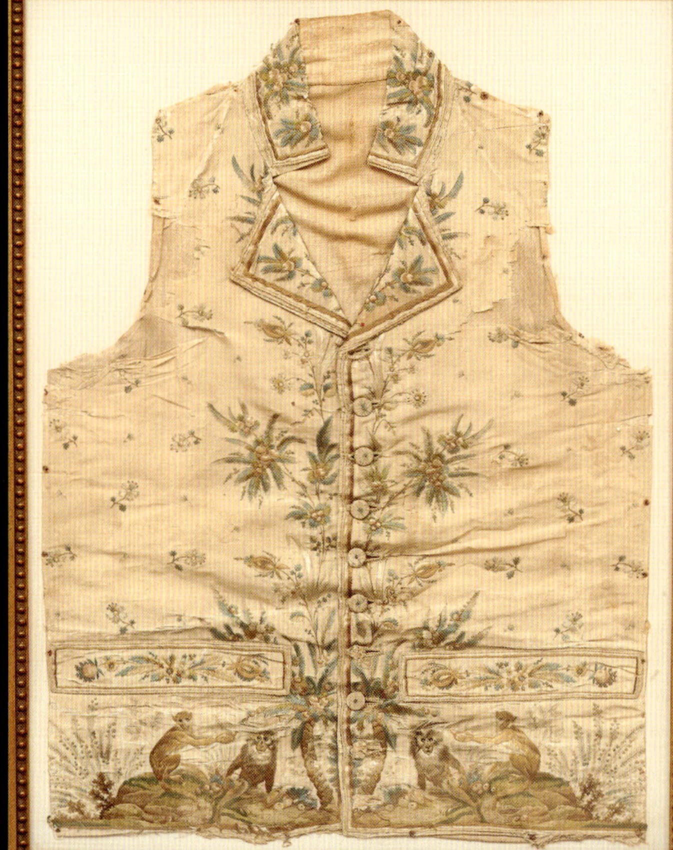

Clockwise from top left:
Still life with flowers, Theude Grönland, 1846.

Grotesques tapestry, attributed to the workshop of John Vanderbank, 1700–1725.

Embroidered Waistcoat, Louis XVI period, 1780–1789.

Oriental scene, Pierre Jollain, 1754.

tapestries from 1689 to 1717. Similarly delightful is the Louis XVI-period embroidered *Waistcoat*, 1780–1789, with its monkeys under coconut trees. The design for this waistcoat survives at the *Musee des Tissues* in Lyon, as well as a waistcoat at the Victoria & Albert Museum, London.

No room in David's home is complete without a painting of a dog and above the door is a fine example by Jakob Bogdany (Britain 1660–1724) of a *Papillon*, c. 1710. Better known for his paintings of exotic birds and flowers in the late baroque-taste (similar to the Vanderbank tapestry), this image captures the preferred lapdog of royal courts. The papillon (butterfly dog) is set in a landscape alongside a red squirrel, great tit and somewhat peculiarly, a still life of fruit. Likely commissioned by a member of the English royal court, the painting in the late 20th century belonged to the animalier collector, Count Alarico Palmieri of Italy. Above the fireplace is a fine Pierre Jollain (France 1720–1762) painting of an *Oriental scene*, 1754, illustrating musicians in rich brocades with exotic objects. The small Theude Grönland (France/Germany 1817–1858), *Still life with flowers*, 1846, was acquired by David two months before he passed away. Like many paintings, a new bespoke frame was made by Charles Hewitt Frames of Sydney. Sadly, David did not see the finished product.

Below: *Papillon*, Jakob Bogdany, c. 1710.

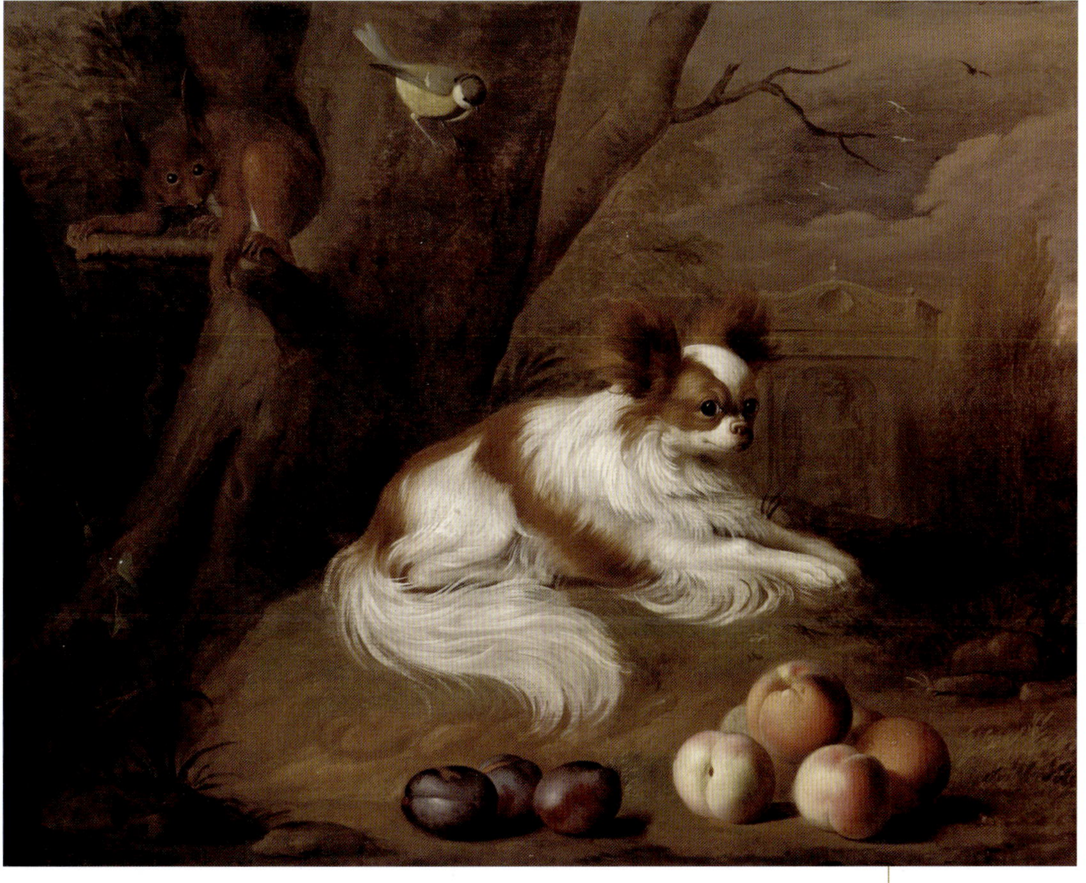

THE MILITARY DINING ROOM

Instantly impressive with its red paper and walls adorned with portraits of officers, the Military dining room has long been a feature of David's home. The flock, floral paper dates to the 1970s, when Angus Foulds worked for David, and also maintains simpler, less extravagant green curtains from the period. David often spoke of replacing the paper with a deeper coloured, more masculine paper. He also looked at many military-themed marble fire mantels, but did not find one of the necessary, diminutive proportions. He did however call upon painter Steve Baliga to create a grand, faux-marble door surround, replete with pediment in 2000. David acquired a range of military-inspired objects and clocks for the room as well. Although always his formal dining room adjoining the kitchen, it saw very little use, with David preferring the Roman room for entertaining.

Furniture

The dining room contains a range of English Regency furniture, and from the same period a rare matched pair of Russian attributed *Vitrine cabinets*, c. 1810, which David modified to house his porcelain tablewares. A feature of these Graeco-Roman-Egyptian revival vitrines are the reeded columns decorated with ormolu mounts. Standing in the hearth are a *Pair of Pole screens*, c. 1810, to Thomas Hope's design of Roman shields, held aloft by spears. The room contains the only musical instrument in the collection, a John Broadwood & Son (Britain established 1728), *Sofa table piano*, 1803, to a Thomas Sheraton design. Sold at the closure of the Broadwood museum, the piano exists in the same form at Ham House, a National Trust property in Surrey. The large and imposing *Side cabinet*, c. 1810, attributed to designer George Bullock (Britain 1777–1818), was acquired in 2002. Veneered in

Right: *Sofa table piano*, John Broadwood & Son, 1803.

Opposite page: Military dining room featuring a *Side cabinet*, George Bullock, c. 1810, and Trophies of *war mantel clock*, Laurent Ridel, c. 1780. The topmost painting is of *Captain Peter Everard Buckworth*, Mather Brown 1787–1793; centred below hangs *Captain Percy Burrells' horse 'Peninsula'*, David Dalby, c. 1826.

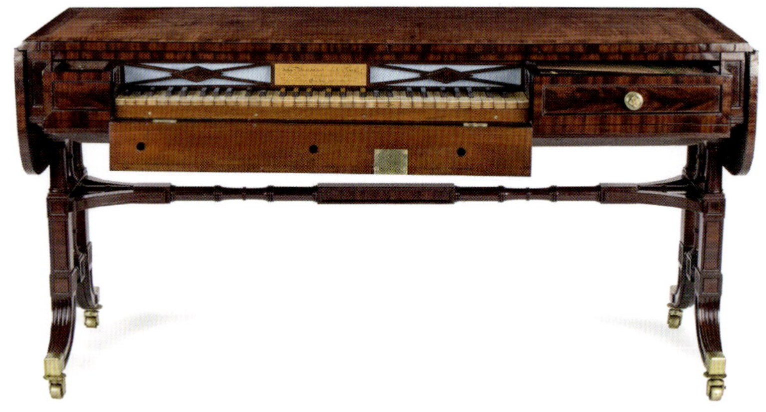

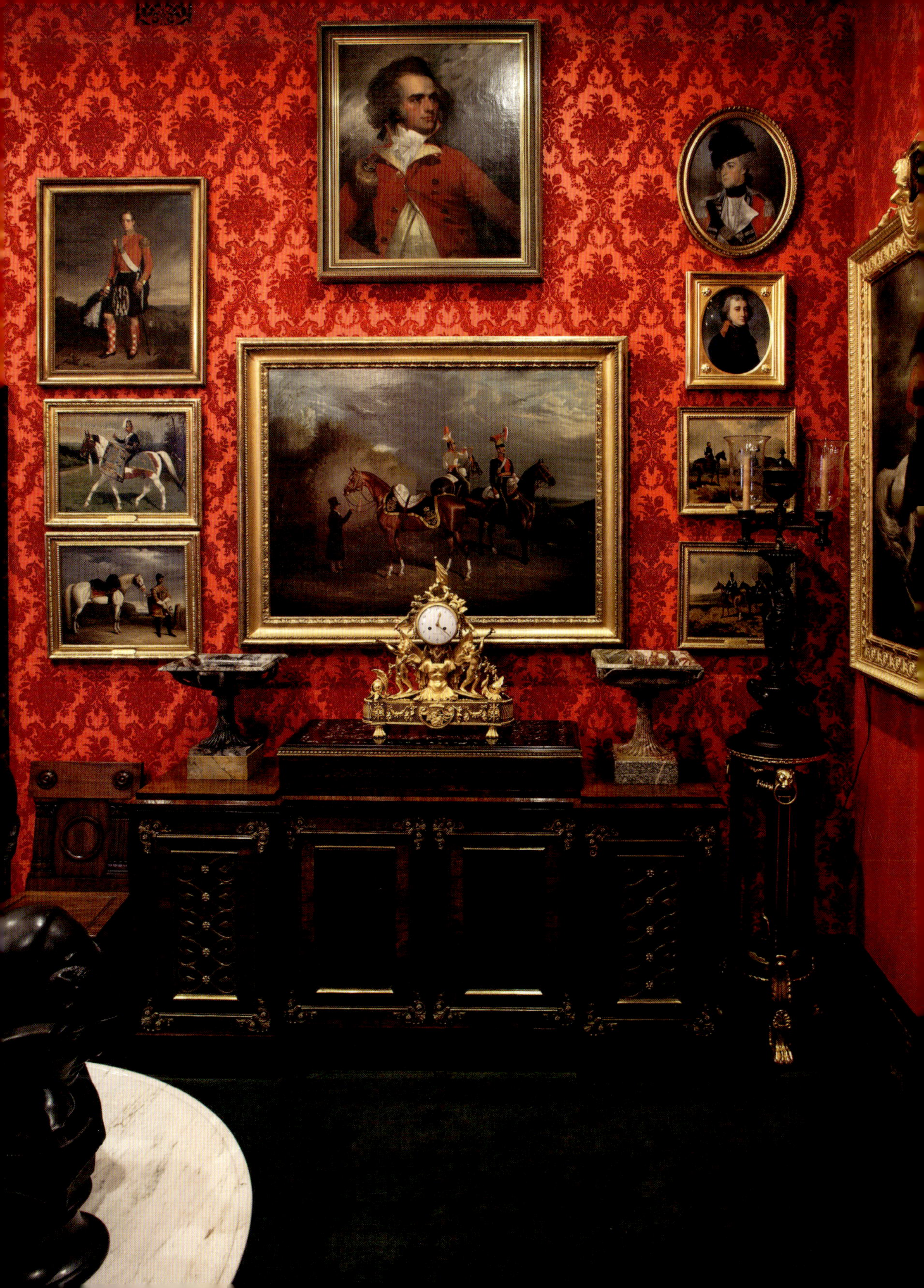

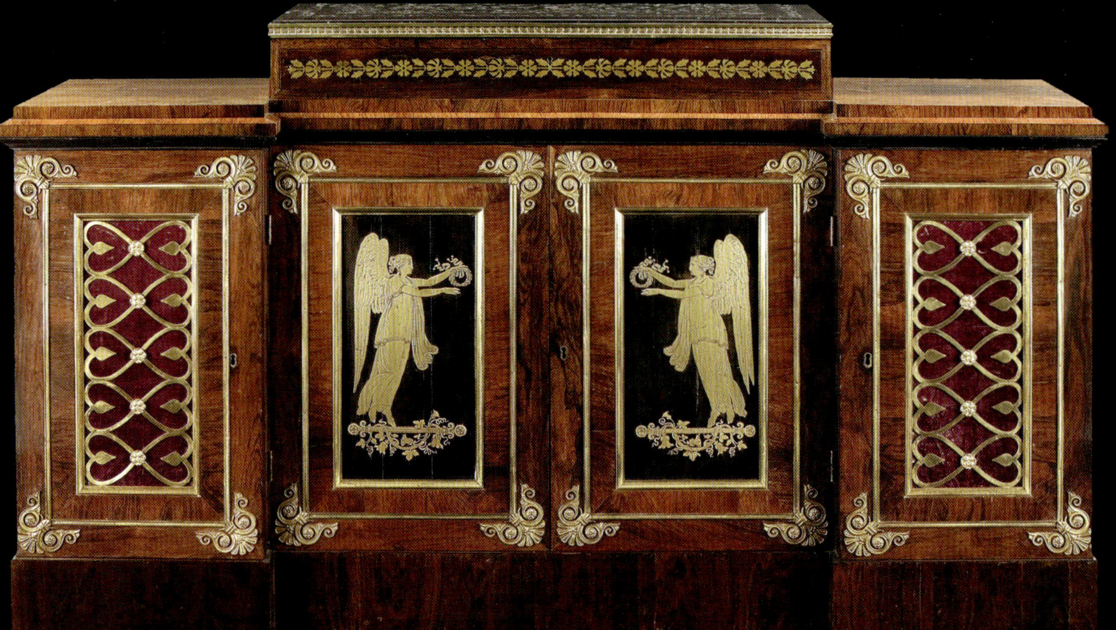

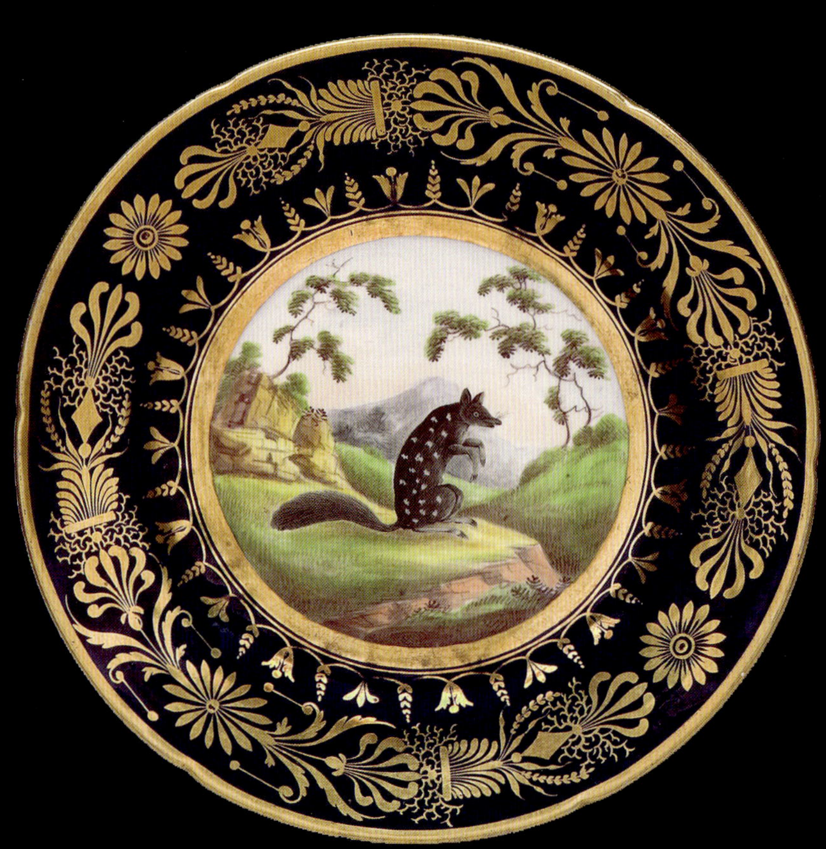

rosewood and ebony, and embellished with brass and gilt mounts, the main feature of the piece is the two striking images of the winged female figure of Nike, goddess of victory, with outstretched arms holding a laurel wreath. The Regency *Breakfast table* (not always displayed), c. 1825, was acquired by David c. 1969 from an antique dealer in Ballarat, and features an attractive brass inlaid border. Of superlative quality are the set of *Six Regency dining chairs*, c. 1820, in carved rosewood, after the ancient Greek *klismos* form. Acquired for the room, but not always displayed in-situ, is the large *Fall-front desk (Secrétaire à abattant)*, c. 1805, in the manner of Thomas Hope. In the French Imperial manner, it carries a brass label: 'Cabinet given to Sarah, Countess of Jersey, by Prince Poniatowski'.

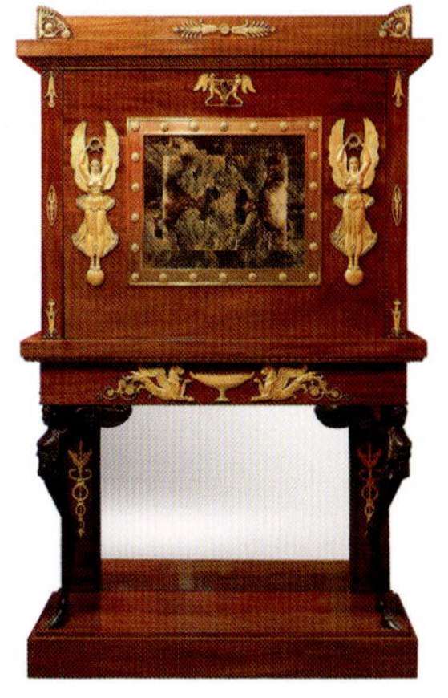

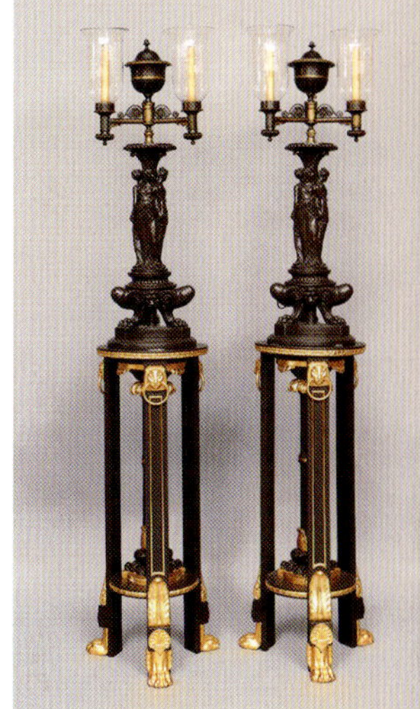

Opposite page:
Top: *Side cabinet*, George Bullock, c. 1810.

Bottom: *'The Spotted opofsum of new south wales'*, plate from a *Zoological part dessert service*, Coalport Porcelain, 1800–1805.

This page:
Top: *Fall-front desk (Secrétaire à abattant)*, in the manner of Thomas Hope, c. 1805.

Bottom: *Pair of argand lamp torchères*, Robert Shout, c. 1802.

Lighting

Of great interest is the large gilt-metal *Argand chandelier* (Colza-oil), c. 1805, attributed to George Bullock, which David acquired for the room in 1996. The original commission is unknown, however Bullock is known to have supplied high-quality lighting to Viscount Cobham at Hagley Hall, Worcester and Cholmondley Castle in Cheshire. The Robert Shout (Britain 1764–1843) *Pair of argand lamp torchères*, c. 1802, once part of the Charles and Lavinia Handley-Read Collection in London, were acquired in Sydney in 1994. Faux-bronze plaster, ebony and gilt, the torchères sit on their original tripod form bases. In the Greek revival style, the three Graces form the decorative stem supported by crouching paw feet.

Principal Objects

The dining room was the main setting for David's English porcelain collection of table-wares and contains items from the manufacturers of Worcester, Derby, Coalport, Spode, Bow, Longton Hall and Chelsea. They range in style from the rococo and chinoiserie to the neoclassic and Regency tastes. Like many collectors, David acquired a Derby Porcelain William 'Quaker' Pegg (Britain 1774–1851) painted *Botanical plate*, 1810–1820, of a double Anemone. Amongst a wide range of Worcester Porcelain are a handsome *Pair of ice pails*, 1770–1775, with solid blue grounds and floral sprays on white reserves. The Coalport Porcelain *Zoological part dessert service*, 1800–1805, was acquired from The James O. Fairfax Collection sale in 2003. David's primary interest was in one plate, which illustrates an Australian marsupial. In red script to the reverse of the plate it reads: 'The Spotted opofsum of new south wales'. David was delighted by it.

On the Bullock side cabinet stand two *Tazza* in coloured marble, 1820–1840, attributed to the Benedetto Boschetti workshop (Italy c. 1820–1879) after the antique. In the same vein, David acquired the bronze reductions of the *'Furietti' centaurs*, c. 1840, the originals of which were

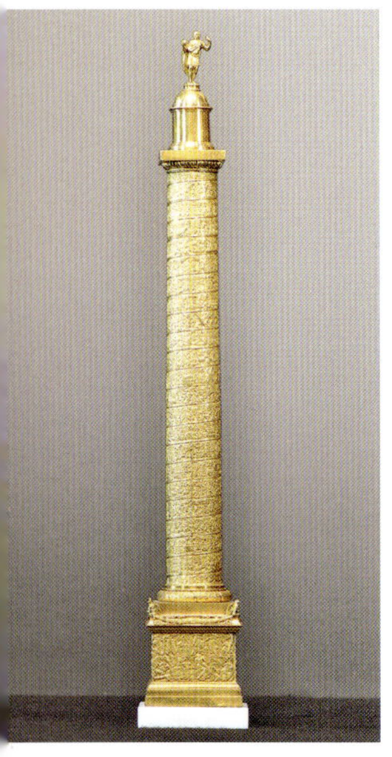

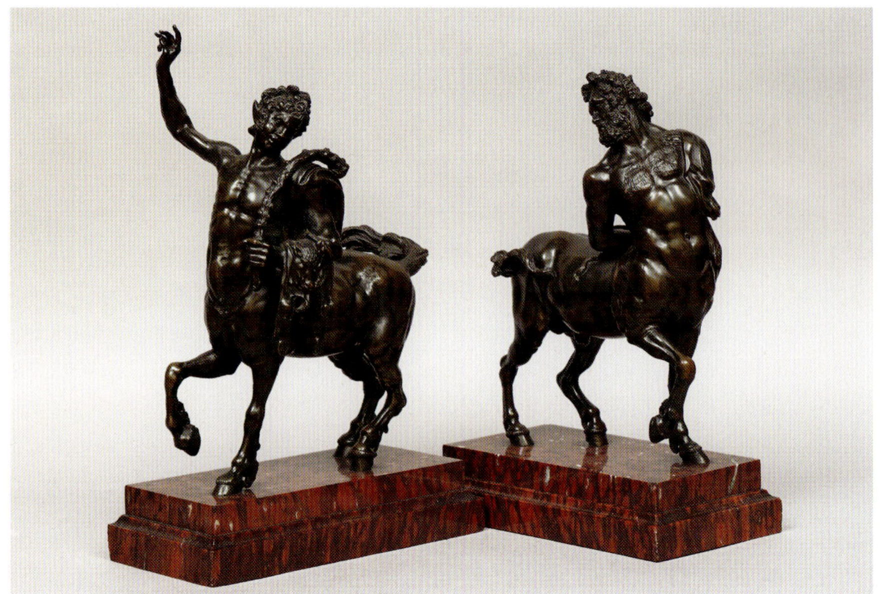

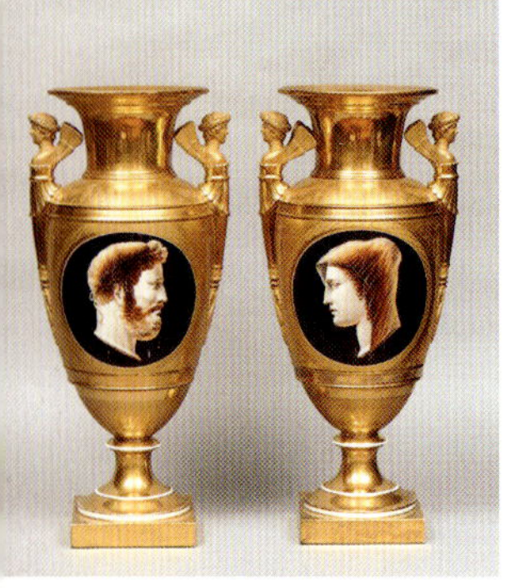

Clockwise from top left: *Trajan's column*, attributed to William Hopfgarten and Benjamin Jollage, c. 1810.

Pair of 'Furietti' centaurs, Italy, c. 1840.

Pair of vases 'Love always overcomes Wisdom' attributed to Louis Socrate Fouquet, painter, and Perche Factory (Paris), c. 1830.

unearthed at Hadrian's villa at Tivoli in 1736, and much copied as their fame spread from the Capitoline Museum, Rome. Another Grand Tour favourite were reductions of *Trajan's column*. This Roman triumphal monument was the source for Napoléon's *Vendôme column*, 1806–1810, which inspired foundries to reproduce both in the early 19th century. David's *Trajan's column* dates to c. 1810 and although not marked, is attributed to William Hopfgarten (Germany/Italy 1779–1860) and Benjamin Jollage (Germany/Italy 1787–1837). Alternately, it centred David's dining table or found a place in the Roman room. Purely French, and continuing David's fascination with Napoléon, is the Ferdinand Barbedienne (France 1838–1892) silvered *Napoléon entering Cairo*, c. 1897, after Jean-Léon Gérôme (France 1824–1904). Made to celebrate the 100th anniversary of the event, Gérôme's model met with great enthusiasm and was reproduced in several sizes by Parisian foundries.

Clocks, an integral part of every room in Fermoy House, pervade the dining room and are military inspired. The French *Empire obelisk clock*, c. 1810, on the mantel-shelf takes an Egyptian form; embellished with Graeco-Roman 'Trophies of War' ormolu mounts. The imposing Laurent Ridel (France active 1770–1790) *Trophies of war mantel clock*, c. 1780, was acquired from the Mrs Robert Lehman Collection in New York in 2010. The iconography of the ormolu decoration is symbols of 'Victory in Battle' with cherubs trumpeting success. Allusions to the classical were widespread throughout Europe, including Russia, and David was keen in his later years to represent the skills and quality of their art. The Russian *Pair of vases with canephorae*, c. 1810, highlight the quality of their metalwork, influenced by the classical volute crater. Also known for their prowess in glass making, the Russian *Twin handled vase*, c. 1840, imitates cut and polished agate with ormolu handles.

Principal Pictures

David spent many years collecting European military portraits and regimental paintings for his dining room, always upgrading as he went and enjoying learning about the lives of the people depicted. A favourite was the George Dawe, RA (Britain 1781–1829) portrait of *General Don Miguel Ricardo Alava* (Spain 1770–1843), 1818, who was present at the two major battles of the Napoléonic Wars: Trafalgar and Waterloo. Highly decorated, the cross of the Order of the Bath hangs from his neck and on his chest he wears the red cross of the Order of Santiago. In 2006, David was anxious to acquire a second Dawe, this time of *Prince Leopold of Saxe-Coburg, Duke of Saxony* (later Leopold I, King of the Belgians), 1820, when it came up for sale in North Wales. Successful, David had the canvas restored and a bespoke frame made. Leopold is depicted wearing an English uniform (he married Princess Charlotte, daughter of the Prince Regent), seated on a rearing white charger. He distinguished himself in the Russian army fighting against Napoléon and the painting's composition deliberately references Jacques-Louis David's *Napoléon Bonaparte, crossing the Alps* of 1803.

Other portraits of note include Charles Paulin François Matet's (France 1798–1870) *Auguste Laurent Casimir-Périer* (France 1811–1876), 1840, a French diplomat and political leader, who wears the uniform of a Chargé d'Affaires, with the neck badge of the Spanish Order of Isabelle the Catholic and the officer's cross of the French Légion d'Honneur. The subject of the imposing Robert Lefèvre (France 1755–1830) is *Anatole Demidoff* (Russia/Italy 1813–1870), 1820, and is housed in its original frame. Later, it was owned by Prince Alexander of Yugoslavia (Britain b. 1945), before being sold to David in 2005. Young Anatole wears the uniform of the Russian Hussars. From an immensely wealthy Russian family he would, like his father, become an art collector, spending his time living between France and Italy. Lastly, attributed to Niels Simonsen (Denmark 1807–1885), a depiction of *'Bao', an Algerian Spahi*, c. 1840, is a very rare example illustrating a member of the light cavalry regiment of the French army in Algeria. Simonsen travelled to the region and was struck by the exotic nature of much of what he saw, recording his impressions in drawings and studio paintings.

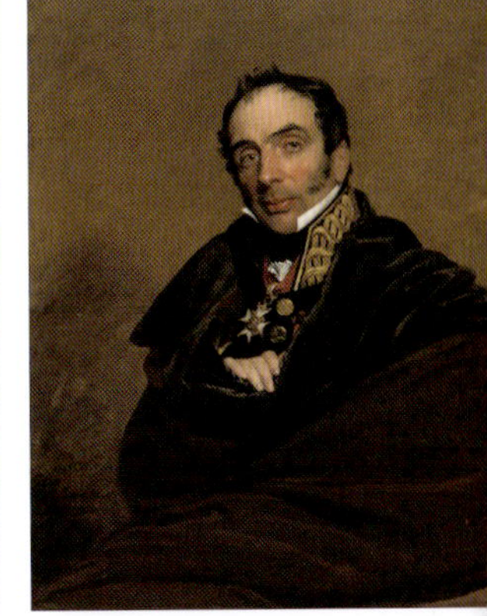

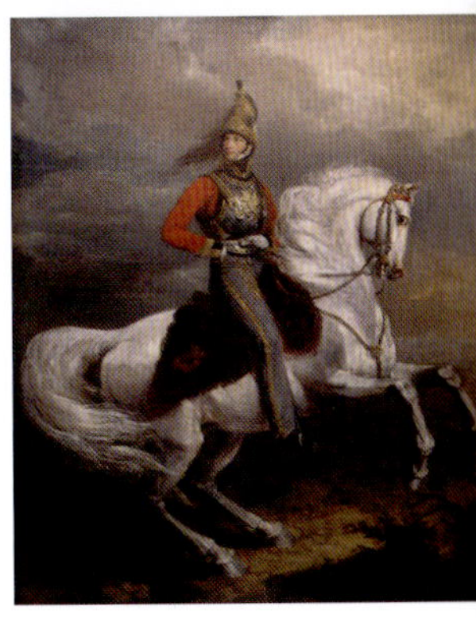

Top: *General Don Miguel Ricardo Alava* (Spain 1770–1843), George Dawe, RA, 1818.

Bottom: *Prince Leopold of Saxe-Coburg, Duke of Saxony* (later Leopold I, King of the Belgians), George Dawe, RA, 1820.

Following spread:
Left: *Anatole Demidoff*, Robert Lefèvre, 1820.

Right: *'Bao', an Algerian Spahi*, Niels Simonsen, c. 1840.

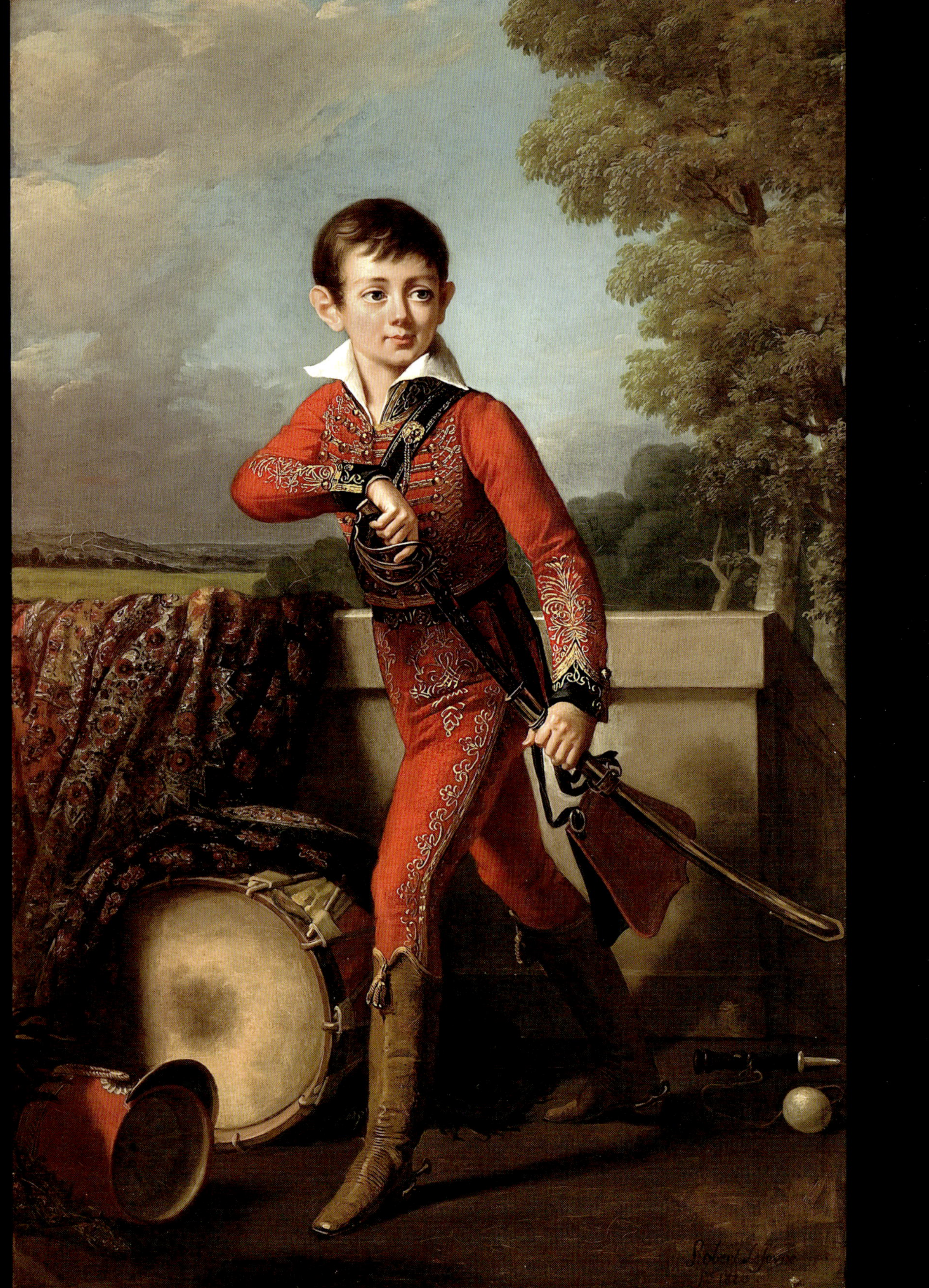

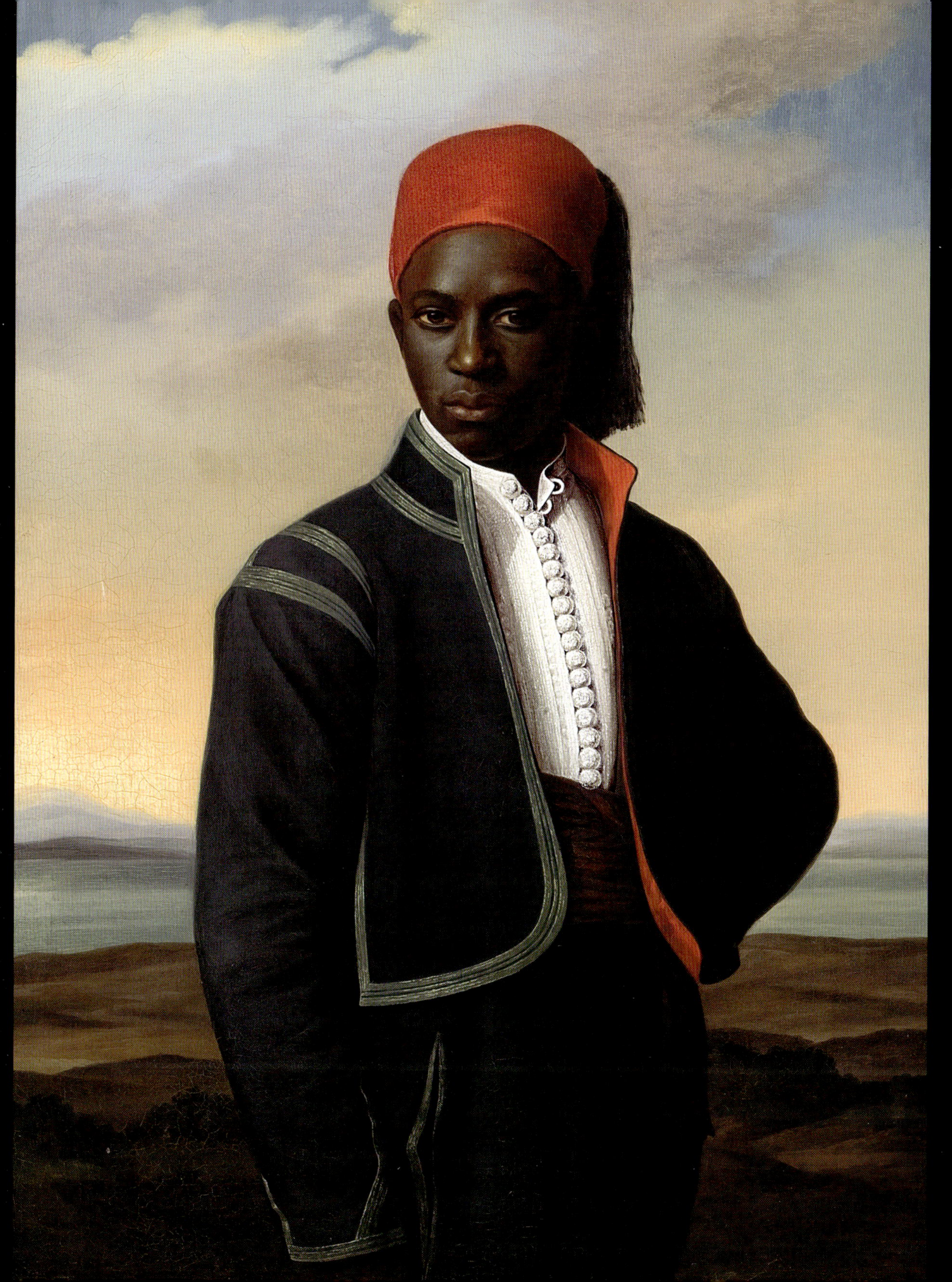

THE KITCHEN

David's kitchen is truly the hearth of his home, lined with mementoes from childhood, travels, and good times. David and his mother chose the block-printed hessian in the early 1970s from Commission Dyers, Adelaide. The walls support a showcase of nursery pottery, animal paintings, folk and naïve art, framed embroideries, Dutch and Staffordshire pottery as well as a range of novelties and knick-knacks. The country-style dresser was used by David to display boxes, toys, mechanical moneyboxes, pottery mugs and toile ware. A much-used room for casual morning teas – crackers with Vegemite and cheese or tomato – and for midnight sorties to the fridge for his favourite ice cream, it also houses David's old enamel stove which was regularly used to cook meat for the dogs in the kennels. The kitchen window originally looked across to the kennel door. David could see the coming and goings of staff and dogs and give his own instructions as desired through the window! Today, the kitchen is a source of enchantment for visitors and the most common comments include: 'Was it really like this?' and 'Who did the dusting?'

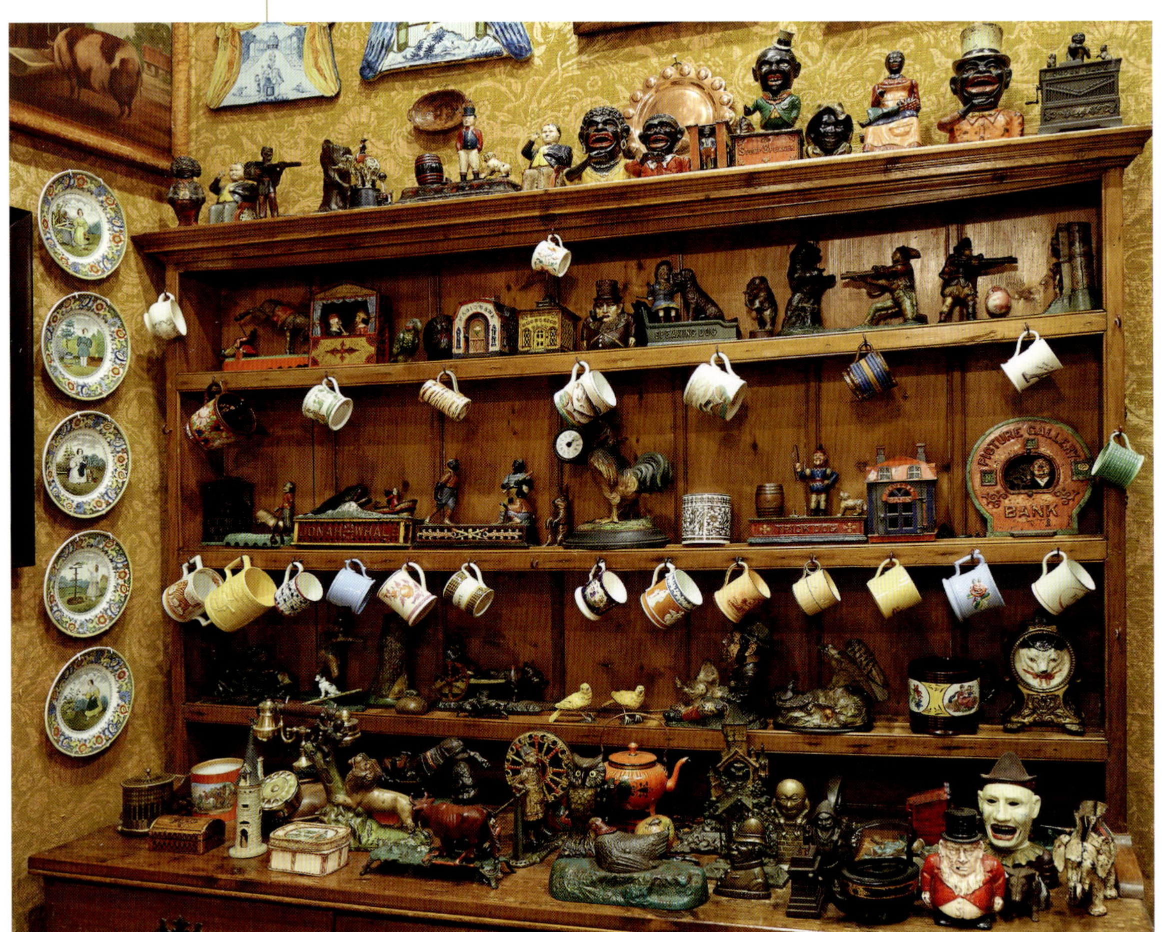

Below: The kitchen dresser with British and American moneyboxes as well as English mugs and other knick-knacks.

Furniture

The *Breakfast table*, c. 1880, is the only piece of Australian furniture in the collection. Made of cedar, it belonged to David's parents and was kept for sentimental reasons. Likewise, the *Cockfighting stool* in saddle form, c. 1950, was his father's shoe polishing seat. The *Four federal style chairs* are 1970s reproductions after Lambert Hitchcock (United States 1795–1852). The squab fabric and matching curtains are a Pierre Frey (France established 1935) cotton 'La Basse Cour' (The barnyard) which David selected from their store in Paris. For a period of time the curtains were changed almost seasonally and include the patterns 'Minton' of teacups and 'Staffordshire' from the Clarence House Collection of pottery figurines, both by Frey.

Lighting

The two faience lights in the kitchen were bought from an auction in New York in 2009. A *Square hall lantern* and a converted *Bird-cage lantern,* they are possibly Hungarian and date 1870–1900. They reminded David of the lights he saw in traditional Viennese coffee houses.

Below: The kitchen decorated with a range of pottery plates, framed embroideries, foil pictures and many other objects.

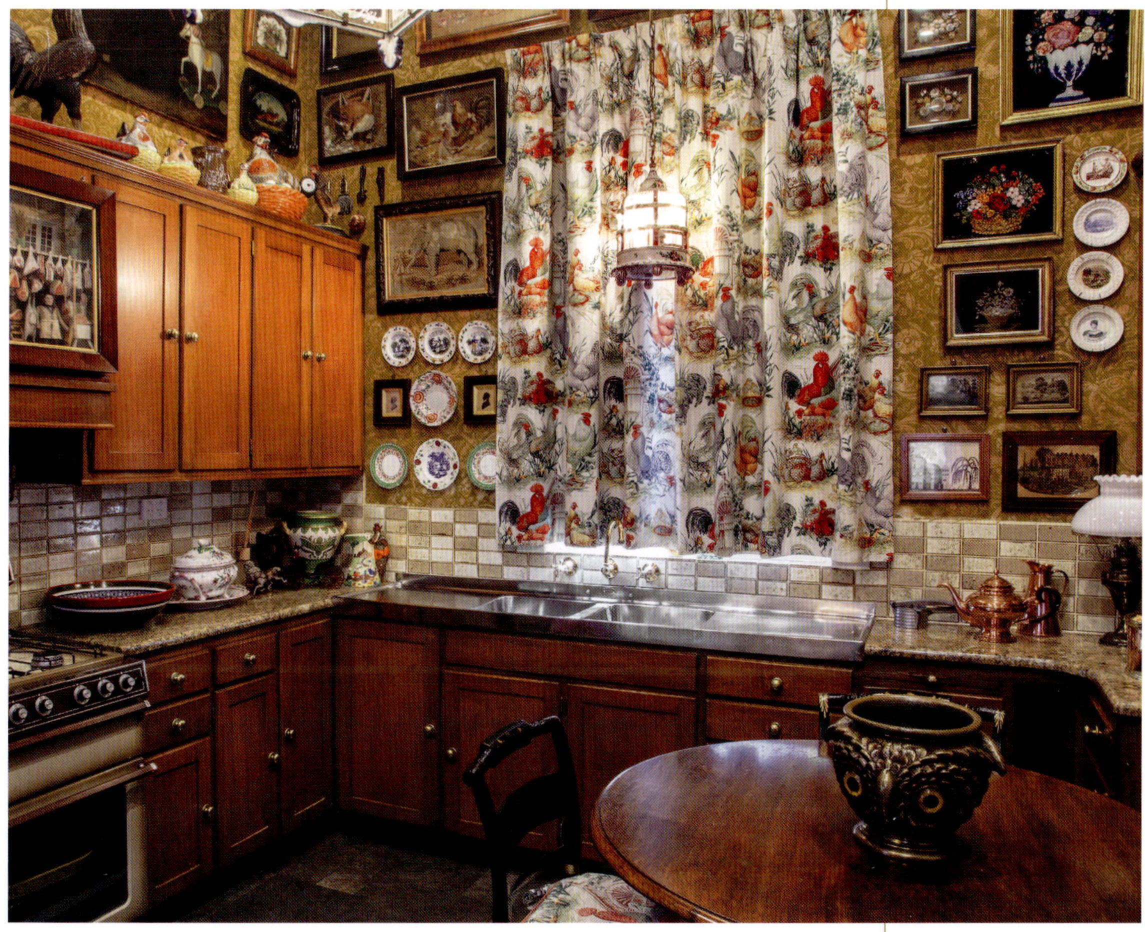

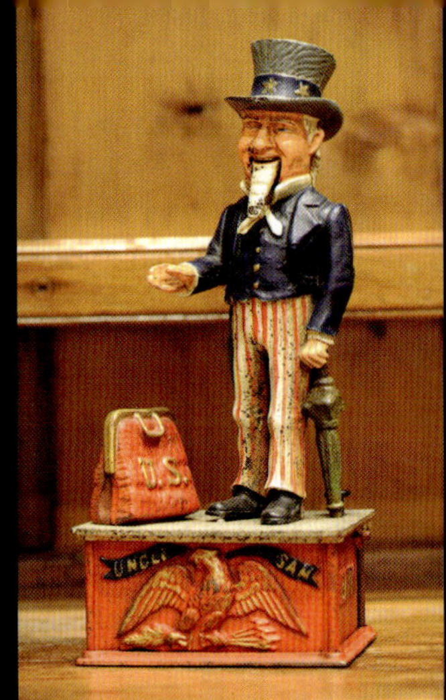

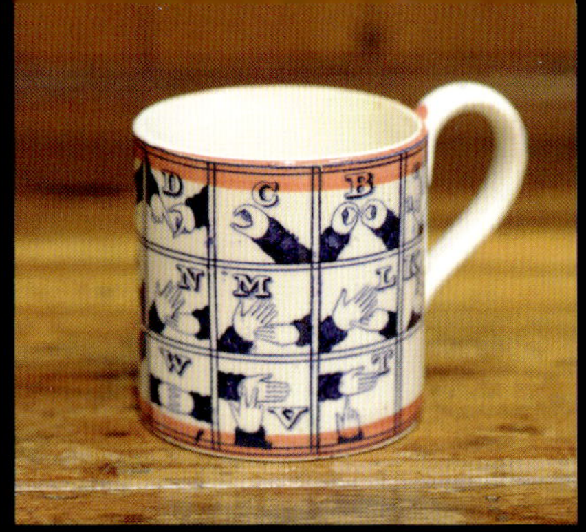

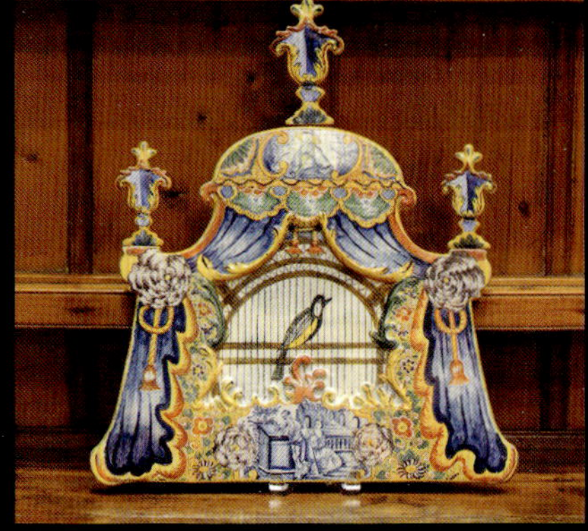

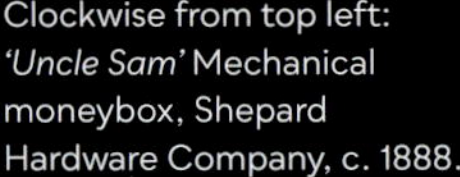

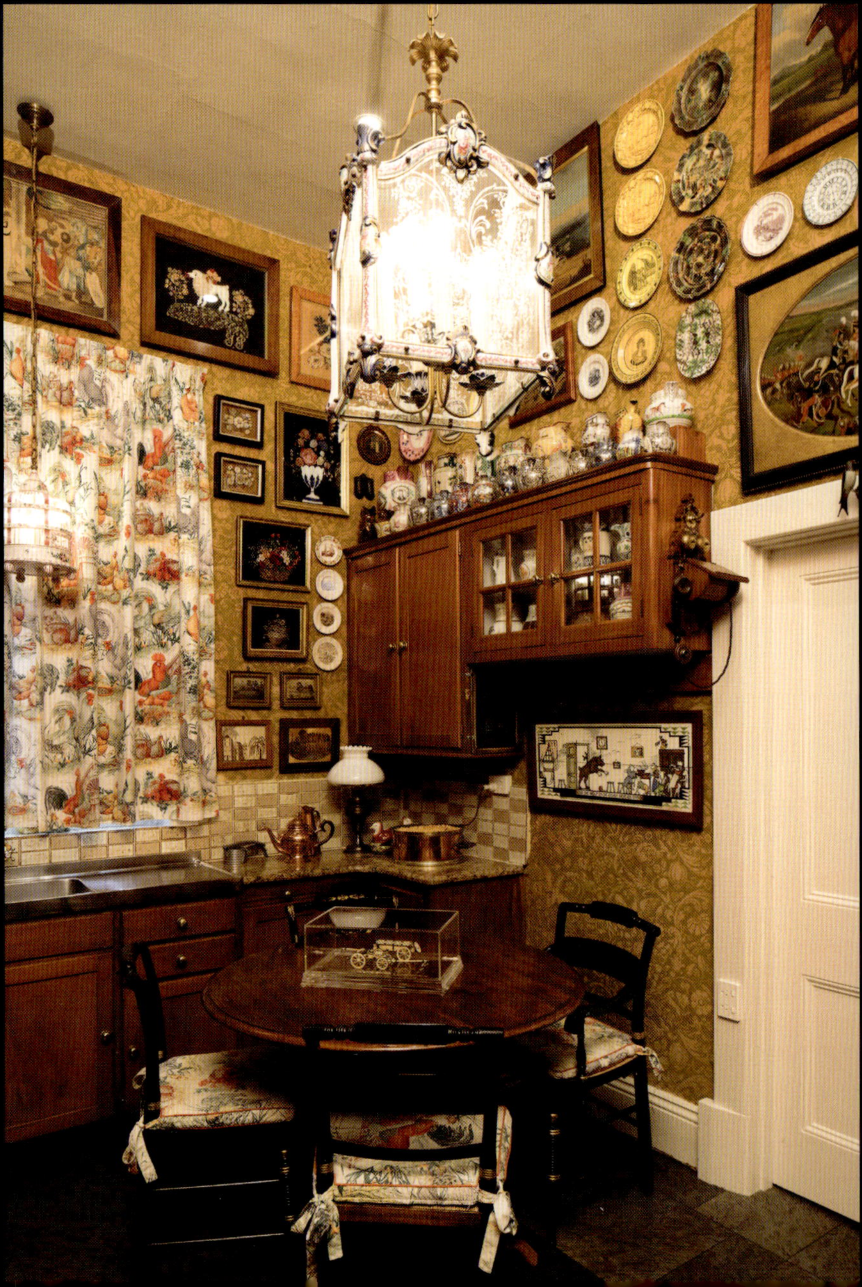

Clockwise from top left: *'Uncle Sam'* Mechanical moneybox, Shepard Hardware Company, c. 1888.

Child's mug (British Sign Language alphabet), Staffordshire Potteries, c. 1820.

Trompe l'oeil *Bird-cage plaque*, Dutch Delft, 1760.

The kitchen with a *Square hall lantern*, 1870–1900, possibly Hungarian, and an Australian cedar *Breakfast table*, c. 1880, with *Four federal style chairs* after Lambert Hitchcock, 1970s.

Principal Objects

More was more for David's kitchen; he enjoyed collecting groups of objects as well as individual examples. Price was not an important factor, rather, condition was, and adding to the themes he developed around nursery plates, English lustre jugs, chook tureens, Delft plaques, animalier plates, English mugs and American mechanical moneyboxes. His moneybox collection numbers 36, including the manufacturers Shepard Hardware Company (United States 1866–1892); Hubley Manufacturing Company (United States 1894–c. 1969); Kyser & Rex Company (United States 1879–1884); and J. & E. Stevens Company (United States 1843–1950). Examples include the *Moneybox 'Punch & Judy'*, c. 1884; *Mechanical moneybox 'Uncle Sam'*, c. 1888; as well as a range of animals, banks, African-American mechanical banks and the rare *Mechanical bank 'Girl Skipping Rope'*, c. 1890, which was made in limited numbers due to its complexity. David always kept a jar of copper coins and enjoyed playing with the banks, especially when staff brought their children to visit.

In the top cupboards, above where the fridge used to be, are David's 19th century English lustre jugs with hunting scenes, chinoiserie themes, figures from history, and topical commentaries. The Sunderland Potteries (Britain c. 1800–1900) *Jug (William IV & 1832 Reform Act)*, c. 1832, and *The Iron Bridge at Sunderland*, c. 1815, are two examples responding to current events, the latter often coupled with maritime-themed limericks. Sitting above the other cupboards are a wide selection of Staffordshire hen tureens and a rare early 19th century Staffordshire *Pair of Cockerels*. On the walls are a range of English and French plates, some for the nursery and decorated with the alphabet, clock face, or names with corresponding objects. Above the old country dresser is a selection of rare Dutch Delft trompe l'oeil *Bird-cage plaques*, 1740–1760, acquired mainly in London from 2007 to 2011. On the dresser are a range of English pottery mugs; some are 'novelties' hiding frogs or pictures within pictures, while another is an early Staffordshire Potteries *Child's mug (British Sign Language alphabet)*, c. 1820.

Of the many items displayed on the country dresser the red Pontypool ware *'Black Jack' Slade's campaign teapot and brazier*, 1780, is a standout. The teapot base is inscribed: 'This kettle was used by General Sir John Slade, Bart GHC, during the war in Spain from 1808–1813', which just seemed so perfectly English to David. Smaller objects include a simple *String box*, c. 1800; a 19th century German *Pressing iron*; and a Regency painted wood *Truncheon* decorated with the Royal Coat of Arms with 'GR' cypher and '1817'.

From top:
Mechanical bank 'Girl Skipping Rope' J. & E. Stevens Company, c. 1890.

String box, Britain, c. 1800.

'Black Jack' Slade's campaign teapot and brazier, Pontypool ware, 1780.

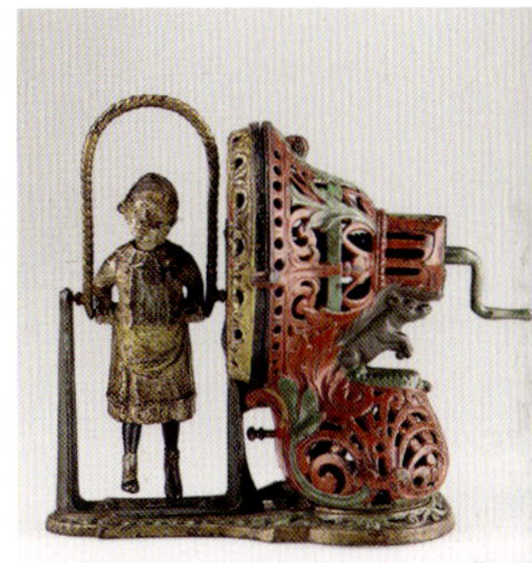

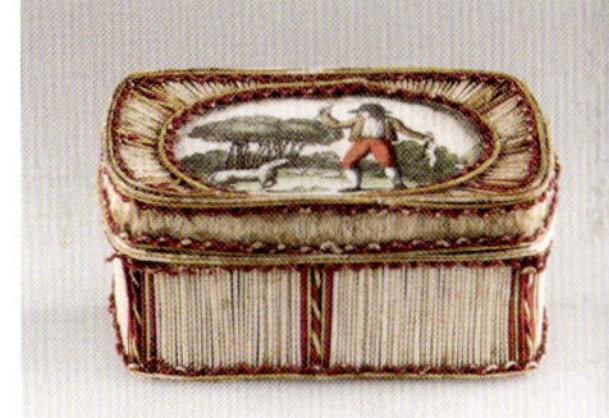

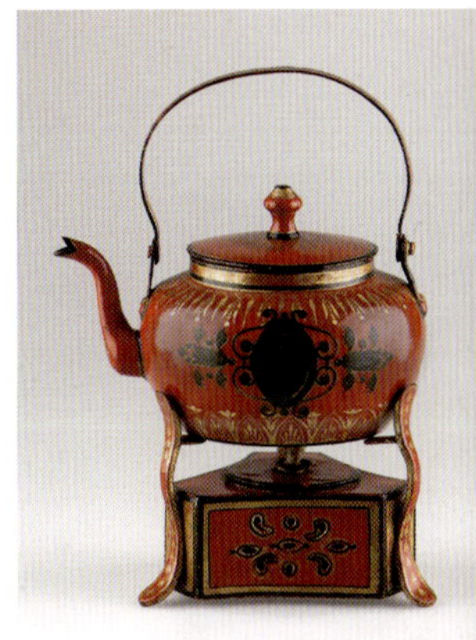

Opposite page:
Clockwise from top left:
Butcher's shop diorama, Britain, c. 1850.

Sand picture of Percherons in harness, attributed to Benjamin Zobel, c. 1810.

'Jack' a Wessex saddle back pig, Henry S. Cottrell, 1848.

Travelling menagerie from the Strand at Exeter Change, London (with kangaroos), Britain, 1800–1810. The kangaroos are in the extreme right cage.

Cat with fish, William Buelow Gould, c. 1851.

Principal Pictures

Every nook and cranny in the kitchen is a delight to behold and David's pictures are no exception. Animals feature regularly by professional, amateur and naïve artists, reflecting David's interest in breeds of pigs, pigeons and horses through to exotic animals. For example, Andrew Beer (Britain 1862–1954) made a reputation from his paintings of racing pigeons, with David acquiring '*Look Out*', c. 1928; '*Southern Belle*', c. 1928; and '*Spanish Pilot*', c. 1926. William E. Jones' (Britain active 1849–1871) *Berkshire pigs in sty*, 1866, was a favourite of David's, both for the handsome sty and this rare breed, a favourite of Queen Victoria. Herbert H. St John Jones' (Britain 1872–1939) *Champion tandem team*, 1907, is a fine rendering of Hopwood Spark and Hopwood Horace, International and Richmond winners at Tandem horse racing. Another distinctive painting is *Cat with fish*, c. 1851. A gift from David's mother, the painting is now attributed to the Australian convict artist William Buelow Gould (Britain/Australia 1803–1853), who worked in Tasmania. It is, however, the *Travelling menagerie from the Strand at Exeter Change, London (with kangaroos)*, 1800–1810, which fascinated David the most when he bought the painting in London in 2007. Two kangaroos feature in their own cage, to the far right of the image. Exotic animals of the world were a regular feature of the upper floors of the Exeter Change from 1773–1829, where they wintered while travelling around Britain.

One of the pleasures of the kitchen is the varied assortment of mediums translated into works of art. These include embroideries such as the two *Needlework samplers*, 1840s; a Berlin work *Rooster*, c. 1860; and a woolwork *Elephant*, c. 1850. There are also 19th century English shell work pictures of baskets of flowers; hair-work landscape pictures; American-coloured foil pictures of flowers; and an *American eagle* feather picture, c. 1860. There is also a rare selection of French prisoner-of-war works made in England during the Napoléonic period, including a hair-work picture *Architectural landscape with trees*, c. 1810; a *Marquetry straw port scene* (possibly a box lid), c. 1800; and a carved bone *Model of a field cannon and limber with trains*, 1793–1815. A highlight of the room is the English *Butcher's shop diorama*, c. 1850, above the old enamel stove. David bought and upgraded many of these over the years until acquiring this very fine example in 2005. Carved and painted, it illustrates the range of meats available from the shop as well as delighting in capturing the butcher and his assistants in action.

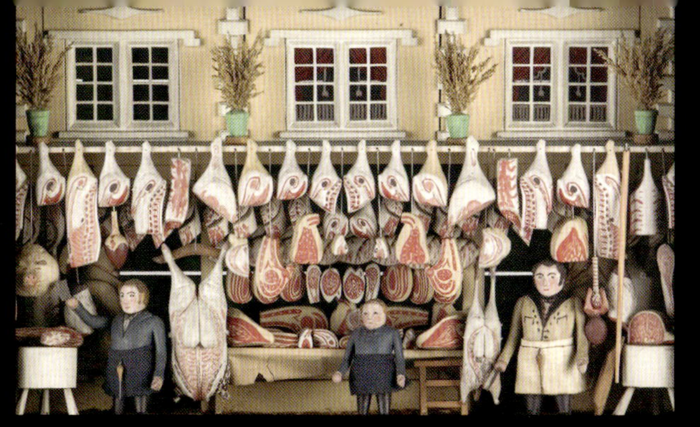

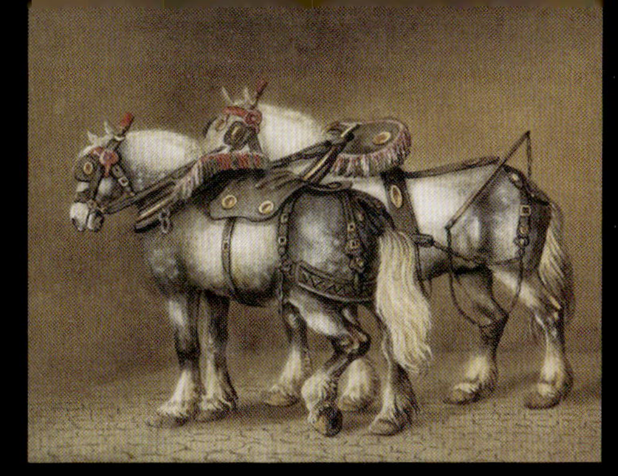

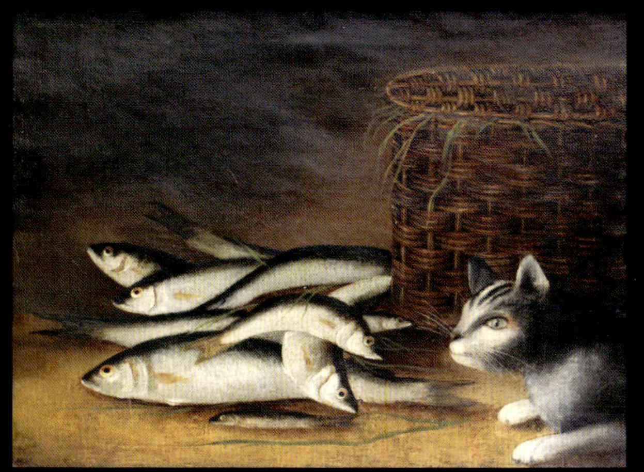

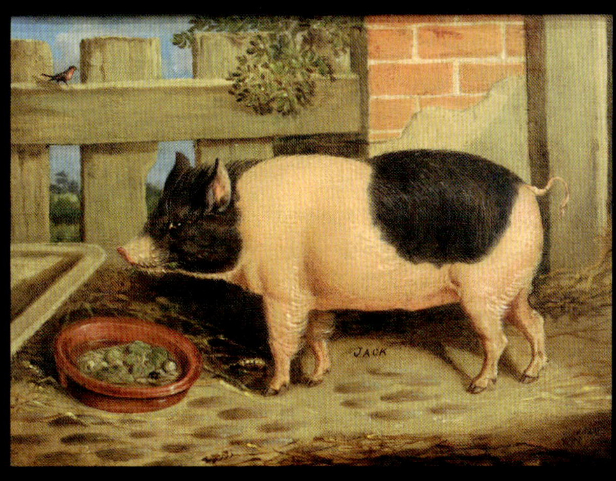
JACK

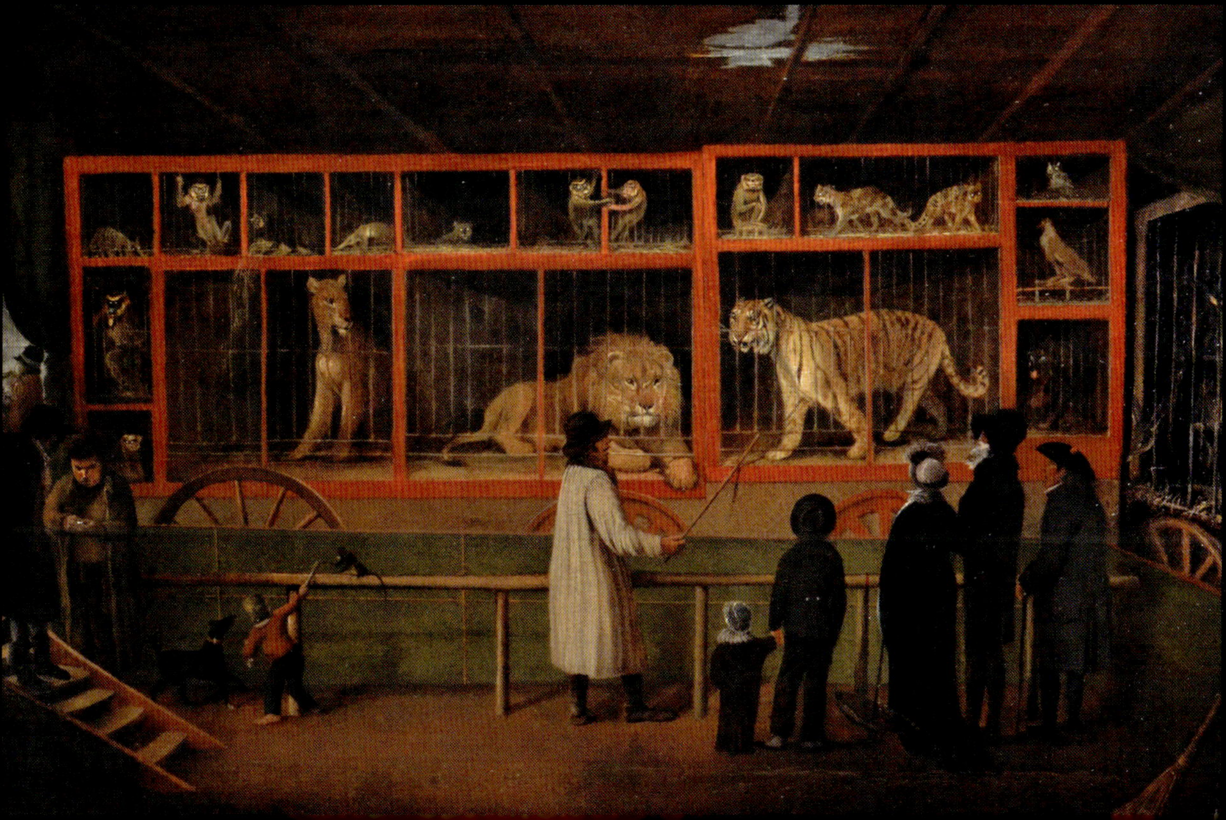

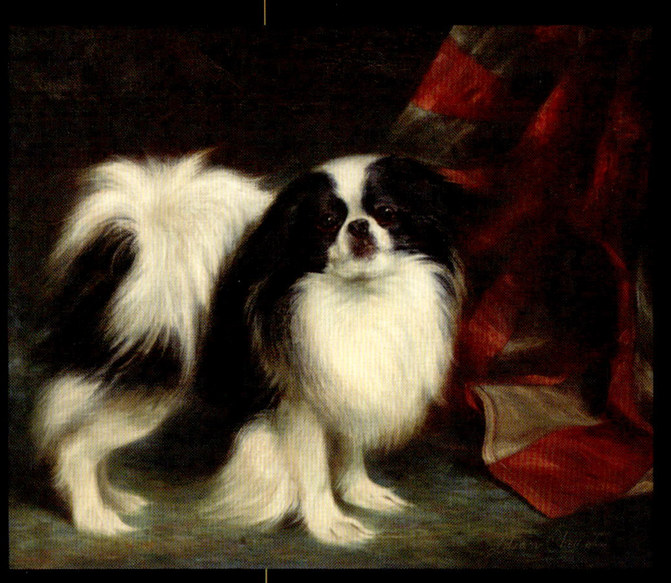

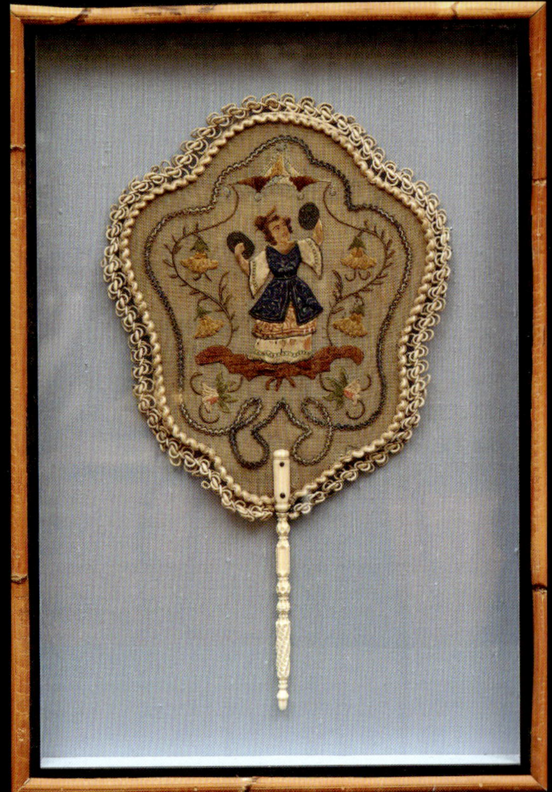

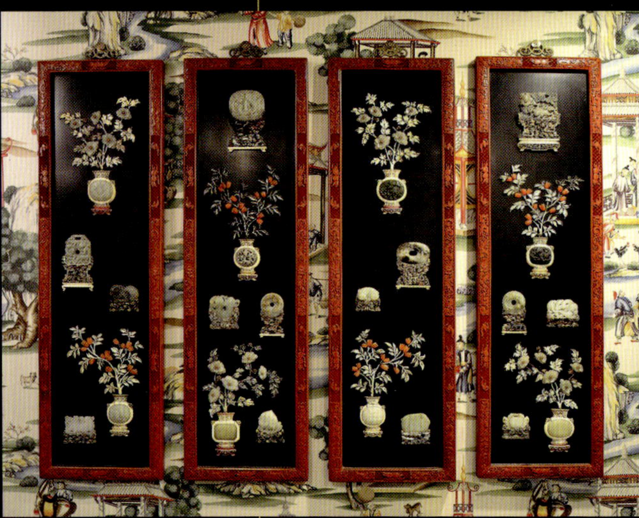

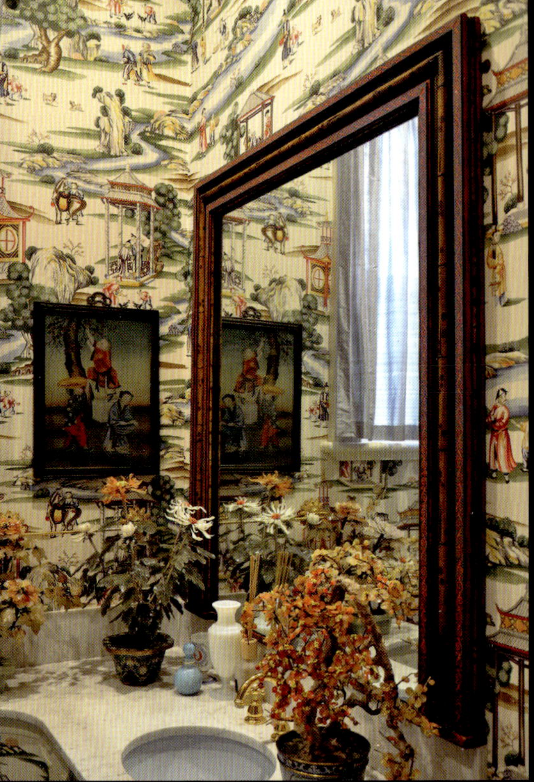

Clockwise from top left:
Japanese Chin, Lillian Cheviot, c. 1920.

Regency *Chinoiserie face screen* (one of a pair), c. 1820.

Mirror frame, John C. Crace, designer, 1802–1804.

Panels with applied hardstone ornaments, China, Qing Dynasty (1644–1911),

THE MAIN BATHROOM

The walls were papered with Scalamandré's (United States, established 1929) celebrated 'Shanghai' pattern in 2000, while the floor is in blue mosaics. The room is decorated in the chinoiserie taste with glass and jade pictures, an Edwardian *Pagoda lantern*, c. 1910, and a faux-bamboo framed mirror.

Principal Objects

A highlight of the bathroom is the English Regency *Mirror frame*, 1802–1804, designed by John C. Crace (Britain 1754–1819) of the same faux-painted bamboo type and period as those supplied for the Glass Passage at The Royal Pavilion in Brighton. David bought the mirror in 1994 specifically for his bathroom and enjoyed the 'royal' link. Also acquired for the room in 2000 are the rare *Pair of Regency chinoiserie face screens*, c. 1820, illustrating Chinese entertainers – a male juggler and female cymballist. Silk embroidered, with additional metallic threads and painted silk elements, the face screens are marvellous examples of the Regency love for exotic looking objects and interiors.

Principal Pictures

To decorate the bathroom walls, David chose to acquire a Chinese Export reverse glass painting *Three figures picking fruit*, c. 1890, from the Gianni Versace Collection sale in 2001. Above the door hang four Qing Dynasty (1644–1911) cinnabar-lacquer framed *Panels with applied hardstone ornaments*, dating from the 18th and 19th centuries. Acquired in Adelaide with a German provenance, the shape of the carved jade plaques indicates that many were once part of ceremonial Ruyi sceptres. When sceptres fell out of fashion, the jades were reused, and here become part of a larger design of flowering pots made of stained ivory and carnelian, or to form parts of gu vases and globular long-necked bottles. No room in David's home was complete without at least one canine painting and the Lillian Cheviot (Britain c. 1876–1936), *Japanese Chin*, c. 1920, was a perfect choice. David acquired the painting from a Canadian dog judge and breeder, and it features on the back cover of the publication *The Complete Japanese Chin*, 1997, by Pamela Cross Stern and Tom Mather. Traditionally, the Chin was a prized lapdog for Japanese royalty before becoming available in the West after 1853.

THE ROMAN ROOM

The Roman room dates to the early 1970s when David decided to extend the back of his Federation villa. He engaged the architect Dudley Campbell Smith to create one large open space for casual living and dining with French doors to the garden. The room was centred by a parquetry dance floor surrounded by decorative Portuguese tiles, which in later years largely disappeared under early 20th century Persian rugs. This light-filled room was home to many potted plants and orchids as well as a large decorative French aviary, acquired in the early 1980s for long-tailed finches, Gouldian finches and canaries. Most visitors (and David himself) entered the home from the Roman room landing and looked across the room and out into the back garden with its swimming pool and temple folly. It was the main area used to entertain and dine guests. Filled with many precious objects, furniture and paintings, these were moved into the villa and the adjoining museum wing in 2016.

Since the redevelopment of Fermoy House in 2015–2016, the old Roman room has been refurbished as a reception room for visitors and as a facility for evening lectures. It houses mainly marble sculptures in the 'antique' style. The three life-size sculptures of *Creugante*, 1884, *Meleagher and the Calydonian boar*, 1885, and *Discobolus*, c. 1885, are from the studio of Charles Francis Summers (Australia/Italy 1858–1945) in Rome. They were brought back to Australia by Summers. The first two are copies after Antonio Canova (Italy 1757–1822) and graced the eastern entrance fountain garden of the Melbourne Royal Exhibition Building from 1886 to c. 1940. David placed them in his front garden in 1998, while *Discobolus,* after an ancient Greek

Right: The Roman room in 2012 with a Russian commode, a range of malachite objects and one of a pair of Russian chandeliers. The pair of chairs are attributed to Marsh & Tatham, c. 1805.

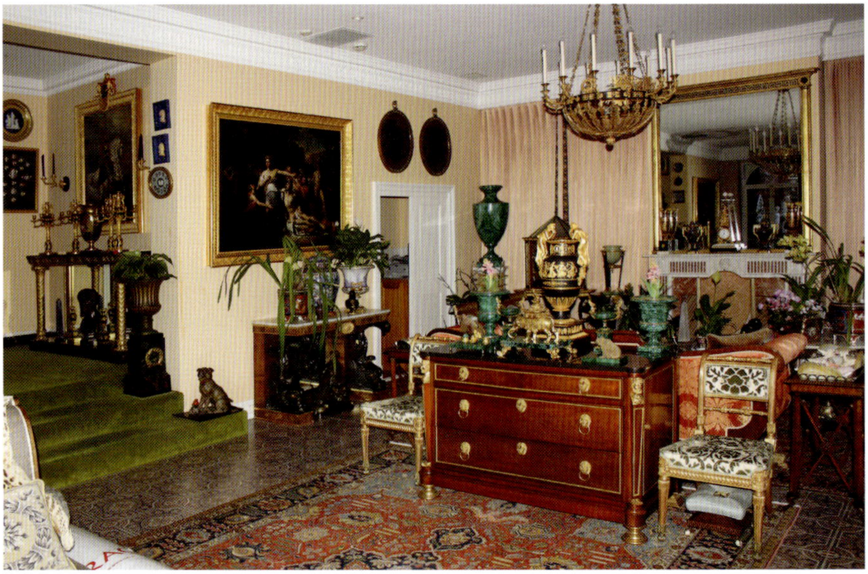

Following spread: The Roman room in 2016. On the landing is a painted terracotta *Allegorical Figure of Autumn*, after Antonio Canova, c. 1900. In the background are a Russian *Gueridon table*, c. 1820, and a marble statue of *Diana hunting*, c. 1859, attributed to the Giovanni Benzoni Workshop. On the south side, a marble sculpture of *Creugante*, Charles Francis Summers, 1884, and one of pair of Italian Grand Tour *Borghese vases*, c. 1780. Against the back wall is a bronze of *Caesar Augustus of Prima Porta, Adlocutio*, Morelli & Rinaldi Workshop, c. 1900.

sculpture, was placed in a niche on the portico to Fermoy house in 2005.

The Canova theme continues with smaller marble busts, including *Venus Italica* (as Pauline Borghese), c. 1840, (previously in the Collection of Leo Schofield, AM, at Bronte House, Sydney) and a nice quality bust of *Perseus wearing the cap of Hades*, c. 1830. The *Pair of 'Borghese' vases*, c. 1780, were acquired in Italy and are handsome late 18th century examples of Grand Tour art, so admired by David. Many of the pedestals in the room are scagliola or period pieces from the late English Regency and Russian Empire. Particularly fine is the Edward Holmes Baldock (Britain 1777–1845) *Ebonised and gilt metal pedestal*, c. 1825.

The only remaining item of furniture in the room from David's occupancy is the William IV *Centre table*, c. 1830, in rosewood with a laminated marble top, brass bound, and attributed to T. & G. Seddon (Britain 1753–1868). It is one of the longest standing items in the collection, acquired by David in the mid-1950s from Theodore Bruce Auctioneers and reputedly from Sir Samuel Way's (1836–1916) Montefiore House in North Adelaide. Two – from the *Set of six chairs*, c. 1775 – for this table can now be seen on the Roman room landing. Acquired in 1991 from the sale of Alan Bond's art collection, David bought these George III period chairs because they came from Althorp House in Northampton. The ancestral home of the Spencers, these chairs were sold during the period of the 8th Earl Spencer, father of the late Diana, Princess of Wales (1961–1997). As a young man, David had the occasion to meet Johnnie Spencer when he served as Aide-de-Camp (1947–1950) to the Governor of South Australia.

Left: The Roman room in 2012 with a *Lion X-frame stool*, Thomas Hope (designer), 1810–1815, and a white marble bust of George IV, Samuel Joseph, c. 1831, on a pedestal behind.

Middle: The Roman room in 2016 with an Anglo-Irish chimney-piece, c. 1780.

Below: The Roman room in 2016 with a marble sculpture *Discobolus*, Charles Francis Summers, c. 1885.

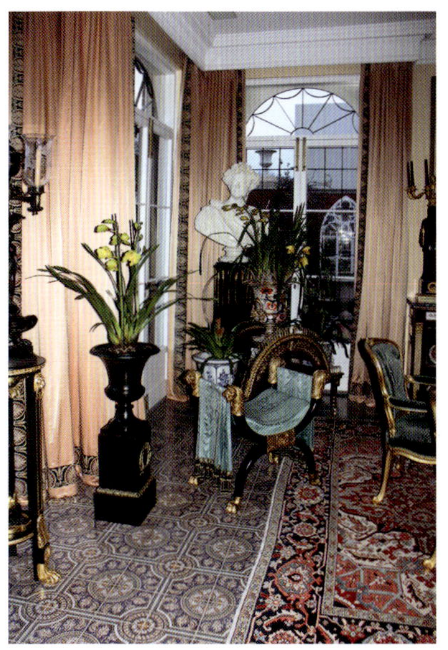

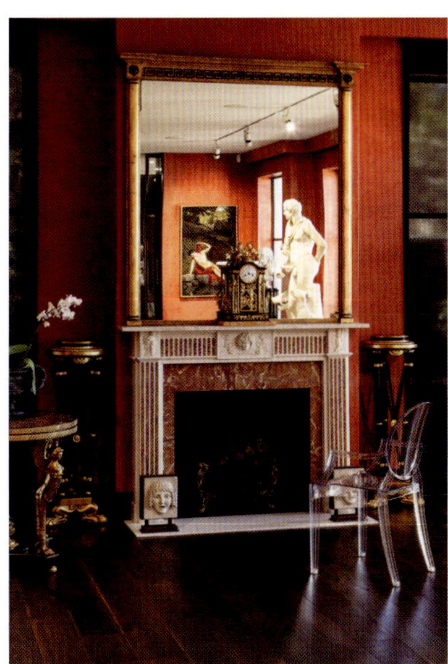

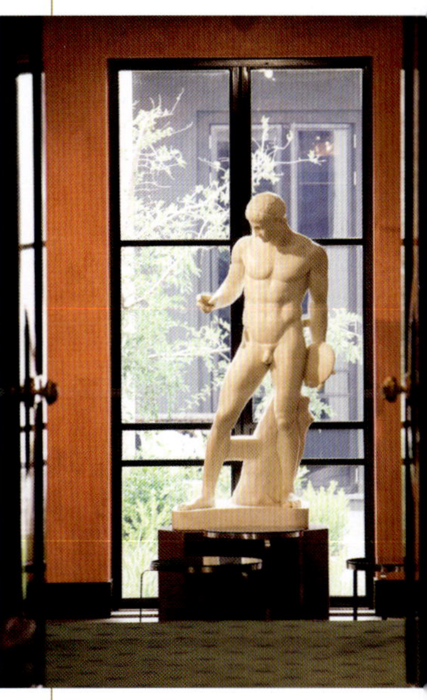

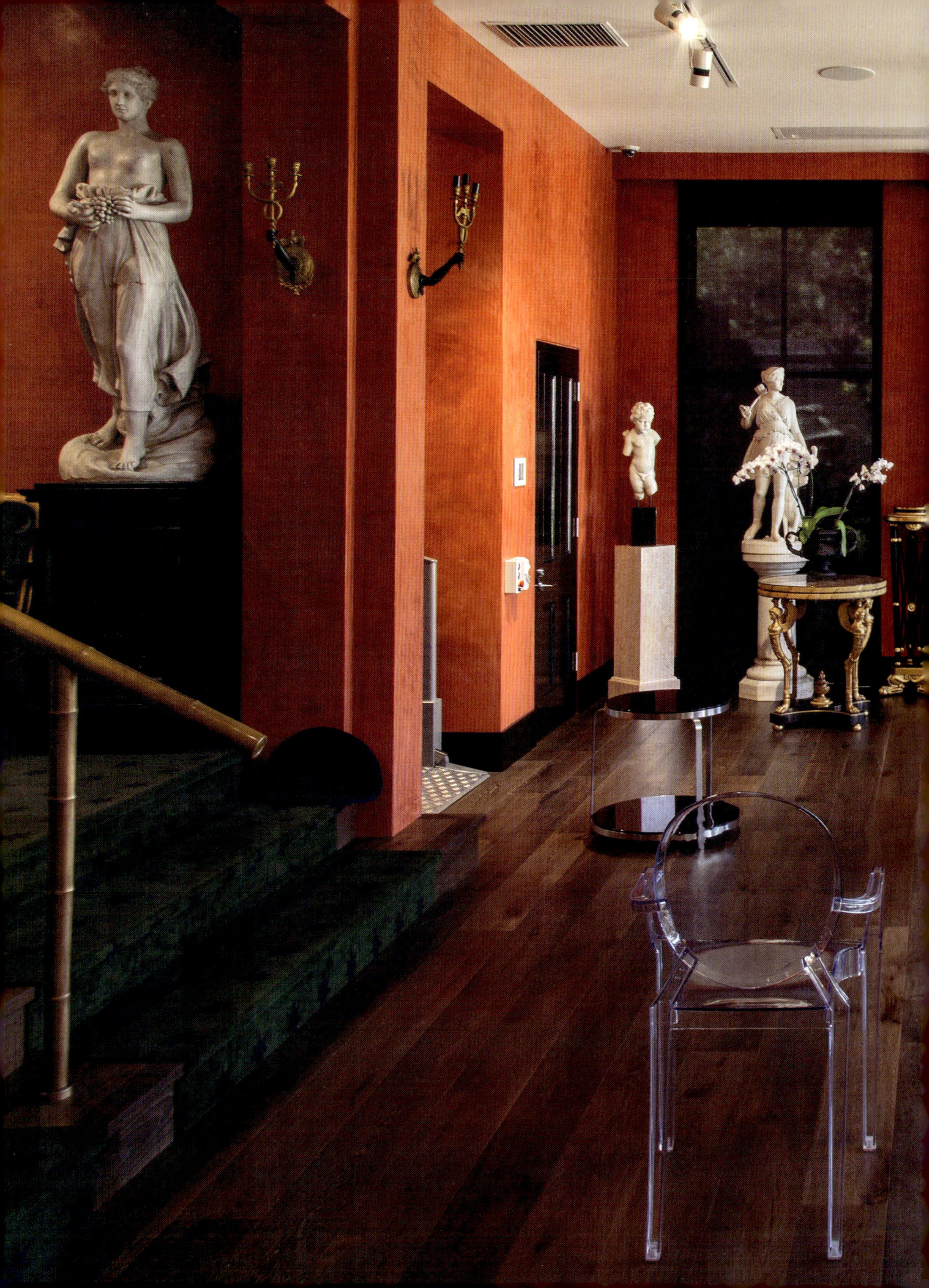

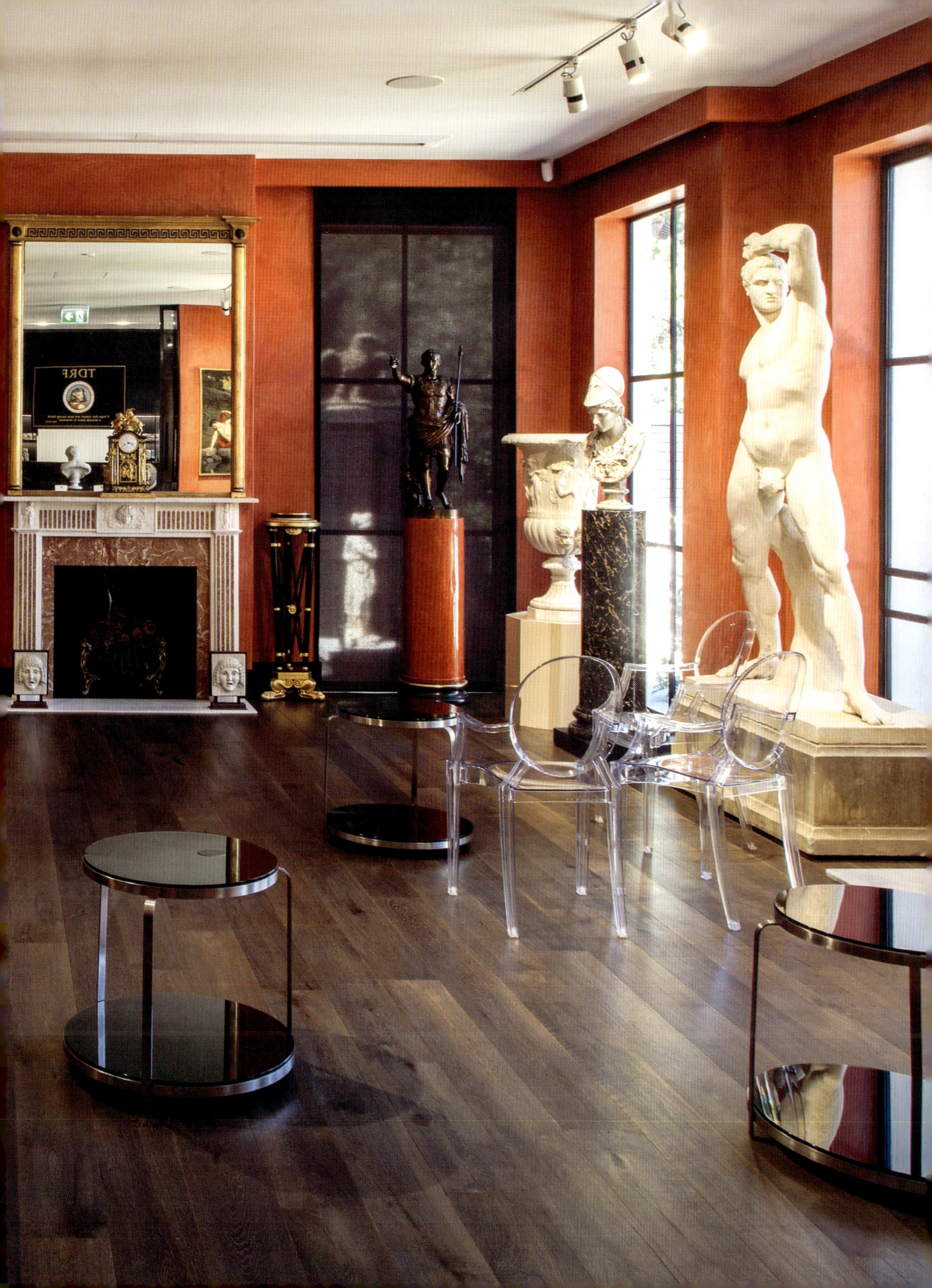

THE GARDEN

Only the garden in front of Fermoy House maintain a resemblance to those created by David, who was passionate about his garden and employed professional horticulturists to develop and maintain the grounds. Influenced by English gardens, especially Hampton Court Palace, and French formal gardens, David's garden had a strong formal structure and clipped hedges with more whimsical perennial elements inside. The rose in the front garden, Yellow Bunny, was a particular favourite. Alongside the plantings, David added marble garden sculptures, cast-iron planters and seating as well as water features, cobblestone paving and decorative elements to the garden and house walls. The French bronze *Lion wall fountain*, c. 1820, in the front garden was added after 1991 and the pair of early 19th century Italian marble *Lions* in 2007. David acquired the large Regency cast-iron *Dish urn* in the lawn, in Dublin, 2001.

Below: The back garden, looking toward the Roman room of Fermoy House, 2013.

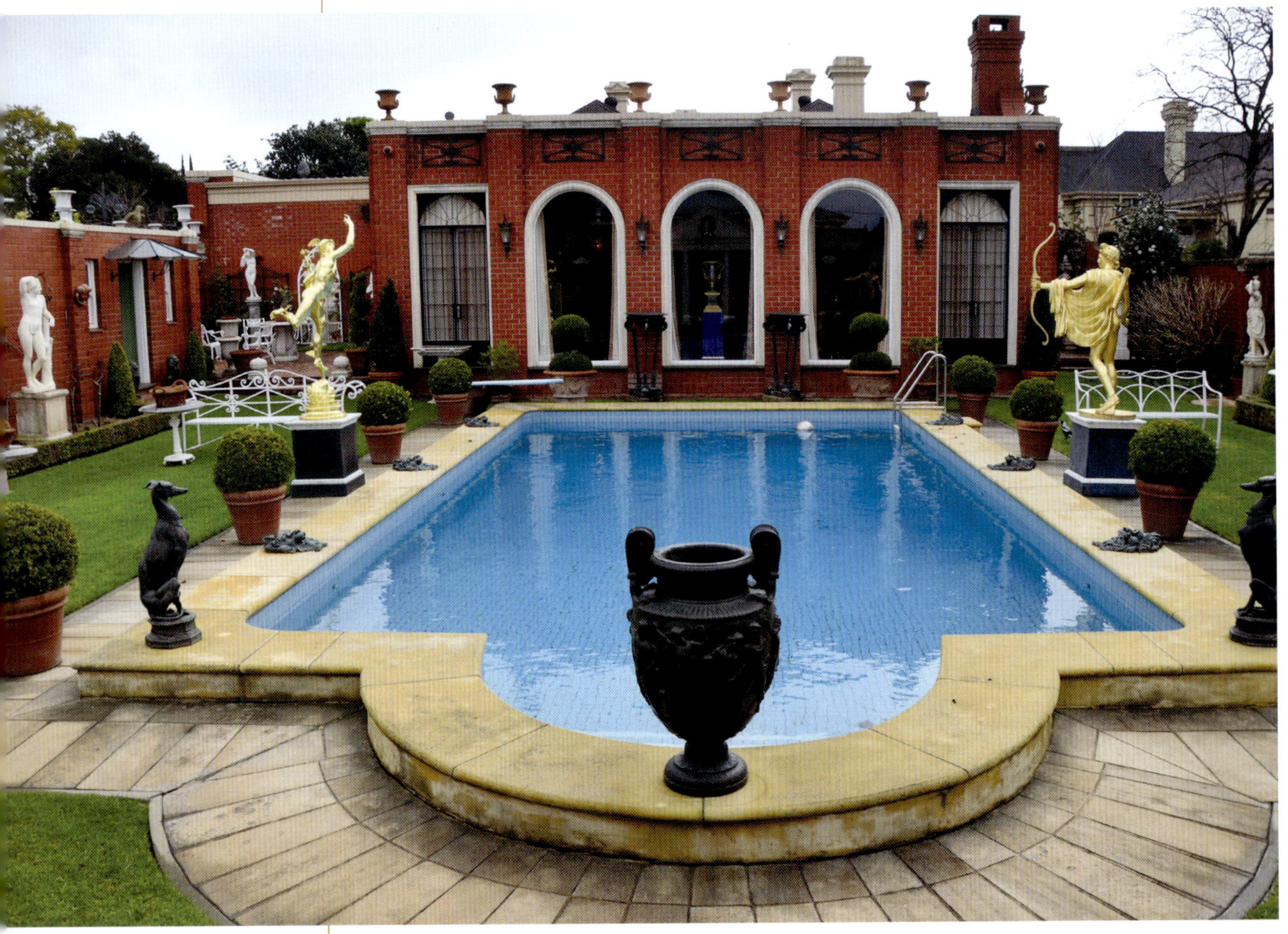

The back garden was replaced by a sunken courtyard garden of clipped hedges and statues in 2015 following the redevelopment of the site and the building of the new museum wing. David redeveloped his back garden in the 1970s after the addition of a large living-dining extension, the Roman room. The focal point was a central, blue-tiled rectangular swimming pool, c. 1972, with lawns either side. The garden borders had formal edges and a range of changing colour within from foxgloves, delphiniums and tulips. With high brick walls, the climbing roses of Pierre De Ronsard, Camille Pissarro and William Morris were selected as well as climbing clematis. The main feature at the end of the garden was a Grecian-style temple portico folly, containing the pool changerooms and offering the perfect setting for classical statues and urns. Demolished in 2015, the metal wreath from the temple was transferred to the pediment of the museum wing. Like the interiors of David's house, the garden was always evolving with seasonal plantings and garden features that complimented the English aesthetic he was wishing to achieve.

Left: The back garden of Fermoy House, 2013.

Below: Looking through the Russian *Vase on pedestal*, 1830, to the temple folly at the end of the swimming pool.

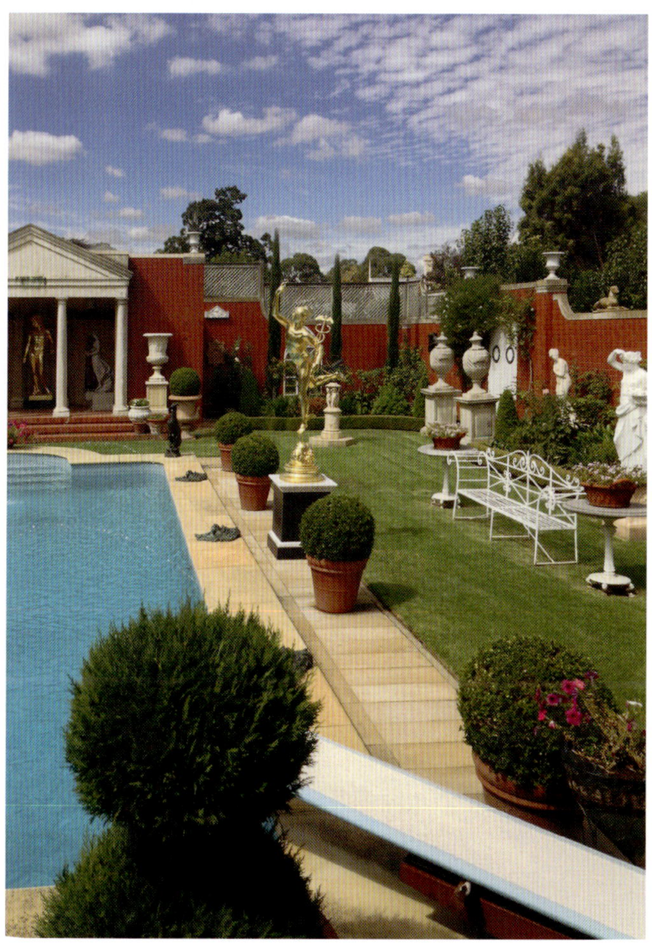

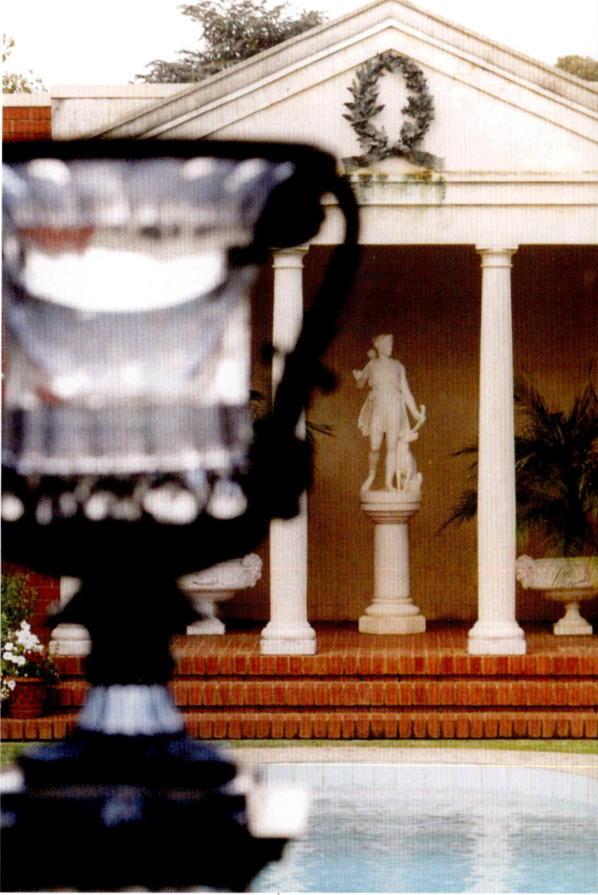

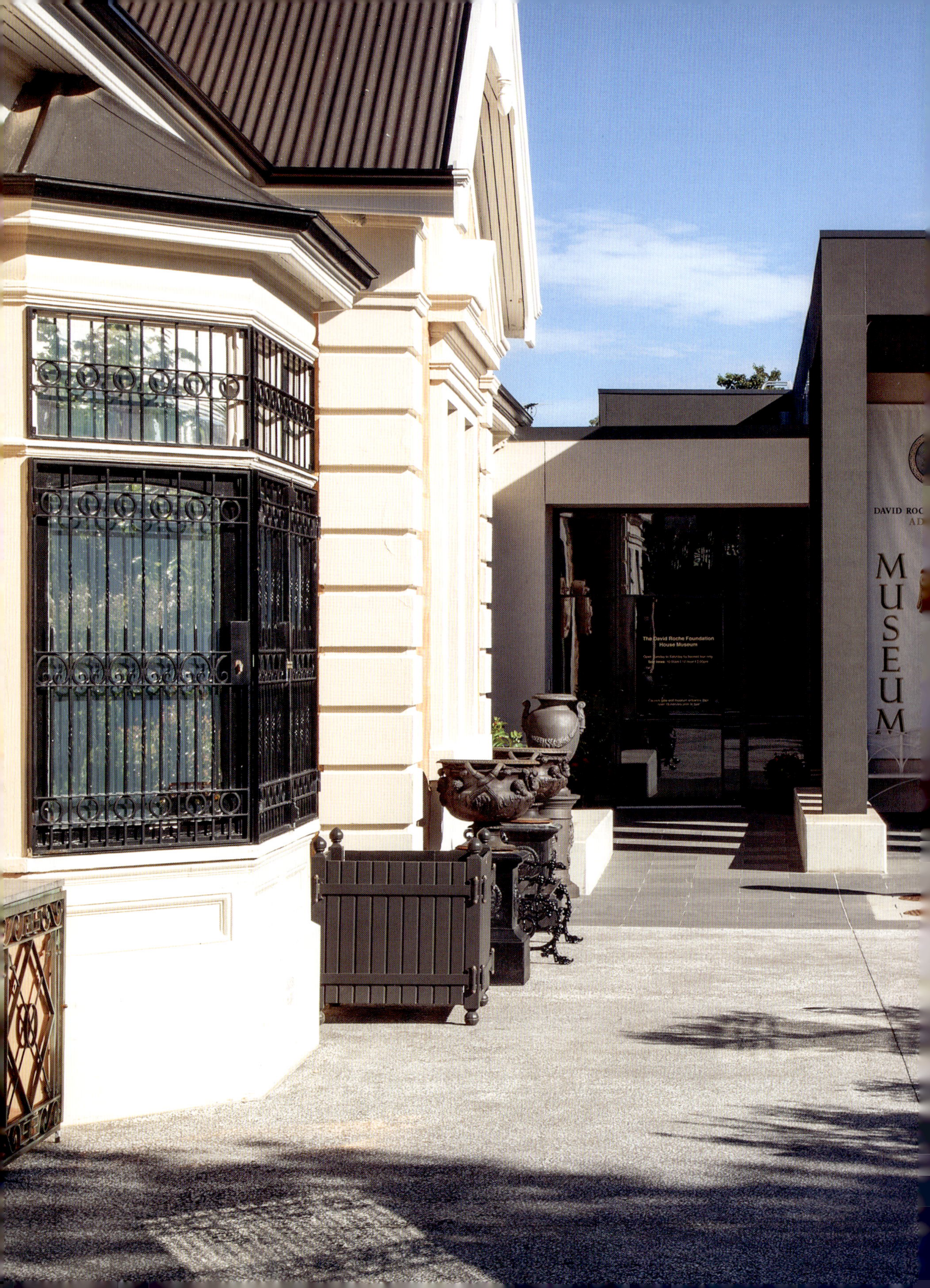

MUSEUM
The David Roche Foundation
House Museum

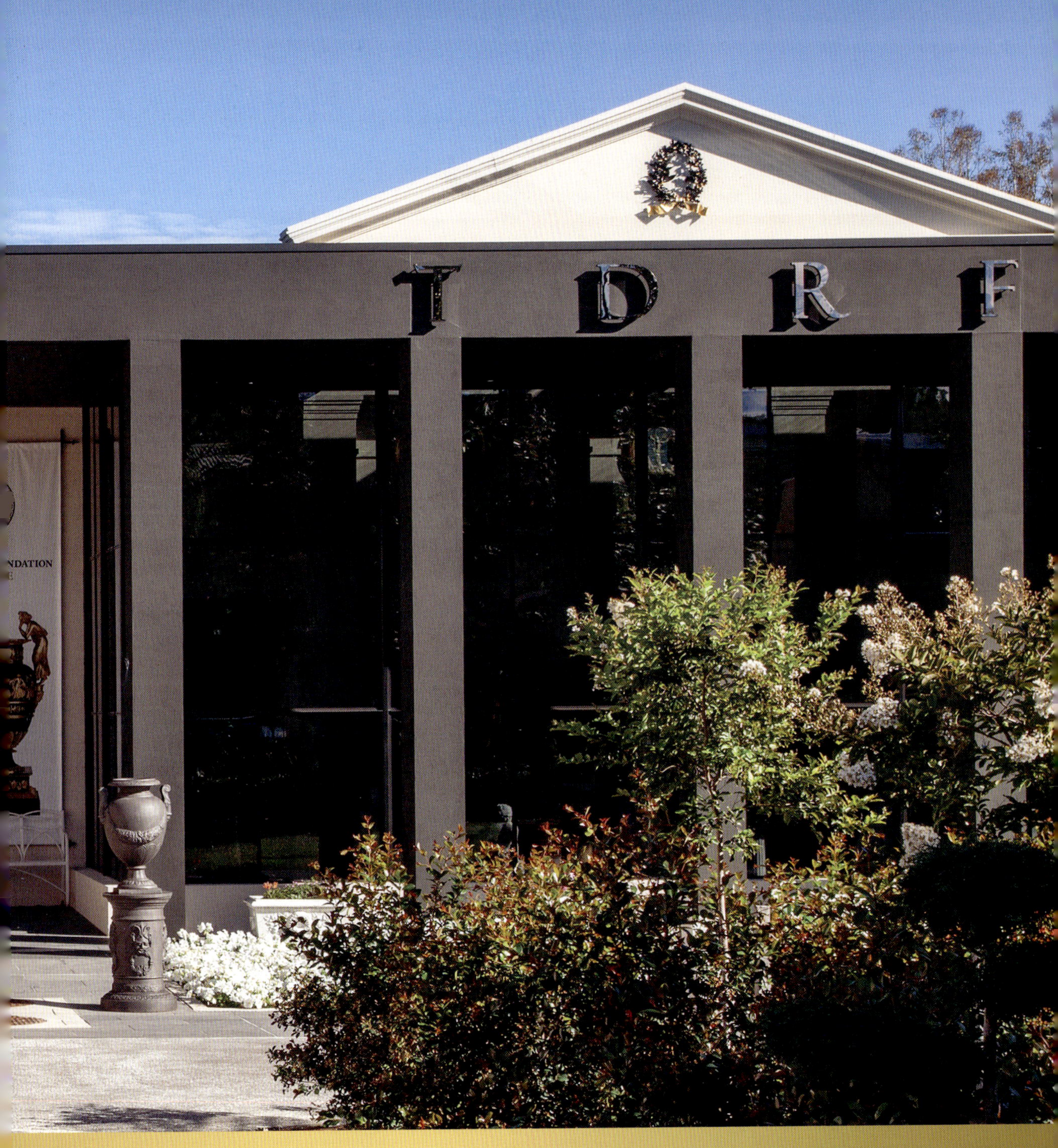

A TOUR OF THE *Museum Wing*

When David Roche acquired Fermoy House in 1954, he was fortunate to acquire the land on the western side as well, which was largely vacant. It was on this site that he would build what became the famous Fermoy Kennels until its closure following David's death in 2013. David imagined that this area would be redeveloped to display aspects of his collection and that a new garden would be laid out. Working with his foundation that he established in 1999, initial plans were drawn up in the early 2000s. Primarily, he wished to open his collection in the tradition of the great 'House Museums' of Europe, but he always felt ambivalent about the process as it would happen after his death. David was familiar with many examples, but one that particularly resonated was Mario Praz in Rome. This unassuming museum is filled with French and Italian Empire Period furniture and a raft of curious objects reflecting the owner's collecting passions. By intimate guided tour, David could envisage his collection being similarly enjoyed.

Ultimately, David decided to leave the redevelopment in the hands of his trustees, including Martyn Cook, his friend and antiques advisor for more than 30 years. The starting point for the architect's brief was German neoclassical architect Karl Schinkel. Both his buildings and interior furnishings had captured David's attention and admiration, especially Glienicke Palace and Charlottenhof Palace. A modern, pared-back version of Schinkel's architectural style was presented by Williams Burton Leopardi – Architects of Adelaide, and selected as the winning design. The new purpose-designed museum commenced construction in 2015 and finished in early 2016, creating three spacious galleries, a sculpture foyer, an internal sunken courtyard garden and all the amenities and back-of-house facilities required to run a museum. The 'black-box' galleries create the perfect foil to David's richly gilded collection and were in-part inspired by the dark, moody interiors of David Nightingale Hicks' apartment in the Albany, central London, which David knew well.

David Burton, architect, wrote of the project:

Any building to house David Roche's collection needed to encompass what was clearly a very personal journey . . . The rigour and proportion of Schinkel, his approach to classical planning, and the importance of his buildings' relationship to landscape and courtyard is equally relevant as the classical order or the neoclassic style of many of his buildings.

Opposite page:
The sculpture foyer with Italian gilded statues of Apollo, Antinous and Mercury. Against the far wall is the Fawley House *Lidded urn on stand*, after a Robert Adam design, c. 1800.

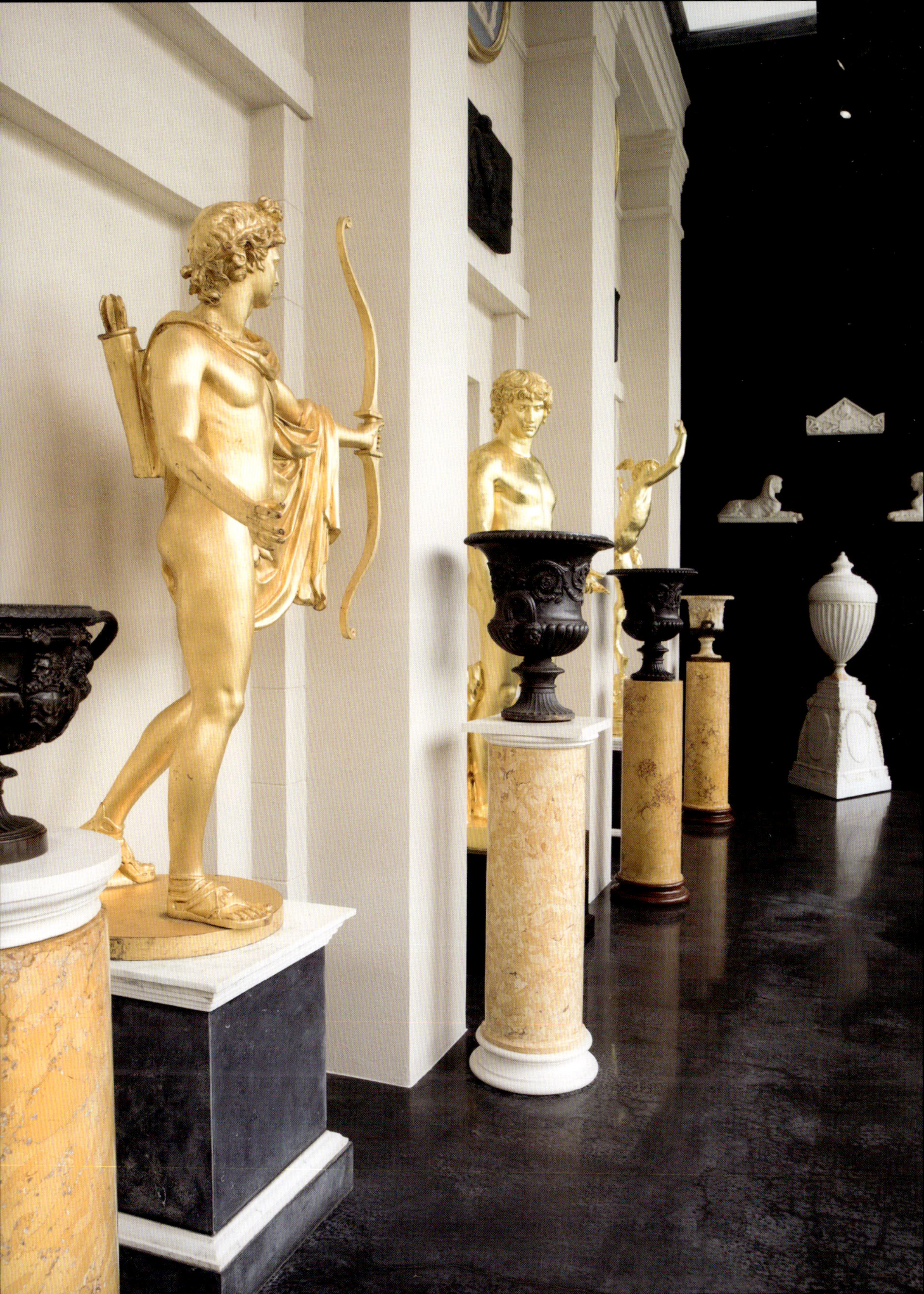

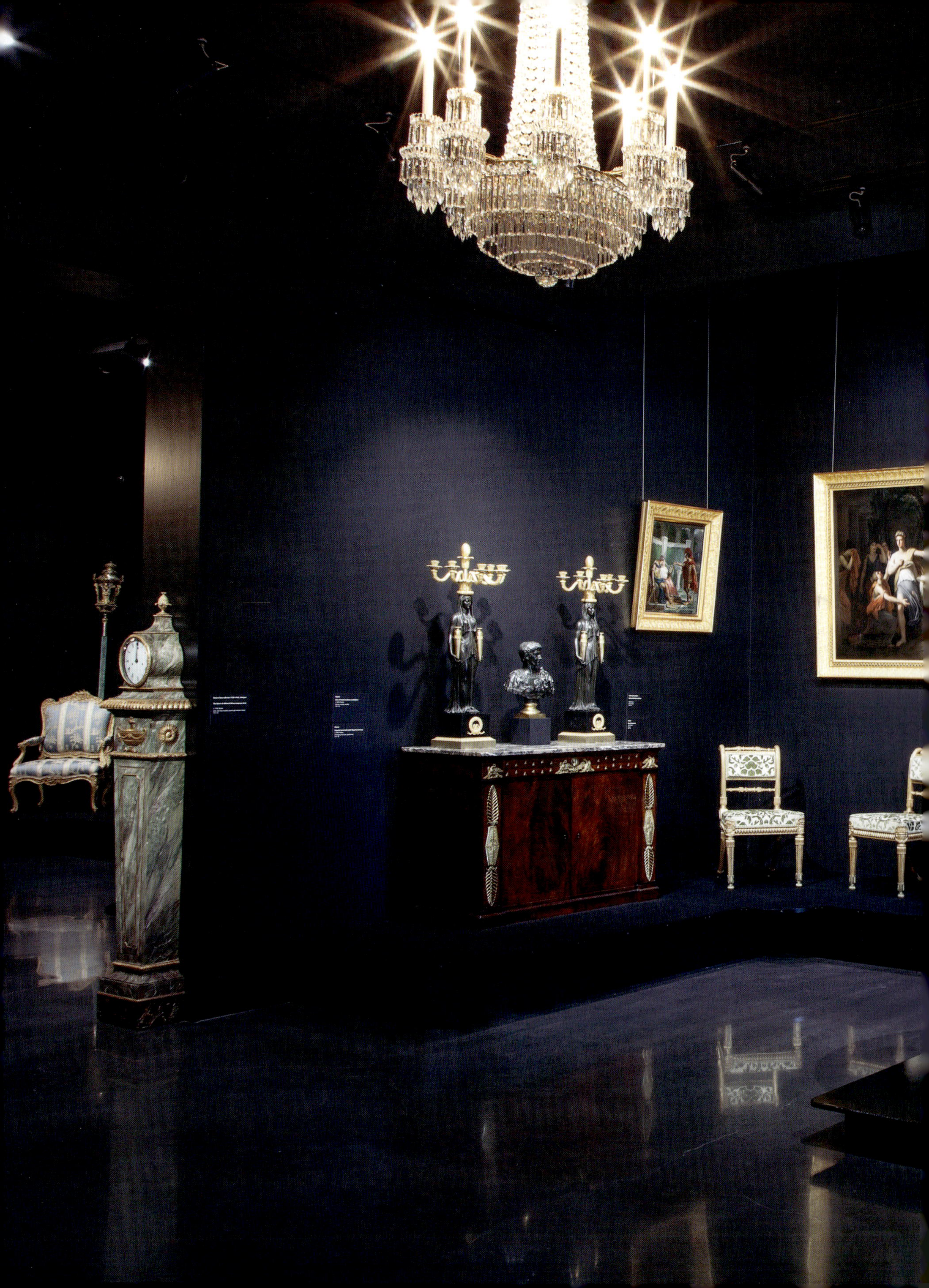

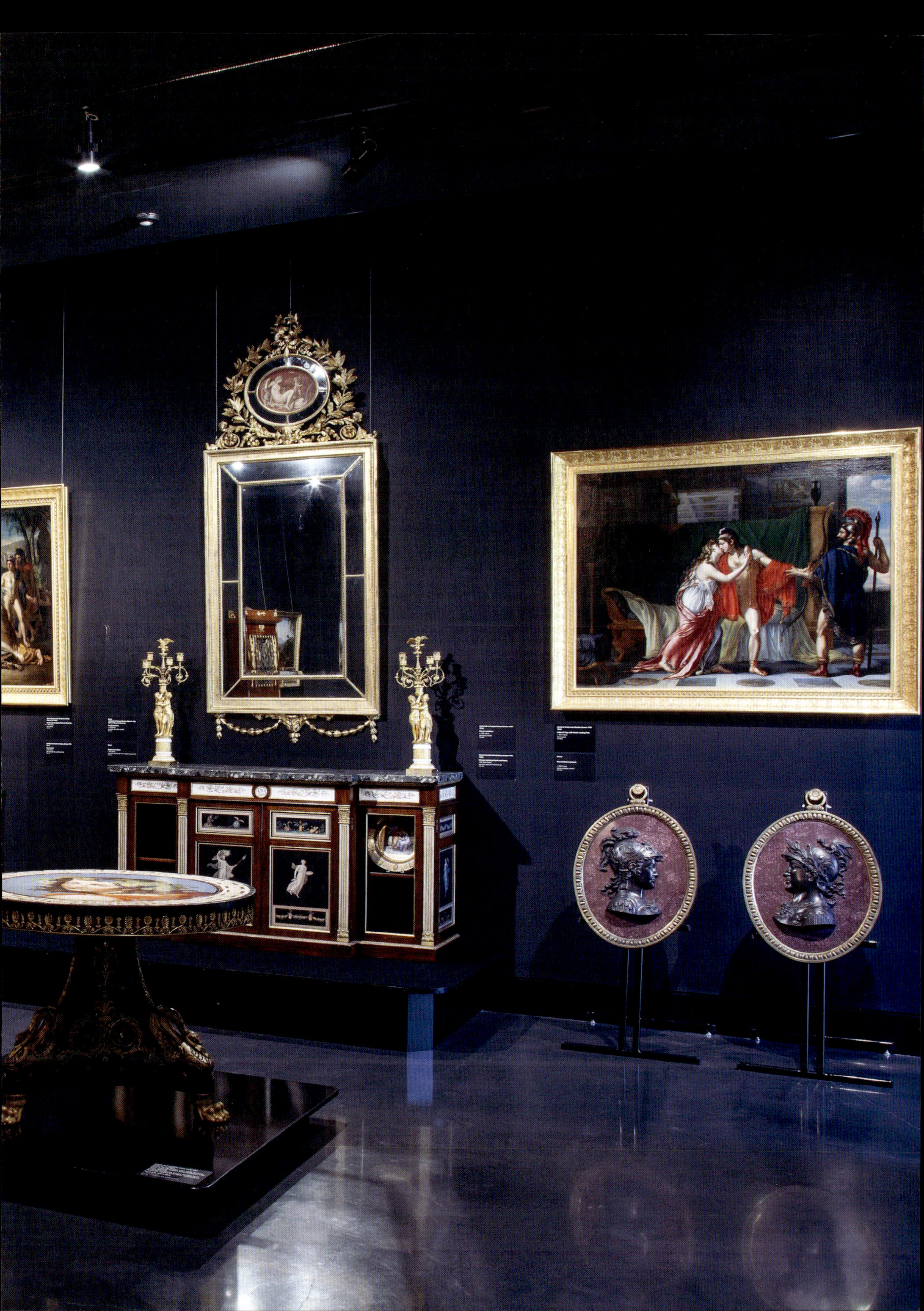

Previous spread:
The Museum wing in 2016, displaying items from the collection including *Helen of Troy, with Hector rousing Paris*, c. 1815, and *Oenone and the death of Paris on Mount Ida*, c. 1790, both Studio of Anne-Louis Girodet; a French Empire *Commode*, c. 1805; and an English Regency *Breakfront cabinet*, c. 1815, set with Italian gouache panels. The Pier glass (mirror), c. 1780, is English and the Chandelier, c. 1820, is John Blades of Piccadilly, London.

This classical rigour permeates throughout the new physical additions to Fermoy House. It has also been used to order the galleries and set a 'Classical context' for sculptural pieces in the Great Foyer fronting Melbourne Street, via a stripped internal Classical facade. This provides a contextual balance for the 'folly' in the lobby, a reconstruction of a pavilion that formally resided as a backdrop to the pool at the rear of Fermoy House and was inspired by Schinkel's Pomona Temple facade, which remained David's favourite building.

The visitor enters between the former Residence and the new Museum, into a light filled contemporary lobby. Fermoy House remains in much the same state as when David Roche was in residence, displaying elements of his collection in the context of his lifestyle. In contrast, the new museum is the antithesis of this with curated displays in a stylised context within a totally black envelope. Appreciating the collection is enhanced by the surprise and delight that is achieved by the simple ordering of space, managing of vistas, and subtle and persuasive nature of controlled light.

Since opening in June 2016, the museum wing has housed neoclassic and rococo art from David's collection and a changing program of temporary

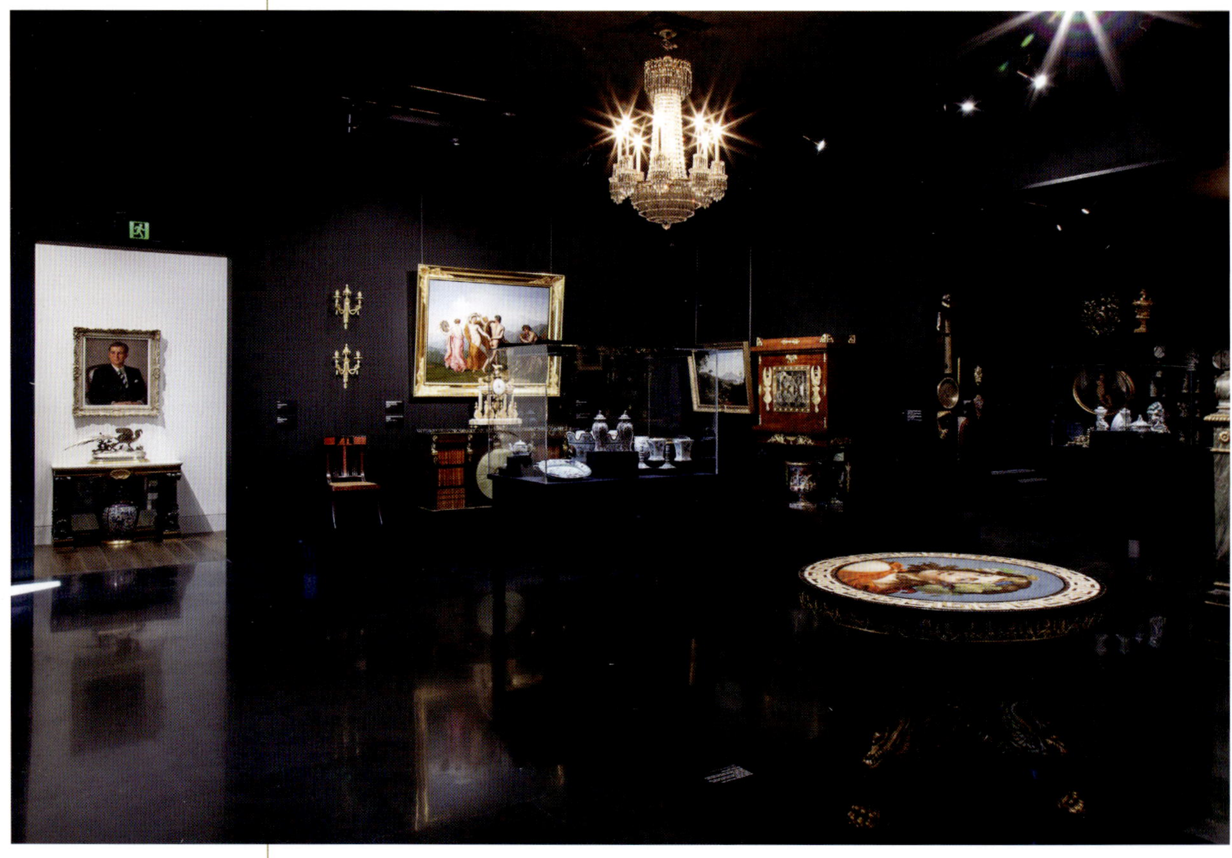

exhibitions. Part of the display comes from items once used in the Roman room, David's open-plan living and dining room at the back of Fermoy House as well as his house in Woollahra, Sydney, which was more sparsely furnished. Items change regularly, but often this is where you will see three large paintings from the Studio of Anne-Louis Girodet. Girodet was a leading French exponent of academic neoclassicism and was trained by Jacques-Louis David. *Helen of Troy, with Hector rousing Paris*, c. 1815, and *Oenone and the death of Paris on Mount Ida*, c. 1790, are both fine examples of Girodet's large narrative paintings which create a staged drama through large frieze-like figures gesticulating and gazing with intent. His painting *Bacchant, Nymphs and Pan*, c. 1809, illustrates a sensuous and softer style where flesh, faces and fabrics are beautifully modelled and figures are given a sense of individuality. The subject and composition relate closely to a ceiling painting by Girodet in the ballroom of the Chateau de Compiegne.

During your time in the museum wing you come to appreciate how different it is to look at David's collection through the lens of a gallery setting versus the domestic setting of his home. Each reward in different ways, revealing collector and collection. Furniture, ceramics, candelabra and objet d'art feature as works of art in the purpose-built galleries, including significant

Opposite page:
The Museum wing in 2016, displaying items from the collection including *Bacchant, Nymphs and Pan*, Anne-Louis Girodet, c. 1809 on the far wall, and *Bacchus table*, Ciuli, Percier & Fontaine, c. 1810, in the foreground.

This page:
The Museum wing in 2016, displaying items from the collection.

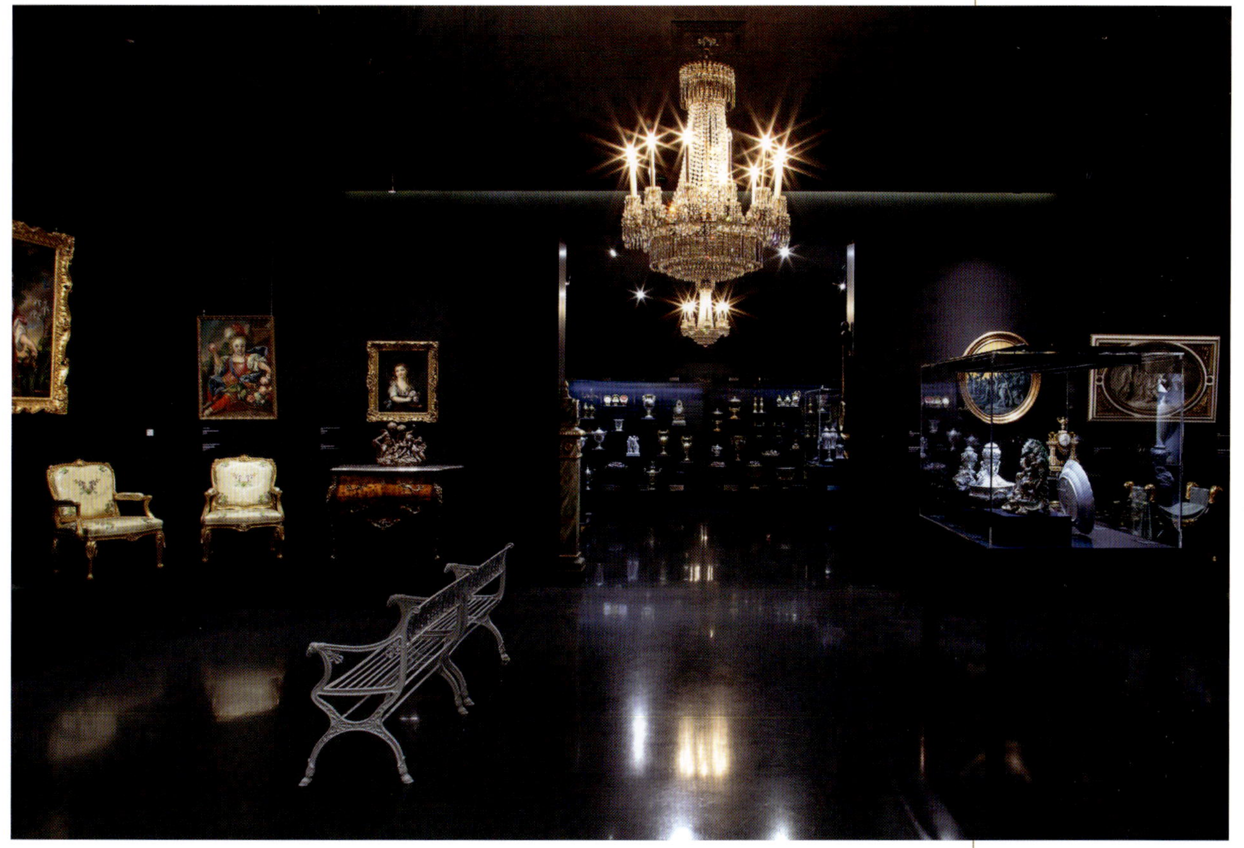

Opposite page:
The Museum wing in 2016, displaying the *Bacchus table*, Ciuli, Percier & Fontaine c. 1810.

porcelain by Chelsea, *The music lesson*, c. 1760; Meissen's celebrated Swan service, with a large *Dish*, c. 1738; a superb Sevres Porcelain *Tea service*, c. 1774, decorated by Jean-Jacques Pierre le Jeune (France c. 1745–c. 1800); and a rare Gardner Factory *Teapot*, c. 1780, previously in the collection of Princess Olga Romanoff (Britain b. 1950), granddaughter of Grand Duchess Xenia Alexandrovna (Russia/Britain 1875–1960). A superb *Pair of Vestal Virgins candelabra*, c. 1815, likely Russian after the French model, sit on a French Empire *Commode*, c. 1805, embellished with gilt bronze mounts symbolising Napoléon. Other furniture of note includes Thomas Hope's celebrated x-frame *Stool*, c. 1810, and a superb English Regency *Breakfront cabinet*, c. 1815, set with Italian gouache panels, English porcelain in the Pompeian taste and finished with a scagliola top imitating *verde antico* marble.

As you move to the front of the museum and into the Great Foyer, a range of marble and metal sculptures from David's garden greet you, including three life-size gilded figures after the classical gods Apollo, Mercury and Antinous (deified after death). David acquired *Apollo* (after Apollo Belvedere) from the Folco Romanelli Foundry (Italy established 1850), which had initially made the sculpture for Princess Margaret, Countess of Snowdon, in 2000 to complement the figure of the Medici Venus for Kensington Palace Gardens. The plaque remains. Other items of note include the large *Pair of urns on pedestals*, c. 1850, by the German terracotta manufacturer Ernst March (Germany 1836–1899), and the marble relief of *Francis I, Emperor of Austria (1768–1835)*, 1833, by Pompeo Marchesi (Italy 1789–1859). The large, elegant marble *Lidded urn on stand*, c. 1800, is after a Robert Adam (Britain 1728–1792) design and came from Fawley House, Oxfordshire. Weighing in excess of 300 kilograms, it is one of the few items shipped by boat, rather than plane, to Australia. David was excited (somewhat morbidly) by the prospect of restoring the urn and using the cavity as the final resting place for his ashes. This was not to be however, as an earlier restoration had stabilised the urn with a vertical metal rod and filled in the cavity. Instead, the imposing Russian *Lidded vase*, c. 1890, of beautifully matched malachite veneers, was to become such a receptacle and can be viewed in the antechamber to the museum wing. Next to it is a portrait by Thomas Percy Reginald 'Rex' Wood (Australia 1908–1970) of *David graduating from Geelong Grammar*, c. 1948. Rex painted David's siblings and parents, but David was not very fond of his portrait and never sat for another.

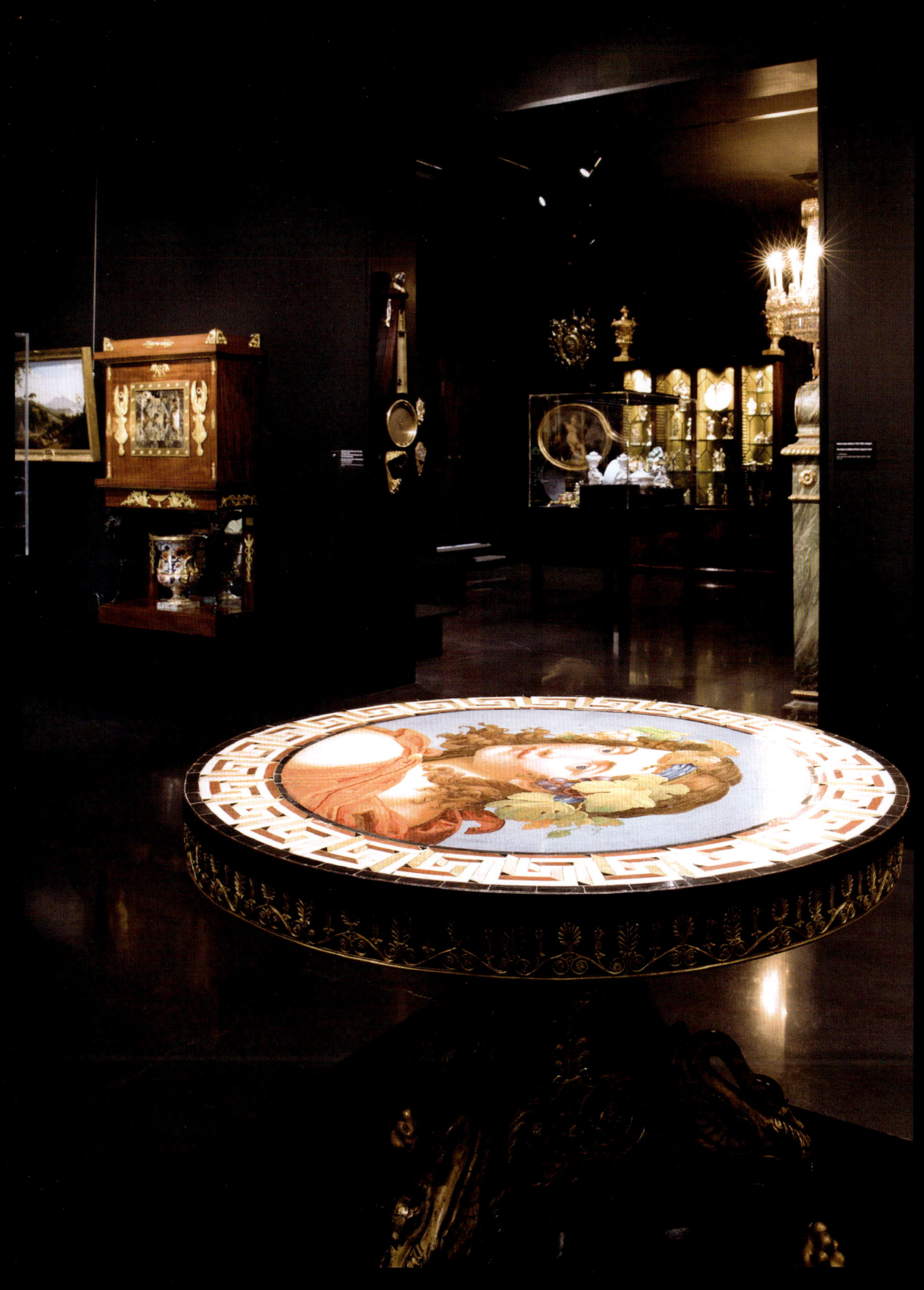

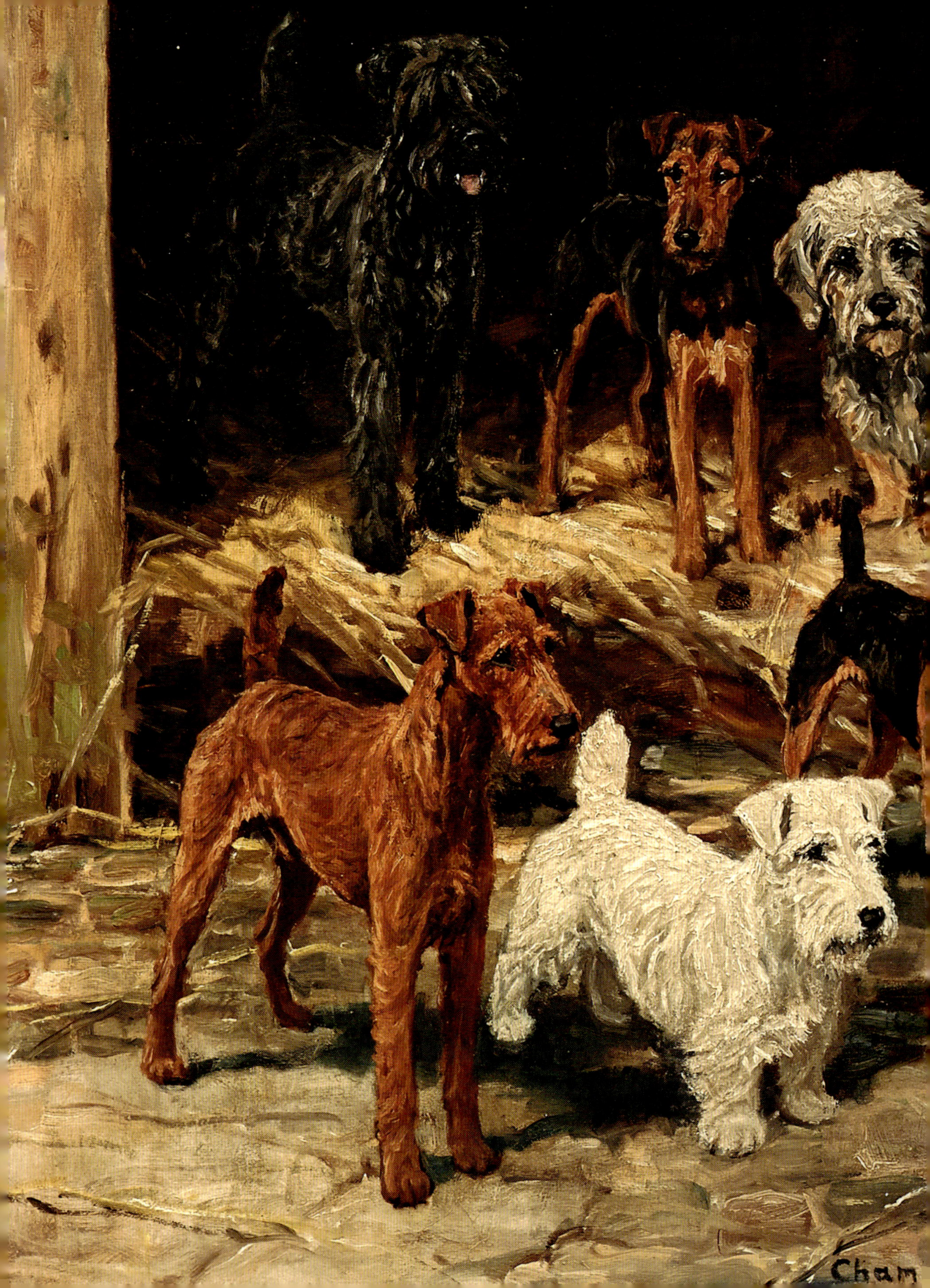
Cham

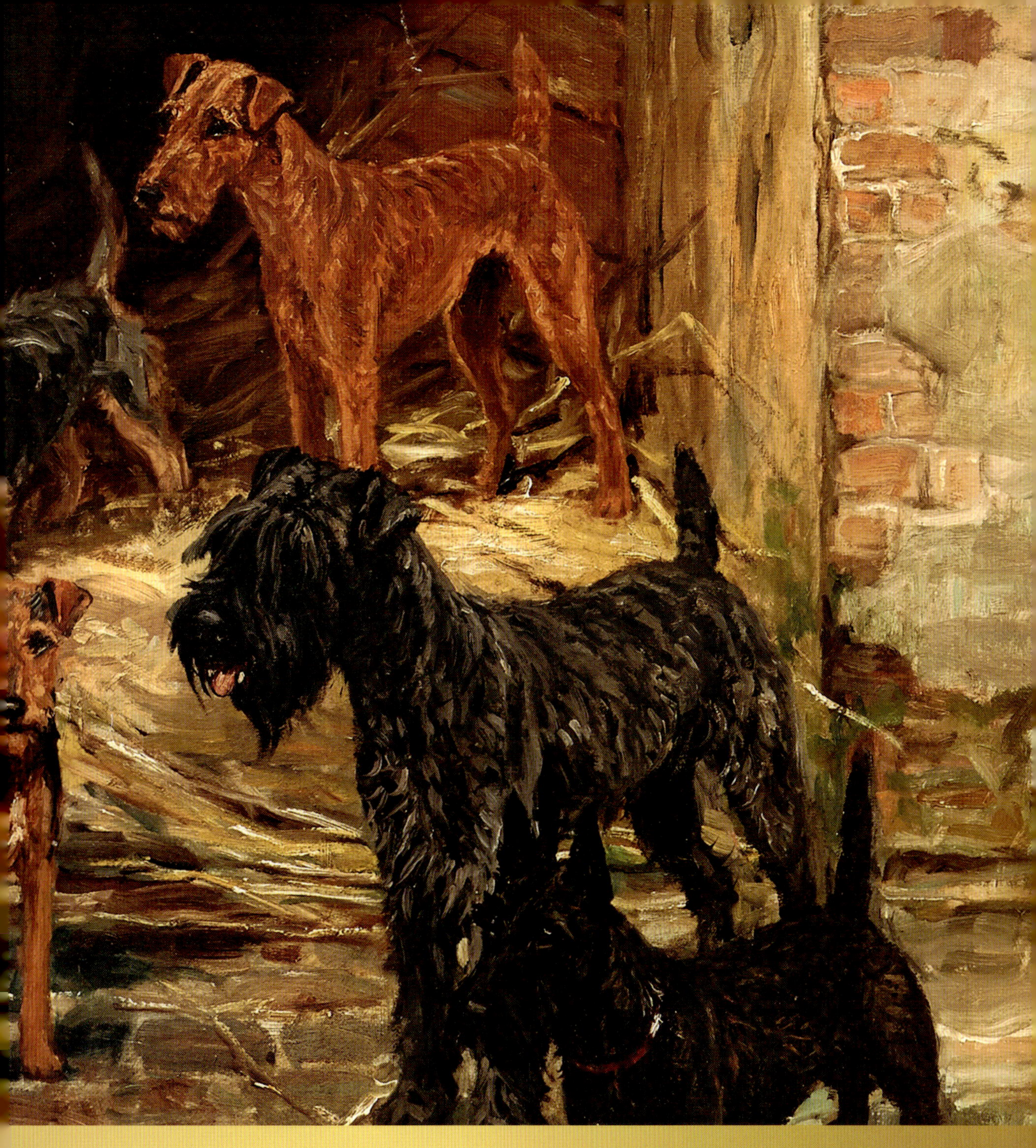

CONSUMING PASSIONS

Fermoy Kennels

THE LASTING LEGACY OF DAVID ROCHE, AM (1930–2013)

David Roche's home is a sumptuous extravaganza of gilded gorgeousness, with fabulous furnishings, luscious colour palettes and an intoxicating ambience. Add to this a cast of charismatic canine characters looking out at you from oil paintings, china cabinets, statuary and classic photographs and, together, you have a magic mixture of David's two most potent passions . . . his antiques collection and his love of dogs. Combine with this the real-life 'in the moment' experience of being up close and personal with those very elements that shaped David's day-to-day existence, and you have an intriguing juxtaposition of past and present, ranging from the opulent to the everyday. You can choose to just look and admire, or let your imagination run riot and drink it all in, with the realisation that so much canine history has taken place right here in North Adelaide.

When David purchased his splendid Australian Federation villa in upmarket Melbourne Street back in 1954, he named it Fermoy House after his French-Irish grandparents. The famous Fermoy Kennels were then built alongside the residence, housing up to 40 dogs at a time in air-conditioned comfort. Breeds included smooth fox terriers, Scottish terriers, cocker spaniels, greyhounds, Italian greyhounds, rough coat collies, pointers, German shepherd dogs, Chihuahuas, griffon Bruxellois and a Boston terrier, as well as those breeds for which he became most famous – Afghan hounds and Kerry blue terriers. In addition to those bred under his own Fermoy prefix, David imported over 130 top dogs from all around the world. His canine charges enabled him to become the most successful dog show exhibitor ever in Australia, including holding the record for having received more Best in Show awards at royal shows than any other exhibitor.

It wasn't just at home that David's dogs soared to dizzy heights. A dazzling example of his mastery as 'king of the show ring' was when he took one of his homebred Kerries, Australian Champion *Fermoy Knight O'Terra*, over to Britain in the summer of 1990. Here, in an incredibly short time, he personally campaigned this dog to his British title, while picking up two very prestigious All Breeds Best In Show awards along the way. The following year this impressive dog added an American Championship to his long list of achievements.

David was already an All Breeds judge when he took up residence at Fermoy House. He was in fact the youngest person in Australian dog history to be awarded an All Breeds judging licence at just 22 years of age. It was from here that he set off for judging assignments all around the world,

Previous spread: *Champions All*, Frederick Thomas Daws, 1927.

Opposite page: David Roche with Champion Berenwode Outrider (Kerry blue terrier) being awarded Best in Show at the 1956 Royal Adelaide Show.

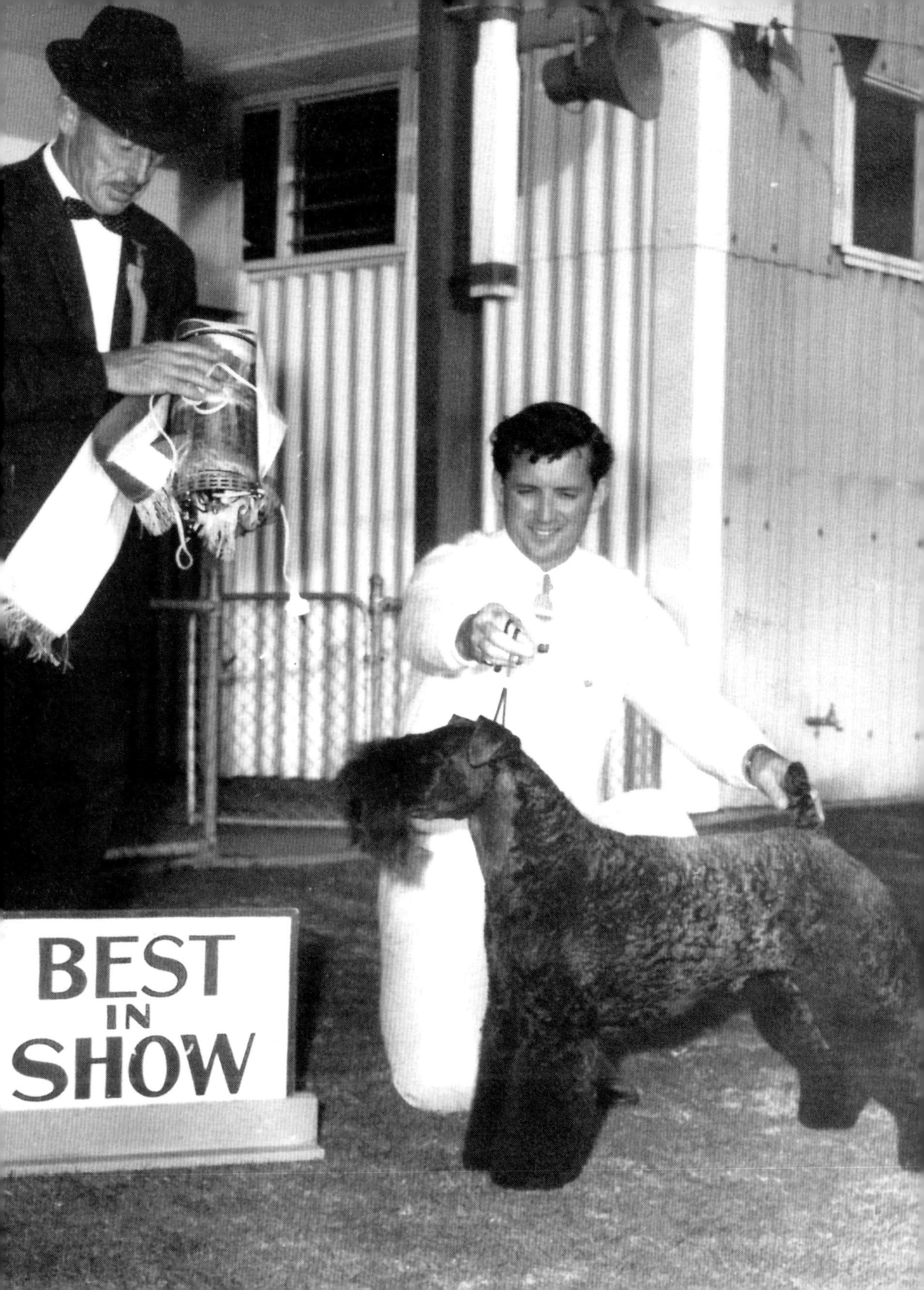
BEST
IN
SHOW

This page:
Clockwise from top:
Fermoy Kennel runs, North Adelaide, 1960s.

David Roche awarding a Kerry blue champion Mareerlane's Minute at the Morris & Essex Show, United States, 1955.

David Roche judging in Boston with handler Jane Forsythe, 1962.

David Roche judging at Goshen, New York, 1952.

Opposite page:
Clockwise from top: David Roche judging at Crufts, Earls Court, 1969.

David Roche showing English, Irish and Australian champion Granemore Shandon, who won Best Exhibit at the Royal Adelaide Show in the mid 1970s.

David Roche exhibiting Champion Fermoy Liffey at a Sydney show in the late 1980s.

David Roche exhibiting Champion Fermoy Liffey under Phyllis Wolfish, United States, 1980s.

David Roche judging in California, 1970s.

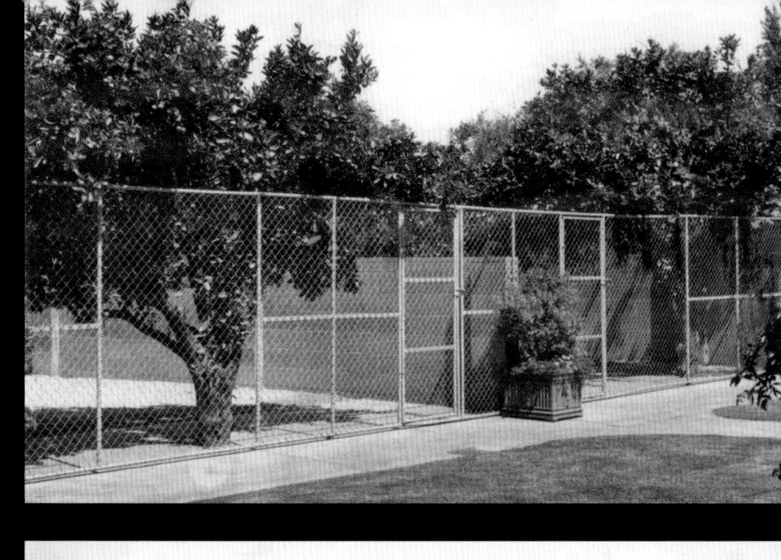

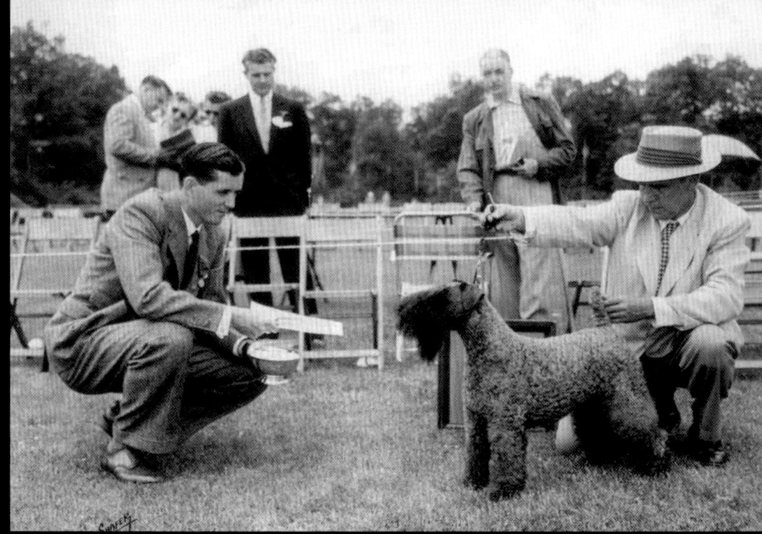

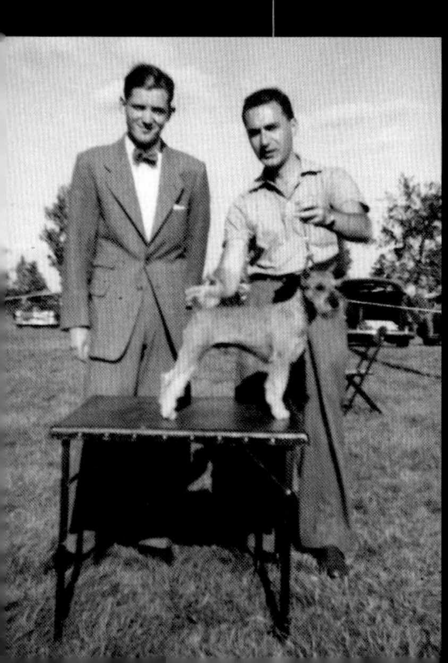

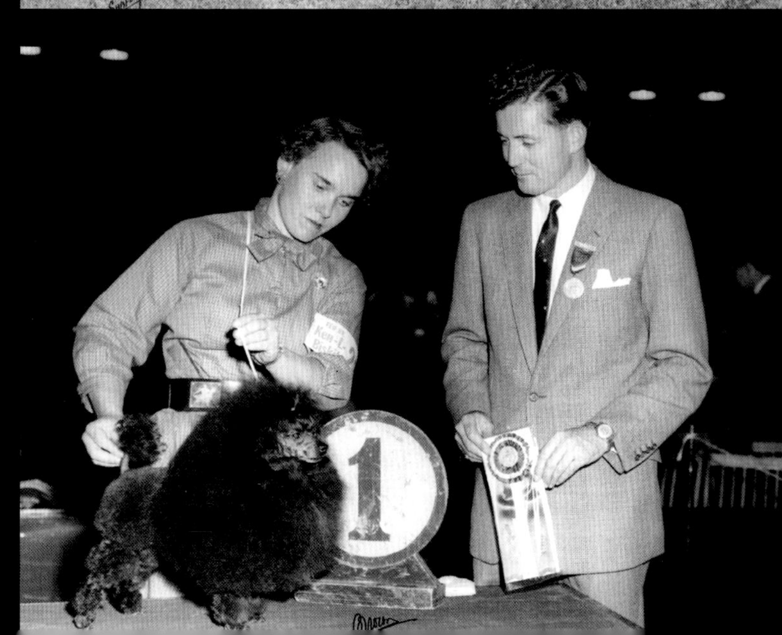

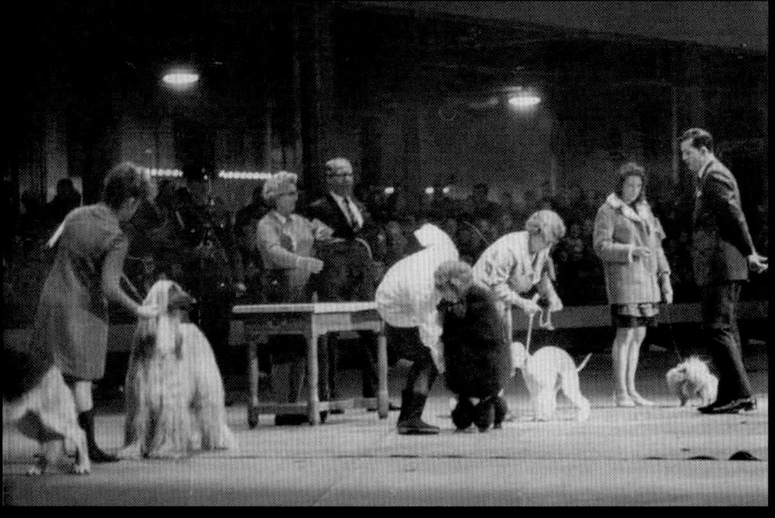

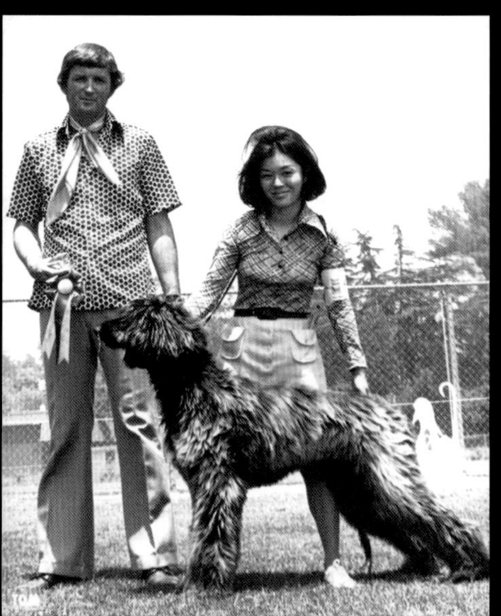

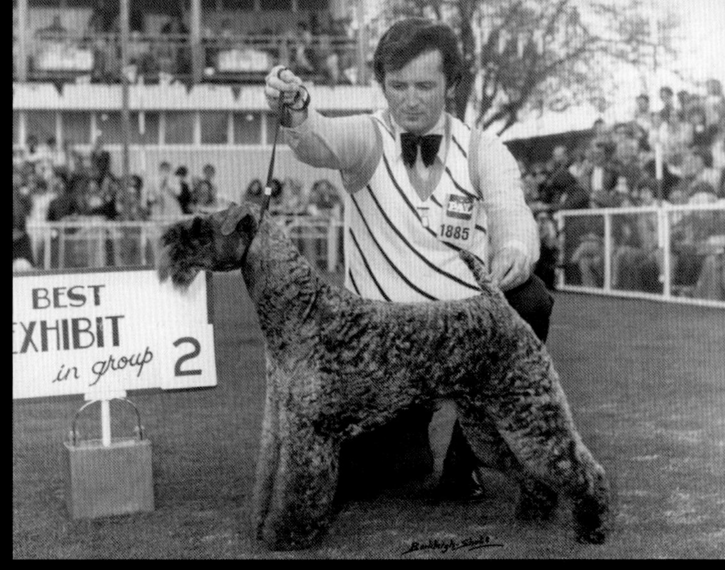
1885
BEST
EXHIBIT
in group 2

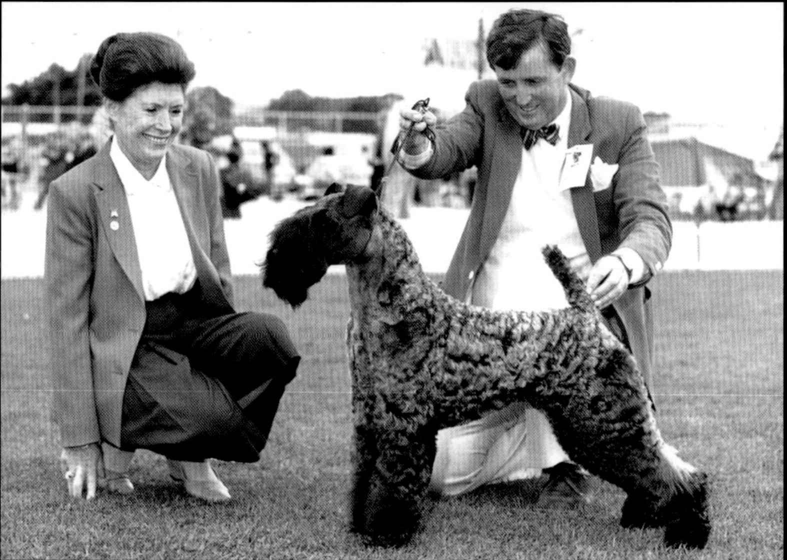

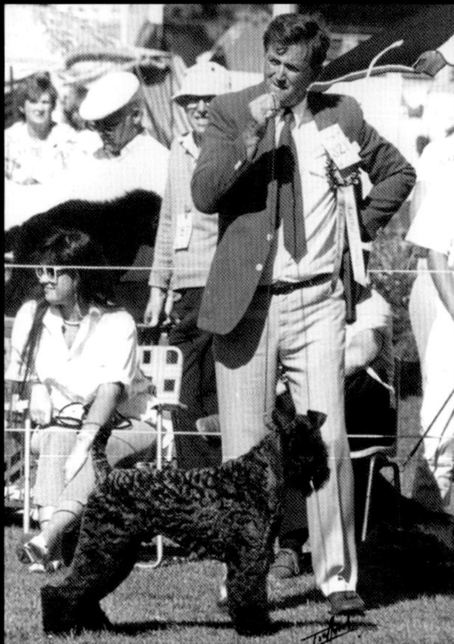

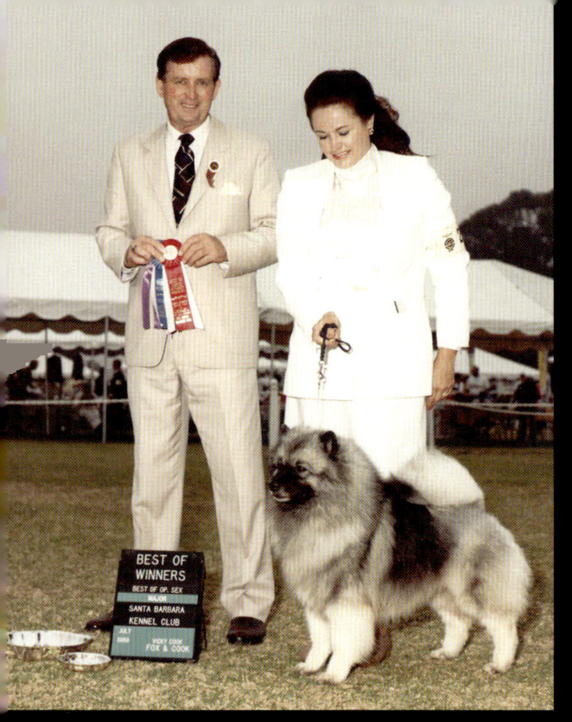

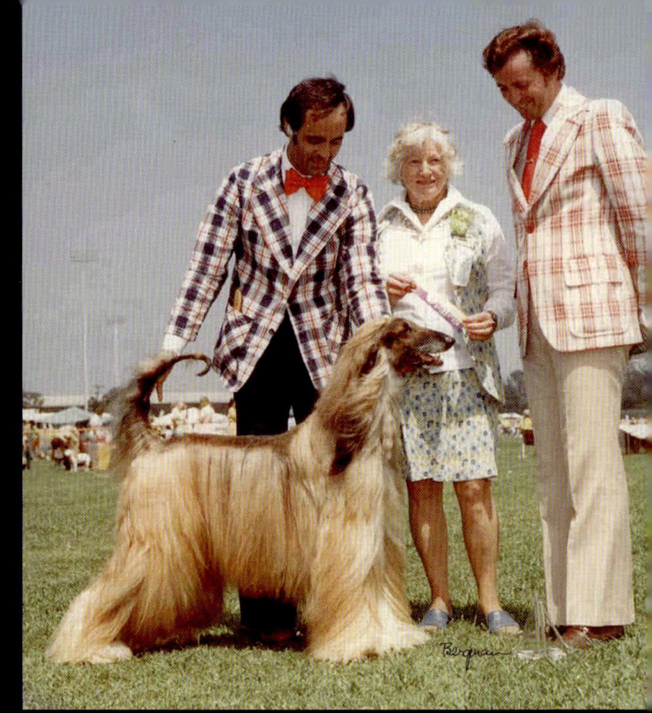

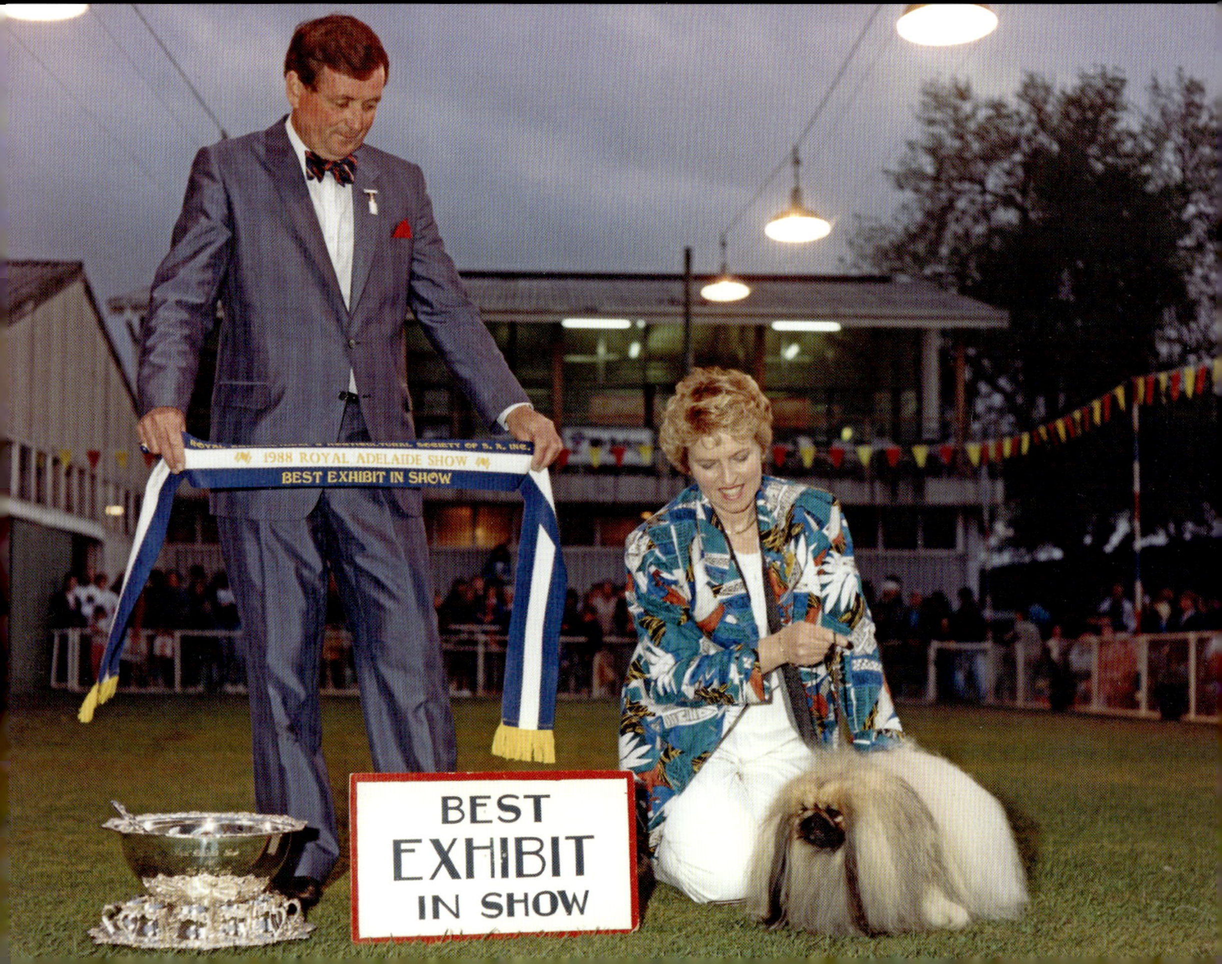

1988 ROYAL ADELAIDE SHOW
BEST EXHIBIT IN SHOW

BEST
EXHIBIT
IN SHOW

officiating in more than 25 countries. One of his all-time favourites was the legendary Morris & Essex in the United States (billed as 'the most beautiful dog show in the world'), where he was the only Australian ever to receive an invitation from the fabled Geraldine Rockefeller Dodge to adjudicate at her ultra-exclusive show. However there is simply nothing to compare with the honour of being the youngest judge ever given the most prestigious gig on the planet – judging Best In Show at Crufts in England – as David did in 1969 at the age of 39. In fact, he was the first non-British judge, and remains one of only very few from abroad to have ever received this plum appointment. So as you can see, many important pages of the canine history book were turned during David's 59-year tenure at Fermoy.

Now the famous kennels have been pulled down to make way for a purpose-built, classically styled structure designed to showcase his breath-taking collection of art. This impressive new building, designed and built in 2015, blends seamlessly into what was David's much-loved home. Just a few footsteps transport you from galleries through to his personal living quarters, and it's no surprise that dogs make a significant appearance along the way.

Paintings of interest abound throughout the home, especially in David's den. Here the stunning Maud Earl *A Pointer in a landscape at sunset*, 1900, predominates, but it has plenty of classic canine company. There are even four-legged fireside friends sitting on the hearth, along with doggy fire bellows, as well as dog cushions on the chairs. Just over the way is David's library of canine books and allied publications, including a comprehensive collection of The Kennel Club's all-important Stud Books. His former dressing room now houses a small sample of the multitudinous trophies and sashes won by his dogs over the decades, as well as a colourful assortment of judges' ribbons. Even the kitchen has a couple of performing pooches in David's quirky mechanical moneybox collection, among other pet pieces.

Certainly dog lovers of all kinds are in for a real treat – be they show-ring exhibitors, art aficionados, armchair cynologists (study of canine matters) or proud pet owners. David's dual interests of dogs and collecting antiques both started very early in his life. He commenced his canine career at just nine years of age, sometimes even taking his cocker spaniel to shows on a pushbike. By the time he was a teenager he had already made his first purchase as a collector – an English bone china statue of a terrier, along with a figurine of Queen Mary's pet dog. Despite the close coexistence of these two all-consuming passions throughout his life, it is interesting to note that it was not until one of the inaugural exhibitions at the museum in 2016 – *David Roche: Kennels and Collecting* – was put together, that these two themes were showcased in tandem for the first time. This fascinating exhibition consisted of paintings, ceramics, photographs and assorted canine

Opposite page:
Clockwise from top left:
David Roche judging at the Santa Barbara Kennel Club, United States, 1989.

David Roche (judging) with Kay Finch, and Richard Souza, handler, with Champion Coastwind Gazebo, at the Santa Barbara Kennel Club, United States, 1989.

David Roche judging Best Exhibit in Show at the Royal Adelaide Show and awarding Pekingese Champion Peregrine Falcon, owned by Loretta Walsh, 1988.

memorabilia that are now found throughout David's residence. Highlights include paintings showcasing a wide variety of breeds such as the English, Gordon and Irish red and white setter, foxhound, Japanese Chin, greyhound, pug, fox terrier, Cavalier King Charles spaniel, pointer, Italian greyhound, Afghan hound, Lowchen, border terrier and papillon. Famous artists include Edwin Landseer, Maud Earl, George Earl and Arthur Wardle. A small oil on board depiction of *Greyhound with pups*, 1895, is by Australia's pre-eminent sporting artist of his time, Frederick Woodhouse.

David also developed a comprehensive collection of Staffordshire Pottery (including a charming pair of begging King Charles spaniel jugs), along with stirrup cups, porcelain miniatures, snuff boxes and decorative ornaments – while photographs in his former dressing room and new reference library document many of David's show-ring triumphs, as well as some of his judging assignments. Among the many Afghans, Kerries and smooth fox terriers, I was delighted to see that my favourite breed, the old English sheepdog, had managed to sneak into the photograph gallery. A miscellany of interesting bits and pieces ranges from a 1968 letter from Crufts Dog Show through to a Breeders Diploma from South Africa. Collectively, the displays in Fermoy House are a little like having a helicopter overview of the life and times of David Roche. They are also of a scale and quality that is unique in Australia.

When David died in 2013 at the age of 83, I predicted in print that our dog world would now be 'less colourful, less grand, and a whole lot less history-making and breaking'. This has certainly proven to be the case. Visiting his house and museum just reinforces for me what a one-off David really was.

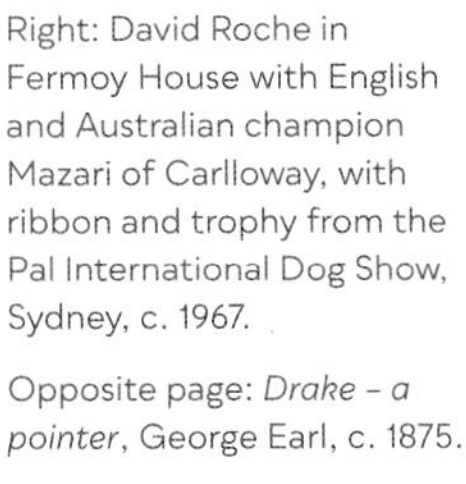

Right: David Roche in Fermoy House with English and Australian champion Mazari of Carlloway, with ribbon and trophy from the Pal International Dog Show, Sydney, c. 1967.

Opposite page: *Drake – a pointer*, George Earl, c. 1875.

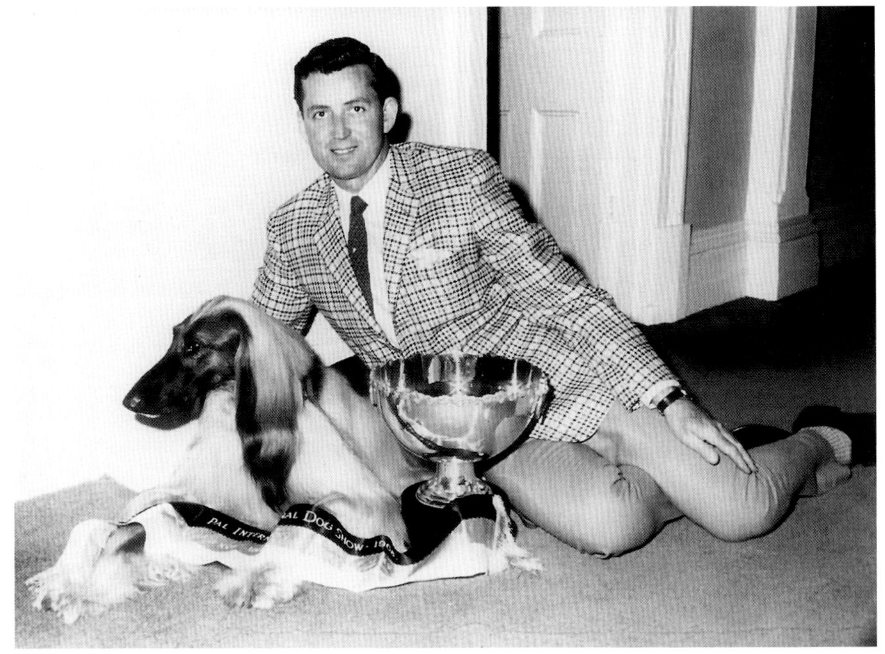

There's never been anyone in the dog world exactly like him, and there will never be anyone quite like him again. To have had one of our own accomplish so much on the world stage certainly enabled us to have a very grand ambassador for Australia. His impeccable canine credentials and his many accomplishments stacked up with the very best of the best. His eminent stature enabled us, by association, to stand tall in the eyes of the international canine community.

David had expressed the desire to have a book published about his lifetime of dog experiences. I thought that this was a great idea, as it would preserve for posterity a very important chapter of our Australian canine history, while giving us all the chance to share in some of David's hysterically funny stories about the many weird and wonderful things that had befallen him along the way. I agreed to write this memoir for him. Regrettably, other issues in his life kept getting in the way of this important project, so it never came to fruition – which I always thought was a great loss for the dog fancy.

Fortunately, we can now all step back into that golden era of dogdom, by visiting The David Roche Collection and experiencing a taste of those historic days, and what this colossus of the canine world contributed to our sport. Not only will you be walking on hallowed ground, but you'll be celebrating the life and legacy of an icon who made a big difference for dogs. I promise you will not leave untouched by the experience.

Judy Chapman
Canine historian, journalist & friend of David Roche

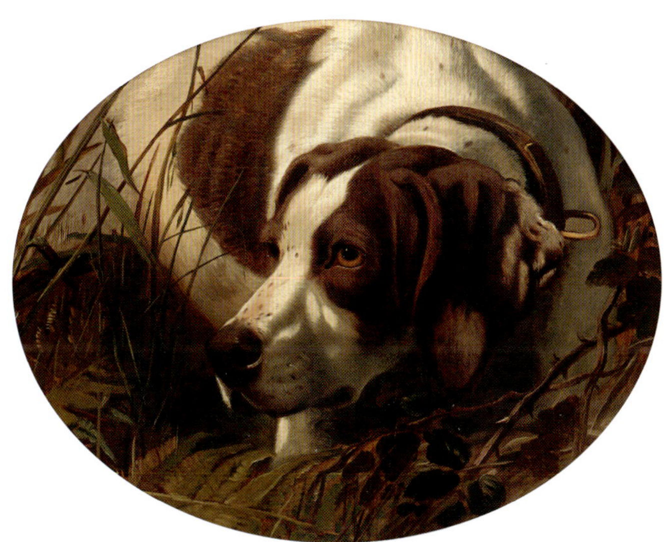

Acknowledgements

Opposite page:
A selection of walking canes, riding crops and parasols displayed in the Roman room landing of Fermoy House.

Acknowledgements

This book has been made possible by the supportive team at The David Roche Foundation – Martyn Cook, Director; Marilyn Joy, Chief Executive Officer; Nathan Schroeder, Curatorial Support Officer; Adam Kromkamp, Site Services Officer; and Jayne Bailes, Administration and Finance Officer. Martyn Cook's knowledge of the collection and memories of David Roche have been critical to the development of the content and I thank him personally for his generosity and patience. Judy Chapman and her chapter on David Roche and his dogs adds a pivotal part of this man's story to the book. Thank you Judy for revising the content and allowing the Foundation to reprint your essay. Geoff Laurenson, archivist, Geelong Grammar School, and Owen Mace, TDRF volunteer, kindly assisted in providing biographical formation.

The book has also been greatly enhanced through the assistance of a number of people who knew and worked for David, particularly June Ashton, Steve Baliga, Chrissie Jeffrey and Ann Preston Flint. The David Roche Foundation is grateful to the many individuals who have assisted cataloguing and researching the collection over many years including the international auction houses Christie's, Sotheby's and Bonhams; and individuals Ronald Pawly, Antwerp; Jenny Spencer-Smith, England; Frank Caldwell, Museums Arts and Heritage, Sandwell, West Midlands; Dr Helen Jacobsen, Senior Curator, Wallace Collection, London; Helen Wyld, Curator, National Museums Scotland; John and Henry Sandon, England; Carlton Hobbs, New York; Bodie Ashton, Australia/Germany; Robert Curtis, Sydney; Ronan Sulich, Christie's, Sydney; Alice Ilich, Sydney; Nat Williams, Treasures Curator, National Library of Australia; and from Adelaide – Jennifer Harris, David Button, Jeffrey Fischer, Helen Roos, Vaughan Cottle and Anthony Hurl.

Robert Reason
Senior Curator

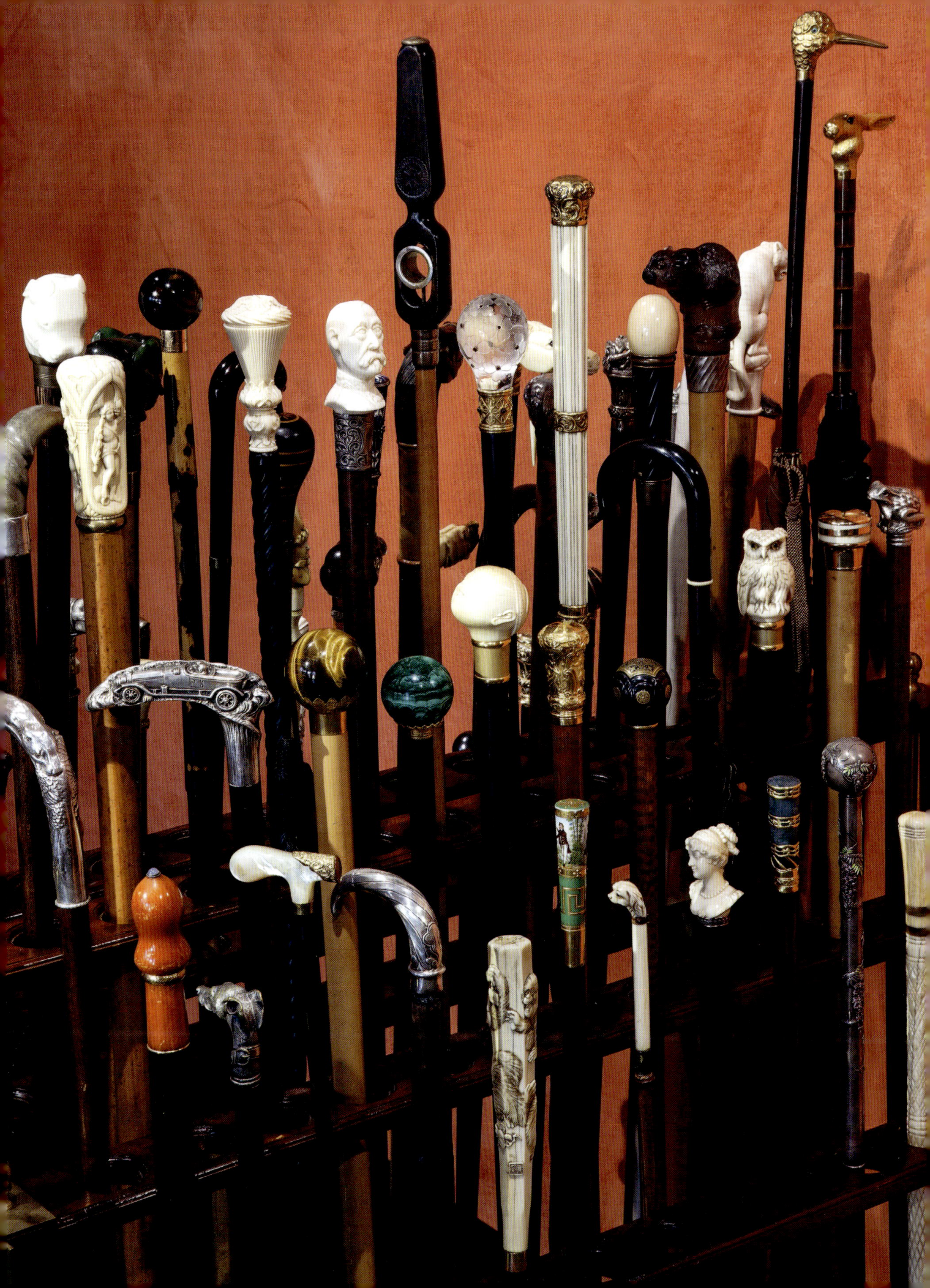

Opposite page: The drawing room with a French Overmantel, c. 1780, and a painting of *Therese Queen Consort of Bavaria*, after Joseph Karl Stieler, 1827–1830. The *Pair of candelabra*, c. 1790, *Pair of lidded urns*, c. 1820, and *Narcissus mantel clock*, c. 1780, are all French.

Following page: *David graduating from Geelong Grammar*, Thomas Percy Reginald 'Rex' Wood, c. 1948. The *Golden pheasant*, Jules Moigniez, c. 1880, sits on an Irish *Dolphin console table*, c. 1825.

Cover image: Detail: *Specimen table*, George Bullock, designer, c. 1815.

Back cover image: David Roche in the Roman room, 2008.

Robert Reason is Senior Curator of The David Roche Foundation, Adelaide. In 2008 he co-curated the exhibition and accompanying catalogue *Empires & Splendour: The David Roche Collection* for the Art Gallery of South Australia. Robert has published widely on the decorative arts and has worked in the Australian cultural sector for over 20 years. He first met David Roche in 2002.

Wakefield Press
16 Rose Street, Mile End, South Australia 5031
Website: www.wakefieldpress.com.au

The David Roche Foundation
241 Melbourne Street, North Adelaide, South Australia 5006
Telephone: +61 8 8267 3677
Email: info@rochefoundation.org.au
Website: www.rochefoundation.com.au

First published 2019

Photography by Max Creasy, London; Randy Larcombe, Adelaide; David Mariuz, Adelaide; Nu Image photography, Adelaide; Roche family archives.
Designed and typeset by Liz Nicholson, Wakefield Press
Copy-edited by Julia Beaven, Wakefield Press
Printing and quality control in China by Tingleman Pty Ltd

ISBN: 978 1 74305 617 2

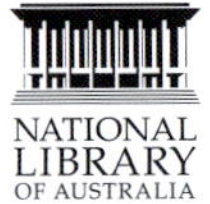

A catalogue record for this book is available from the National Library of Australia

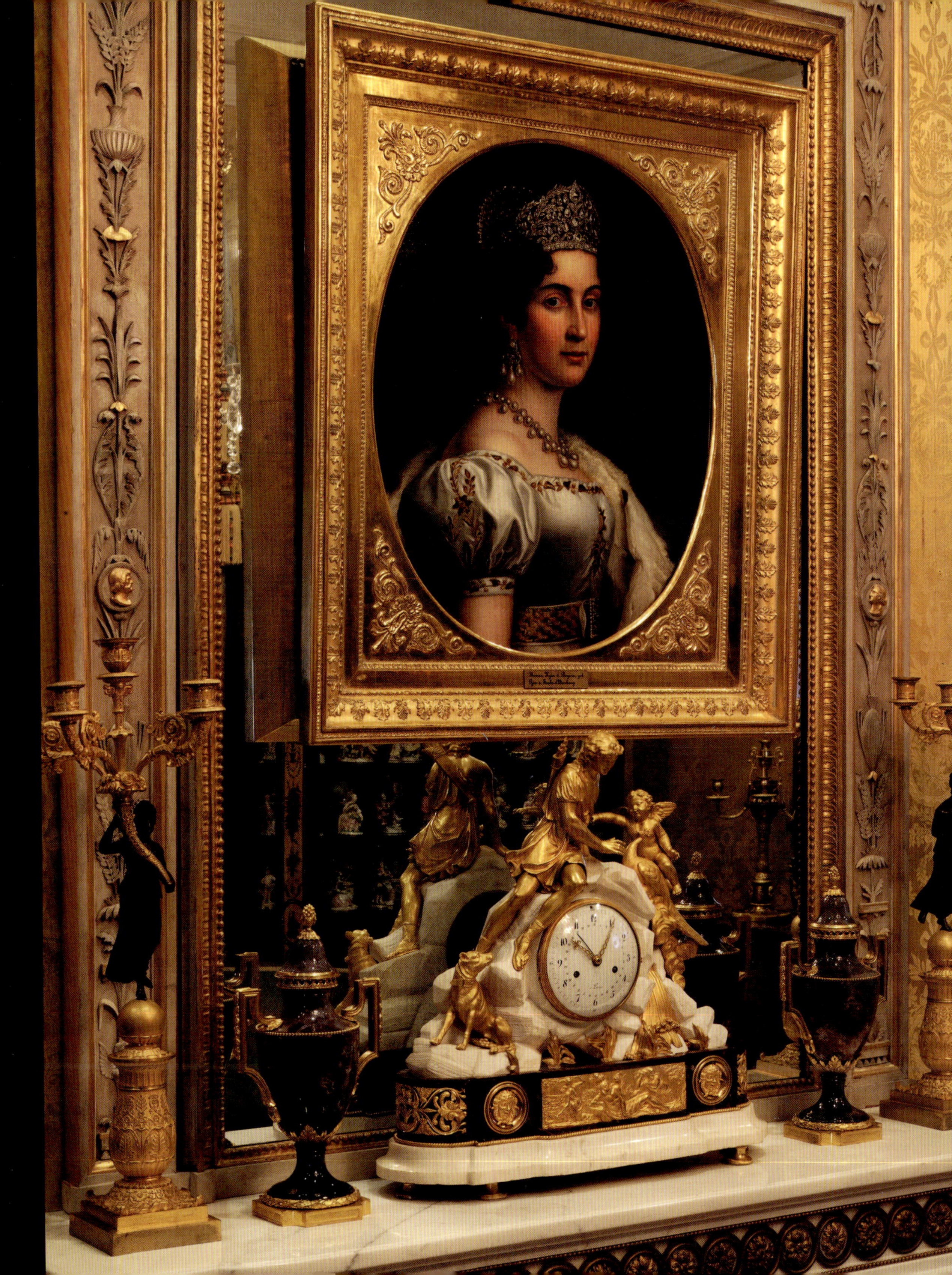

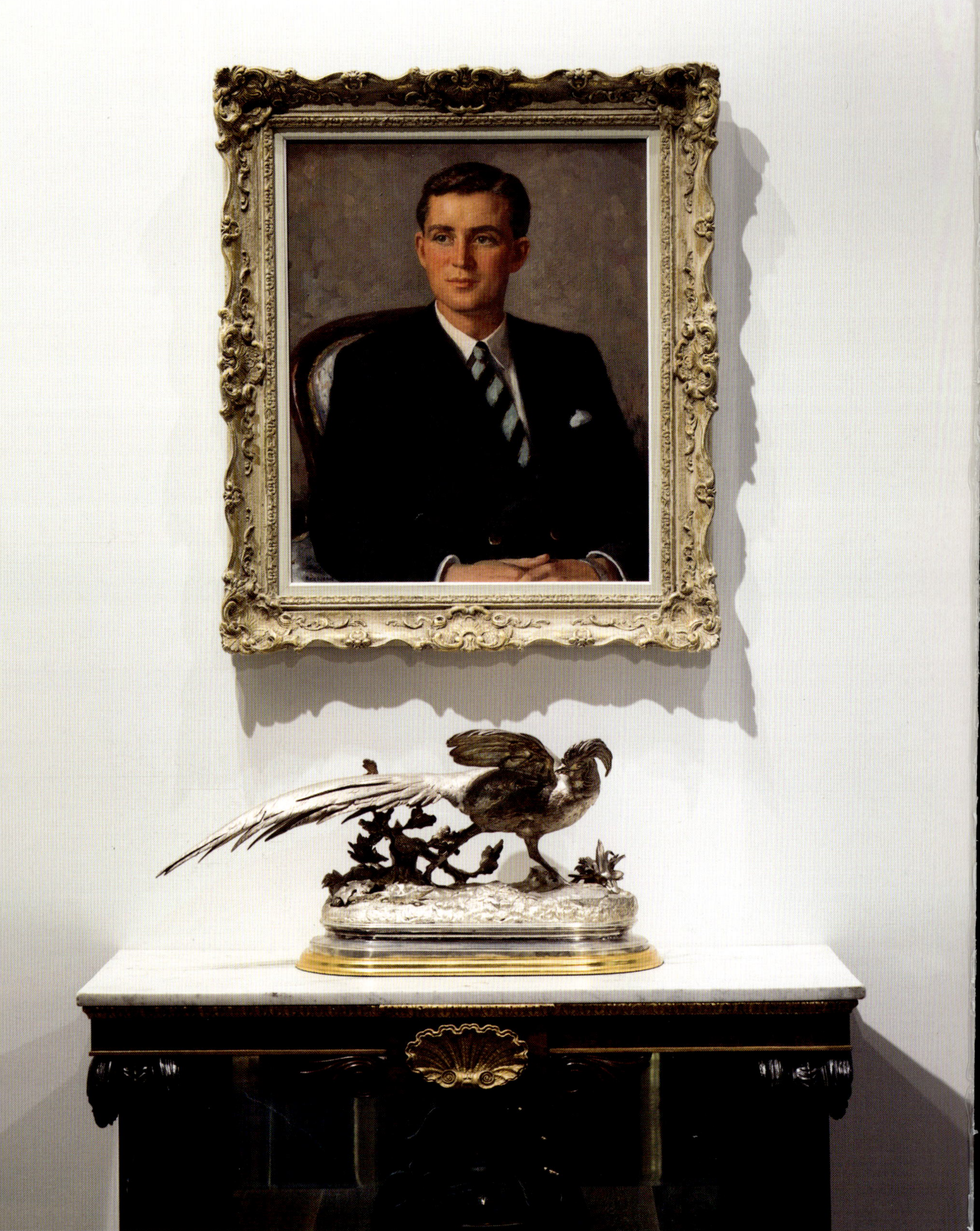